ENGAGING THE PAST

The Uses of History across the

Social Sciences

Edited by Eric H. Monkkonen

Duke University Press   Durham and London

1994

© 1994 Duke University Press
All rights reserved   Printed in the United States
of America on acid-free paper ∞
Designed by Cherie Holma Westmoreland
Typeset in Berkeley Old Style
by Tseng Information Systems, Inc.

Library of Congress Cataloging-in-
Publication Data

Engaging the past: the uses of history across the
social sciences / edited by Eric H. Monkkonen.
p.   cm.   Includes index.
ISBN 0-8223-1440-1 (alk. paper).—
ISBN 0-8223-1431-2 (pbk. : alk. paper)
1. Social sciences—Research.
I. Monkkonen, Eric H., 1942–
H62.H546   1994
300—dc20   93-37086   CIP

CONTENTS

Eric H. Monkkonen

The purpose of the essays in this book is to survey the historical research in each of the different social science disciplines. The set of references included with each essay is designed to guide readers to further works in each field. The authors have sketched both the substantive as well as the organizational loci of their disciplines. They have done so knowing that the sociology of knowledge permeates even the knowledge of social science, and they want these essays to help demarcate how knowledge is produced as well as what is produced. Thus, they have given a sense of some of the institutional as well as intellectual affiliations of the scholars whose work they analyze. Given these intentions, they all understand that their essays will need to be supplemented in the future, for one of the exciting things about interdisciplinary scholarship is that it changes. The essays (in some cases, shorter versions) have been published in *Social Science History,* in a special series originally titled "History and the Other Social Sciences."

While all involved in this project have understood its purposes, the title of the collection itself has proved to be problematic, the difficulty lying in a fundamental ambiguity that remains unresolved in the title of this book. We debated whether the series of articles should have been titled "History *and* the Social Sciences" or "History *in* the Social Sciences" and ended up with "History and the Other Social Sciences." In the subtitle of the collection you hold in your hands, we have tried yet another formulation, "The Uses of History across the Social Sciences."

How one solves this disarmingly simple problem of a connecting term reveals both disciplinary and perhaps epistemological stances. "And" would imply a separateness of history as an intellectual enterprise, setting history off from the social sciences. "In" would imply that the practice of history was carried on within the nonhistorical social sciences and suggests—but not so strongly—that history was also separate from social science.

And both alternate titles drop "*other*"—the role of the "other" in the series title was intended to place history as one of the social sciences, perhaps the primary social science, whereas dropping "other" might carry the implication that one considers history to be a humanistic discipline. No "other" for the humanists; "other" for the social scientists. Historians are divided about this question, as are humanists and social scientists. So too are universities, for in some history belongs to the humanities, whereas in others it is happily ensconced with the social sciences.

The origin of this current division lies in the growth of the scholarly professions in the late nineteenth century, when the disciplines defined themselves, created professional organizations, and then replicated these in university organizational structure. By the end of the twentieth century, these disciplinary divisions seem secure. Millions of college students consider themselves history or political science "majors." Thousands of scholars and teachers care solely about their home discipline. There is an occasional crossover appointment and an occasional combined department, but most training, teaching, and research takes place comfortably within the confines of disciplines now over a half-century old. And thanks to the post–World War II expansion in the size of universities, the sheer volume of knowledge within each of the social science disciplines has expanded so vastly that any hope of an individual mastering the literature of more than one discipline—actually any single discipline—is quixotic.

The disciplinary narrowing is our culture's strategy for dealing with the expansion of knowledge it has produced. The division, which seems so natural now, could have been accomplished in other ways which, had they been implemented, would also seem natural. Other strategies might have been to focus on tools of learning (e.g., algebra), methodologies (e.g., analysis of narrative structures), or topical concentration (e.g., birds, their history, flight mechanics, artistic representation, biochemistry, and religious symbolism). So the division of knowledge into the disciplines is not natural, but a strategy.

A major accrued benefit with this strategy has been the development of professional standards which transcend person, institution, or locale. The scholarly professions have no formal regulatory power or mechanisms—they cannot license, censure in a meaningful way, or even promote model work. But they have multiple informal mechanisms to set and enforce standards—the most important through teaching, book reviews, and the now solidly entrenched practice of anonymous peer review. Reinforced by the peer review practice having filtered into the hiring and firing of professors, high quality research and teaching no longer depends on individual genius or institutional quality alone.

Standards of method, of adequate proof, of conceptualization, or of substantive knowledge get enforced through peer review of publications, in the grant process, and in institutional evaluations. The practice and teaching of social science is regularized and regulated across an enormous spectrum of teaching and research institutions.[1] (Consider, in this regard, that the annual ranking done by a popular news magazine, *U.S. News and World Report,* is watched very carefully by college and university administrators.)

The success of the disciplines has not bred complete satisfaction for all practitioners, however. In particular, many scholars have been dissatisfied with the completeness of their explanatory accounts or even of the disciplinary questions, the broad research goals. Of the many possible responses to this dissatisfaction (from abandonment to radical criticism), an important one has been an interdisciplinary quest for methodological tools, concepts, and differing kinds of empirical evidence from other disciplines. One such cluster of interdisciplinary quests has been between history, sociology, geography, anthropology, economics, and political science. (There are others, the American studies movement, or most prominently in the 1980s, cultural studies—literary criticism, philosophy, and history.)

As the essays in this collection make abundantly clear, such boundary crossing is not new and has occurred quite regularly, usually among the most prominent scholars in each field. In this sense, boundary crossing has never been marginal, but central. The formal attempt to give such interdisciplinary forays a visible home dates from the late 1960s, when scholars created journals (such as *Journal of Interdisciplinary History, Comparative Studies in Society & History, Journal of Historical Geography,* and *Historical Methods*) explicitly dedicated to publishing interdisciplinary work.

These efforts were followed, in the 1970s, by organizational activities—the creation of the Social Science History Association, the founding of the history sections of the American Political Science Association, Association of American Geographers, and the American Sociological Association. On the academic level, there have been far fewer initiatives—most typically positions within the nonhistory fields in historical research for that field. The important aspect of these positions is that they are for historical sociology, say, rather than the history *of* sociology.

Hardly mass movements, these activities nevertheless have captured the interests and commitment of some of the leading scholars in each discipline. In addition, the epistemological tremors caused by various reltivisms—now broadly captured by the concept of postmodernism—have caused many nonhistorians to look to history. The reasons vary, but the turn is strong (McDonald 1992). At the same time, historians originally interested in improving their explanatory skills continue to turn to the social sciences for what they perceive as better intellectual tools, tools honed by years of intense development and usage.

The motives for jumping disciplines among historians differ somewhat from those in the other social sciences. Historians who look to the other social sciences tend to be dissatisfied with what they see as their own discipline's conceptual sloppiness, its reliance on anecdotal evidence, its happy privileging of certain stories over others. These historians like the seeming "hardness" of the other social sciences, hardness in the sense of rigor, conceptual precision, and the explicit prior stipulation of what constitutes an adequate explanation. The social scientists turning to history, on the other hand, are often dissatisfied with those parts of their disciplines which seem the most "hard," that is the most mathematicized and abstract.

Consequently, scholars in the various disciplines who wish to learn from other disciplines find that their counterparts do not show exactly the same intellectual concerns. And few understand the other's discipline, in spite of the best intentions. Three specific misunderstandings may occur. Because they have not been trained in the broader parts of the discipline, they may be unaware of epistemological or methodological conflicts, which are passed on to practitioners through informal cues. A related misunderstanding can come from an incomplete sense of how work is assessed and the reputational status of individuals and their scholarship—a weakness consequent of the way in which research paradigms get discarded rather than outright rejected. And third, while these issues may inform many discussions in the discipline, the interdisciplinary explorer may feel like ignoring some while attending to others, an attitude which makes the resulting research seem quirky to other practitioners.[2]

They find that in spite of apparently similar goals, they are still foreigners in other disciplines (Cohn 1987). The essays in this book express that tone clearly, for although each author refers to many cross-disciplinary works, these are for the most part by scholars within the core discipline under discussion. That is, few historians have influenced economists, historical economics, or even economic history. On the other hand, Rockoff's essay makes clear that major economists and major theoretical arguments have begun in the context of historical research. One might argue that the impact of historical research has been greater in economics than in the other social sciences.

Not only does it continue to be difficult to participate deeply in the dialogues (conversations?) of more than one discipline, but when their research comes to fruition, very few scholars who use interdisciplinary modes of research are willing to publish in a journal explicitly tied to another discipline. Those who do so are, for the most part, those who can "afford" to do so; that is, who can publish in a place their disciplinary colleagues will never see and therefore, in a sense, give up through that publication their participation in a disciplinary dialogue.[3] Young scholars do not dare place their research anywhere but the most central and visible place, so those who expect genuine interdisciplinary activity from the young will be disappointed.

Consequently, in spite of all the substantive reasons which should push interdisciplinary research, it has proved to have formidable internal barriers. The essays in this book are designed to help cross the barriers, serving as guidebooks written by natives to the terrain. The authors of this book have written their essays as guides to the historical social science work in each of their disciplines. The intended audience are the communities of social scientists and historians interested in reading or researching historically informed social science. At one level, the essays constitute a user's guide to other fields. At another, they help show how some of the best and most innovative research has been interdisciplinary, often more so than is remembered.

These essays were stimulated by the now nearly two decades of annual meetings organized by the Social Science History Association. This association has fostered intentionally cross-disciplinary communication and research, forcing people to listen to one another. All but one of the authors have actively participated in the association's meetings, and all have experienced the excitement and frustration of cross-disciplinary exchanges. Long experience has made each author cautious in assessing the potentials for more cross-disciplinary research because each knows the genuine intellectual stretching required.

One aspect of this stretching and intellectual risk taking illustrates how disciplinary subcultures function. Just as there are both formal and informal rankings of institutional quality by departments, there is a similar if even less formal ranking of individual scholars (quantified, if inadequately, by studies of citations via *Social Science Citation Index*).

Students of scientific research use the concept of scientific communities to explain how scientific research is evaluated. The notion is that research and publication occurs within a community, one of whose responsibilities is gatekeeping and shaping research to conform to that community's standards. (Such communities can also wrongly resist innovation or mistakenly keep out good work, of course.)

There are such communities in the social sciences and history profession also, and the deliberate moving out of such communities is fraught with danger. Within subfields, researchers know who is smart, who does good work, whose work cannot be trusted, and who can be counted on for creativity and ingenuity. But in an organizational setting like the Social Science History Association which deliberately breaks up secure subcultural codes, scholars instantly become aware of how much intellectual interchange depends upon trust, stringent conceptual vocabularies, and complex background knowledge. "Is this person who is explaining a research project to me a crackpot or a legitimate social scientist or historian?" "How do we know that an expert is an expert?" "How can I know that this book I am reading is representative of good quality?"

As those who have presented or conducted research in an interdisciplinary setting know, the issue is not at all trivial nor can it be subsumed as a communication problem.[4] In essence, to think or work or read in an interdisciplinary setting one must be a bit of an anthropologist, looking for cues and trying to be open to different ways of thinking. This receptiveness and risk taking also requires an effort at attending to how legitimation works in other fields so that the crackpots can be differentiated from the avant garde.

Each author in this book has been certified as sane, or at least as noncrackpot. Each author participates in disciplinary scholarship, that is, by publishing, teaching, and presenting research at conferences within her or his discipline.

Several thematic issues run beneath the surfaces of the essays.

One with the greatest potential for conflict is the role of quantification, which is conspicuous by its absence. As characterized by Abbott, the issue of quantification in the 1970s worked this way: some historians ran toward it, seeking in quantitative methods the rigor and precision which they felt history lacked, while simultaneously some sociologists (and by extension, other social scientists) ran away from it for what they saw as its false promise of scientificity. When they met, they had confused encounters because what each group wanted from the other was exactly what the other was trying to escape.

Were the issue of quantification one simply of counting versus not counting, the issue might not be worth mentioning. Rather the critique of quantification within nonhistorical social sciences had become one focusing on a social science where the research often seemed to focus on issues designed to fit the assumptions required for a particular statistical technique; the critique attacked this trivilization as a barren way of framing problems. This barrenness came from a rhetoric of pseudotheoretical rigor, with all referents in a research article to theoretical propositions and none to concrete social reality.

The historians running toward social science defined as quantification were not actually seeking the satisfactions brought by doing difficult statistical manipulations (though these should not be denied), but rather were seeking to frame their research questions in ways systematic enough to allow for a modicum of logical resolution or falsification. Such goals are not necessarily realized via statistics, but statistics often enough accompanied the process so that they did become a sign of such logical rigor. Thus the incompatibility first greeting interdisciplinary adventurers has turned out to be less daunting.[5]

A second latent theme is ideology. In the political realm, less rigorous, more historical social science is sometimes associated with leftist scholarship, and some historians have rejected quantitative techniques as being inherently conservative (Green 1972). Although there is abundant evidence to refute these ideas, readers should be aware of this common misconception. In the theoretical realm, questions raised about culture, the question of history as a nontheory driven enterprise, and the big problem of how to understand time also lie beneath the surface. Many scholars are turning to cultural studies, broadly defined, in a spirit of anti-empiricism or anti-positivism. Enlivened by a critique of Western thought loosely gathered under the umbrella of postmodernism, these scholars at one time follow an interdisciplinary urge which might well be "social science history," but they include in their disciplinary travels a heavy portion of cultural (or literary) criticism. How these intellectual currents will fare in future historical/ social science research is not at all clear.

Finally, there is the theme that although not arcane, the literature produced by historians and social scientists crossing borders is not the work of dabblers. History remains fact centered, at least so far; theory plays much less a role than in the other social sciences. "Normal science" in one discipline is not "normal" in another. In spite of the long list of outstanding scholarly exceptions developed in these essays, most mortals will accomplish most of their best work in one discipline. Knowing this, the authors of the essays are all deeply committed to a difficult task. The reading and evaluation of the many books and articles cited here should be done critically, with no special exceptions made. If anything, the work should be held to higher standards, for all of the authors believe that historical social science or social science history is a better way to do things.

Notes

1   Of course, these professionalization and control practices cover the range of knowledge production, but here I wish to concentrate on their implications for the social sciences and history.

2   These three points were suggested to me by Susan Kellogg.

3   I should note here that this is true across a range of disciplines—say, law and the environment.

4   For similar efforts in teaching, see the special issue of *Historical Methods* (Spring 1990: 132–34).

5   If the issue of quantification has proved to be less than important, it may be necessary to add "so far." See the articles by W. Sewall, D. Heise, and A. Abbott in *Sociological Methodology and Research* (May 1992).

References

Cohn, B. S. (1987) *An Anthropologist among the Historians, and Other Essays*. New York: Oxford University Press.

Green, J. R. (1972) "Behavioralism and class analysis." *Radical History Review* (Winter 1972): 89–106.

McDonald, T., ed. (1992) *The Historic Turn*, Ann Arbor: University of Michigan Press.

HISTORIES FOR ANTHROPOLOGY

Ten Years of Historical Research and Writing

by Anthropologists, 1980–1990

Susan Kellogg

The past, once considered the exclusive domain of historians and antiquarians, has increasingly been embraced by anthropologists. Today, it is difficult to find a major anthropological study that does not claim to offer a diachronic, processual, historical analysis. In examining ten years of historical anthropological writing, I cover three broad topics in this essay. First, I explain the emergence of a more historical anthropology as a widespread response to a crisis in the conceptualization of culture. Second, I argue that while there are certain identifiable themes that cut across this literature, in general, it reflects long-standing topical interests within anthropology; I review this literature according to these topics rather than divide it into interpretive or cultural studies versus studies of political economy. Third, I try to assess this body of work critically. I concentrate here on anthropological history as both research and textual practice, as well as briefly examine anthropological uses of the concepts of time, colonialism, and structure and agency.[1]

The first point I make is that anthropologists were never as indifferent to history as it now seems fashionable to assume.[2] First and foremost, of course, there is the long influence of evolutionary thinking on both ethnographies and theory making;[3] second, the persistence of an ethnohistory and cultural anthropology concerned with native Americans (e.g., see Eggan 1966; De Laguna 1960; Spicer 1962; Wallace 1970); third, the research of a group of ethnographers who worked from the 1950s on India or China, with their long indigenous trends of literacy, and who therefore found textual sources useful (e.g., Freedman 1958; Singer 1959; also see Cohn 1987), or who worked on Africa and were interested in social change (e.g., Barnes 1951; Cunnison 1951; Evans-Pritchard 1949, 1962; Smith 1960). Fourth, the developmental cycle literature also brought time (if not history) into analysis (Fortes 1949; Goody 1958).

But interest in history among anthropologists was not confined to these particular fields. Even in the dominant areas of study (structural-functional or cultural-symbolic), history was not wholly ignored. Prior to the 1970s, ethnographers working within these frameworks tended to treat history in three distinct ways. The most common was "history as preface." Anthropologists often began books with a few paragraphs, in a preface or introduction, offering historical background to a particular geographic area or social group. While they might allude to the impact of historical trends or developments treated in the main body of the text, these scholars made little effort to integrate historical themes systematically into the argument. It was also common for anthropologists to use "history as contrast": the distinctiveness of present forms gained resonance by comparison with past ones.[4] Finally, those who drew on "history as data bank" used historical examples precisely because they were assumed not to differ fundamentally from the present.[5]

In retrospect, these three uses of history appear to be ahistorical, in the sense that they do not inject a truly diachronic perspective into anthropological scholarship. Thus, symbolic anthropologists tended not to examine the emergence, maintenance, or transformation of symbolic systems; structuralists tended not to analyze the impact of historical developments on structures; and British social anthropologists tended not to examine how social groups, relationships, or institutions, or social structure itself, are produced, reproduced, and transformed.

The Emergence of a More Historical Anthropology

In the late 1970s, however, history began to acquire a much more important place in anthropological writings. The question then becomes, why. The answer to this question lies in a crisis over representation and authority that anthropology underwent during the 1970s (Marcus and Fischer 1986). This crisis called large parts of both anthropological research and theory into question; indeed, the whole concept of culture was thrown into question. One resolution to this crisis was the adoption of a more diachronic, processual conception of culture, which made history central to anthropological understanding.[6]

Thirty years ago, most anthropologists, regardless of their theoretical orientation, accepted a "normative" definition of culture, according to which culture was a unified, coherent unit of analysis characterized by clearly defined behavior patterns and shared symbols and values. There was general recognition that latent tensions and conflict existed in all societies, but symbols, myths, and religious practices were assumed to mask these tensions and oppositions. But three movements outside anthropology profoundly destabilized the concept of culture within it: Marxist scholarship (Nash 1981; Ortner 1984: 138–44; Roseberry 1988), literary studies,[7] and social history.[8]

At least three alternative ideas about what culture is have emerged in recent anthropological writings in response to these different movements. The first conceives of culture as a multiplicity of groups and voices (Marcus and Fischer 1986; Clifford and Marcus 1986); the second, as a battlefield on which competing groups struggle to define symbols and meanings (Fox 1985; Sider 1986; also see Rebel 1989); and the third, as a process inevitably involving contradiction, conflict, and accommodation and emphasizing actors' agency (Ortner 1989; Fowler 1987). For all their differences, these views each require that some account be taken of temporal phenomena as the sources of multiple social groups, beliefs, symbols, and actions.

This pluralistic conception of culture has been accompanied by a growing sensitivity to the relationship of culture to power and politics (what some call poetics and politics). Thus, many anthropologists attempt to understand how particular aspects of culture reflect, embody, reinforce, or challenge broader social and power relationships within a society. This increased sensitivity has taken diverse forms. For some anthropologists, collective action becomes a means of mediating between more persistent cultural beliefs or ideologies and rapidly changing political and economic structures (e.g., Nash 1979; Comaroff 1985; Fox 1985; Stoler 1985; Collier 1987; Schryer 1990; Taussig 1980, 1987). Other anthropologists, indebted to such figures as Clifford Geertz and Victor Turner, have focused less on power and politics and more on culture as a system of meaning—as codes, grammars, and structures of seeing embedded in rituals, discourse and rhetoric, and methods of socialization and social organization (e.g., Appadurai 1981; Behar 1986; Burkhart 1989; Dominguez 1986; Fowler 1987; Ortner 1989).

A third important development in anthropology has been a rejection of positivistic conceptions of human behavior in favor of the idea that all

human behavior is mediated through the mind and that human perceptions, attitudes, emotions, language, and cognition are therefore integral to
an understanding of human actions. "Data," whether ethnographic or textual, are viewed no longer as reservoirs of fact but increasingly as texts from
which to decipher unstated but culturally fundamental assumptions.

A fourth development lies in the widespread recognition that virtually
no group of people, no matter how pristine and unaffected by colonial or
neocolonial rule and economic processes it may seem, has escaped the impact of colonialism (Asad 1973; Wolf 1982; Roseberry 1989). World-system
theory has played a role in showing how societies have become increasingly
interrelated economically, and anthropologists have contributed detailed
studies of the "local" processes by which interrelationships have formed and
of their effects (e.g., Vincent 1982; Roseberry 1983; Verdery 1983; Stoler
1985; Stolcke 1988). It is widely acknowledged now that anthropological
research is done in a world shaped by power relations in which the societies
where anthropologists tend to work are economically and politically sub-
ordinated (Asad 1973; Thomas 1989a). Augé (1982: 80) points out that, for
anthropologists, "the moral and political problem of practice and the intellectual problem of object and of methods have always been closely linked."
Colonial heritages and contemporary politicoeconomic contexts provide
powerful motivations for more historically oriented ethnographic inquiries.

As anthropologists turn to analyzing how the many different groups
and societies they study have themselves constructed their own histories,
material processes, and social and cultural dynamics, they have also been
moved to examine how anthropologists and historians construct some
broadly shared basic concepts (O'Brien and Roseberry 1991). The practical
effect of each of these developments has been to encourage anthropologists to conceive of culture as a process. Instead of presenting static pictures of societies in an ethnographic present, anthropologists increasingly
have sought to describe a dynamically changing world in which groups
survive by making decisions, altering strategies, and changing, sometimes
consciously and sometimes as an unexpected consequence of previous decisions or actions. The heightened emphasis on history reflects the realization
that all of social and cultural life has historicity.

Thus, "history" began to show up much more openly in anthropological scholarship. One approach was to treat history as interpretive context; it
provided political, social, economic, and cultural background necessary to
understand "peoples" and/or their activities and beliefs (e.g., Guyer 1984;

Smith 1984; Moore 1986; Peña 1981; Warman 1980). At base, this is an updated and expanded version of history as preface. Another approach was to treat history as a developmental process, either a microhistorical process (focusing on life stages, family cycles, or emigration patterns; see the sections on family studies and gender) or a macrohistorical process (assessing the impact of colonialism or capitalist expansion on smaller-scale societies; see the sections on work and production, and politics and power). But the notion of developmental process contains implicit assumptions about intrinsic patterns of change, which troubles other anthropologists. Many have adopted a third approach, treating history as a process of social and cultural construction (Cohn 1987; Dirks 1987; Frykman and Lofgren 1987; Moore 1986; Thomas 1990).

But to say that history occupies an increasingly important place in the field of anthropology is not to say that historians and anthropologists conceive of or practice history in the same way (Medick 1987; Sheridan 1988a; cf. Cohn 1980). On the contrary, historians and anthropologists tend to hold fundamentally different ideas about what history is and how it should be done. *Anthropologists* often use history to understand emergent social or cultural formations, while *historians* tend to be preoccupied with the pastness of the past. This difference both distinguishes anthropological histories from historical histories and shapes them.

In the pages that follow, I examine the subjects that have attracted anthropologists to historical analysis as well as their historical practices. In general, anthropologists have addressed anthropologically distinctive topics—production, politics, religion and belief systems, ethnicity, family and community, gender, and history as a cultural category—and have drawn on historical literature, particularly in Africa, Latin America, and Europe, to write histories, though they do not necessarily address historiographical issues.

From the varied list of topics (by which I organize the summaries of historical anthropological research) it is possible to isolate a few encompassing themes. One is identity formation. Increasingly, anthropologists have asked how national and ethnic identifications are formed and transformed over time and how they acquire different meanings for distinct groups in a society. The tendency has been to see ethnicity, nationality, and race not as fixed classifications but as social and cultural constructs influenced by a broad range of legal and social forces. The processes of social confrontation, domination and subordination, and contradiction and opposition, anthropologists have argued, are particularly important in the shaping of group identity. One point that has received a great deal of emphasis is that political, ethnic, and tribal groups and castes are historical formations, often incorporating people of heterogeneous origins rather than descent groups writ large. Anthropologists have also examined how group and gender differences are both conceived and enacted.

A second very broad theme entails the reactions of peasant societies to colonialism, capitalist transformation, and state building. Anthropologists have often viewed non-Western people as agents as much as victims in this historical process. They have focused on marginalized groups' strategies of coping and resistance, in both domestic life and the world of work, in the face of assaults on land, labor, and religious practices.

Law has also emerged as an important site of conflict and negotiation. Anthropologists have examined shifts in the meaning of specific legal concepts that have occurred as new forms of production and social relations have emerged. Legal anthropologists have also examined the roles of law and the state in the process of establishing group hegemony. Finally, microdevelopmental processes have garnered the attention of anthropologists, who look specifically at the effects that a changing world economic system has on domestic organization in various parts of the world. These processsual interests emerge in many different kinds of historical anthropological research and writing.

Research Topics in Current Historical Anthropology

WORK AND PRODUCTION

This broad topic subsumes a number of interests; perhaps not surprisingly, the emergence or transformation of peasantries is a key focus. Many of these studies use specific organizational units (tribes, ethnic groups, communities, or regions) and look at how local political, economic, and/or cultural systems changed over time as they responded to a changing world economic system (Kahn 1980; Warman 1980; Peña 1981; Vincent 1982; Gewertz 1983; Guyer 1984, 1987; Stoler 1985; Ong 1987; Trouillot 1988; Holmes 1989; Carrier and Carrier 1989; Smith 1989; Gunn 1990; Hefner 1990). Other studies proceed from commodities or industries to examine the changing nature of peasantries or proletarians (Roseberry 1983; So 1986; Stolcke 1988), the changing forms of community organization or solidarity (Nash 1979, 1989; Wallace 1987), the changing uses and meanings of a specific commodity (Mintz 1985; Pomeroy 1988; Weiner and Schneider 1989), or the changing forms of organization and meanings attached to specific kinds of work (Kumar 1988; Sacks 1988; Hansen 1989; Comaroff and Comaroff 1987; Comaroff and Comaroff 1990). A few studies examine transformations in land tenure or use (Snyder 1981; Behar 1986; Rodman 1987; Sheridan 1988b).

Not surprisingly, most of these studies use some form of political econ-omy framework. Vincent (1982) and Roseberry (1983) stand out for the depth of their historical researches, as does Stoler (1985) for the way she consistently connects economic change to varying forms of worker politi-cal organization and expression. Both Holmes (1989) and Kumar (1988) emphasize the varying cultural forms that may accompany changing labor organization or class structure. Through an intensive cultural analysis of changing artisanal "identity," Kumar (ibid.: 189–97) shows how a particular set of ceremonies in Banaras has become specifically lower class.[9]

POLITICS, LAW, AND POWER

These works tend to be shaped by a single overarching framework less than the historical studies of work and production are. Some of them do use a Marxist or political economy framework to analyze the historical relations between states and their component peoples (Fitzpatrick 1980; Geschiere 1982; Bunker 1987).[10] Others look more at how political and legal relations and practices were and are constructed over time.

Both Dirks (1987) and Moore (1986) make this theme central to their discussions of how caste relations in India and "customary law" in Africa are not simply vestiges of precolonial periods but contructs whose changing forms were shaped by the particular political and legal organizational pat-terns that emerged under British colonialism.[11] Fabian (1986) shows how even indigenous languages and their forms of representation could become productions of colonial rule and its political and economic needs. Some of the essays in Starr and Collier's (1989) volume share this perspective. There is a group of studies that looks more at changing forms of political organi-zation or behavior over time, over a wide range of societal types (Fowler 1982; Leacock and Lee 1982; Kelly 1985; Friedrich 1970, 1986; Salomon 1986; Dillon 1990; Thomas 1990).

Just as state-local group relations and emergent politico-legal forms have received attention, so conflict has also been a significant theme in historical anthropological studies. Some of them look at forms of conflict or violence endemic to certain areas over time (Bricker 1981; Rosaldo 1980; Boehm 1984; Gordon and Meggitt 1985; Dennis 1987; O'Neill 1987; Greenberg 1989; Hoskins 1989); others emphasize the political repercussions of specific events. Whiteley (1988), for example, examines the hiving off of a small Hopi group, describing both the sociocultural context and historical events that led to the split and its implications. Schryer (1980) focuses on the role that the *rancheros* in the Sierra Alta de Hidalgo played in the Mexican Revolution and its effects on them.

Collier's (1987) study of the rise of socialism in one rural area in Spain mirrors this focus on event by examining the lasting impact of a series of political killings on the community of Los Olivos. But because he so carefully follows "a particular group as their fate unfolded in time and through space" (ibid.: 204) and so fully describes their history in a culturally rich analysis of changing political, economic, and kinship practices, his book is especially rewarding (also see Mintz 1982; Kertzer 1980).

Three other studies use historical data in essentially dramaturgical analyses of political processes. Geertz (1980) shows how the precolonial Balinese state dramatized the key themes of Balinese culture. Kertzer (1988) argues that political rituals create and reinforce political legitimacy, thereby enacting system solidarity. Taylor's (1979) book on the myths surrounding Eva Perón makes more room for alternative and conflicting "local" analyses of political symbols. Persistent or changing meanings of symbols, as well as practices associated with symbols of domains other than politics, have constituted an important theme in historical anthropological works.

RELIGION, SYMBOLS, AND BELIEF SYSTEMS

A number of studies of religion privilege the idea that core sets of cultural beliefs persist. It receives perhaps its most dramatic exposition in Ohnuki-Tierney's (1987) study of monkey symbolism in Japan. She argues that the monkey has been an enduring symbol of the Japanese self, although its uses and enactments as a symbol have changed (also see Ohnuki-Tierney 1990). James (1988), considering how the Uduk's understanding of their preagricultural past continues both to motivate their behavior and to furnish cultural knowledge, has written eloquently on persistence within a changing and politically charged interethnic context. Whereas James searched for evidence of past beliefs primarily in contemporary behavior and practices, Valeri (1985), in his massive semiotic study of precolonial Hawaiian sacrifice and religion, depends entirely on historical documentation. Like Appadurai (1981), he focuses on the interrelationship of the religious and political realms through the figure of the king. Other studies that make arguments for persistent patterns depend on both ethnographic and historical evidence (Carrithers 1983; Tambiah 1970, 1976, 1984, 1987; Babb 1986; Bloch 1986; Howard 1981; Stewart 1987). Sangren's (1987) careful history of a Taiwanese village, in regional perspective, rests on his examination of the spatial and temporal contexts of a core set of persistent religious ideas. By showing how certain key cultural oppositions can be used in struggles within social relationships, he offers an explanation of transformational potentials within this cultural system.

Other anthropologists emphasize change and transformation in religious beliefs and practices under colonial rule. Fox's (1985) study of Punjab Sikhs and the Third Sikh War—a careful treatment of the intersection of a regional colonial political economy, a distinct set of religious beliefs, and collective action—analyzes how an essentially religious movement became an urban reform movement that culminated in a powerful rural protest movement. Other works look less at the political economy of colonialism and more specifically at missionary activity. In his study of a Church Missionary Society mission among the Kaguru of Tanzania, Beidelman (1982) focuses on both the changing ideologies and worldviews of the missionaries and their everyday interactions with the Kaguru. Huber's (1988) book deals with missionaries in the Sepik region of New Guinea and Burkhart's (1989) with missionary activity among Nahua speakers in sixteenth-century central Mexico (also see Mandelbaum 1989; Fabian 1990; Kipp 1990).

Comaroff (1985) proceeds from a similar point (missionary activity), but she emphasizes the way in which the development of a syncretistic religion provided both a compelling belief system and a means of expression for political resistance (also see Comaroff and Comaroff 1986). Appadurai (1981), in a painstaking ethnohistorical and ethnographic study of the religious and legal history of a single South Indian temple, argues that the impact of colonial rule was weakest on beliefs about the temple as a cultural institution and strongest on the social organization of authority relations within and surrounding the temple. Ortner's (1989) study of the rise of celibate monasteries among the Sherpas of Nepal is based less on archival documentation and more on oral history. She asserts that the Sherpas

felt the effects of British colonialism in India and the Himalayas only indirectly and that these effects were primarily economic and positive. Her
study of Sherpa history through their religious history shows how religious
institutions gave rise to struggles over power, authority, and legitimacy as
the introduction of wage labor ameliorated some traditional inequities in
status.

How people at the bottom of hierarchies resist and manipulate systems of class or status differentiation is a theme that runs throughout these
discussions of religion and symbols. It is especially prominent in Taussig's
(1980) study of devil symbolism and in Sallnow's (1987) study of pilgrim-
ages and cults in the Cuzco area (also see Weller 1985; Seligmann 1987;
Bloch 1989). Both share a concern with the impact of colonial and postcolo-
nial economic and religious structures on indigenous beliefs and the ways
in which beliefs express cultural forms of resistance. Taussig (1987) looks
more at the cultural effects of forms of terror used to reinforce labor extraction in Colombia. His interpretive Marxism offers powerful readings of
indigenous responses to the dominant colonial and neocolonial frameworks
that have surrounded indigenous peoples. Another book that emphasizes
the poetics of a colonial experience is Fisher's (1985) primarily ethnographic study of madness as a cultural symbol and social phenomenon
in Barbados. While his book draws only slightly on historical or archival
sources, Fisher's exposition of Britain's colonizing practices advances a historical "master symbol" that shaped an important domain of culture and
beliefs (also see Laguerre 1987; Low 1988).

Nutini's (1984, 1988) highly detailed studies of the *todos santos* and
ritual kinship complexes among Nahua speakers and their descendants in
Tlaxcala, Mexico, examine the social, symbolic, and practical consequences
of these sets of beliefs and practices (also see Nutini and Bell 1980). Nutini
looks at these practices not as expressions of resistance but as expressions of
a long-term accommodation and syncretism of two powerful belief systems
that have long been meaningful. John Kelley and Martha Kaplan (1990)
have provided an overview of anthropological studies that place rituals in
historical context and point to the tension over how best to understand the
simultaneous capacity of rituals to express and reproduce structures and to
undermine and transform them as well.

Another set of studies that has relied heavily on symbolic analysis are those that examine identity and ethnicity as emergent processes and constructions. Such studies often use this kind of analysis to probe the meaning of ethnic identity in varying contexts. Several works examine groups with historically weak or problematic identities in complex societies or identities that have emerged only recently. Karen Blu's (1980) study of the Lumbee Indians of North Carolina sets a standard with its clear articulation of the basis of Lumbee identity—which, she argues, the Lumbee locate in certain behavioral rather than cultural traits—and with its careful ethnographic and historical research. Virginia Dominguez (1986) provides an equally interesting study of the social and racial classification "Creole" in Louisiana. She particularly emphasizes the changing ways in which law has been made and interpreted in the development of social classifications. She used creative historical research to track down clues to the changing definitions of this identity. Drake (1987) argues that cultural conceptions of blacks in the ancient world changed after the beginning of a capitalized slave labor system. He draws not only on historical literature but on a wide range of photographs of Egyptian artifacts. Art and music are increasingly viewed as symbols of emerging or changing patterns of ethnicity (Briggs 1980; Fenton 1987; Waterman 1990).

Other studies that look at emergent identities include Fardon's (1988) on the Chamba of West Africa and Friedlander's (1975) and Hawkin's (1984) on indigenous groups in different parts of Mesoamerica. The latter two books make an interesting pair. They both deconstruct the "Indian" identity in this part of the world, Friedlander through a class analysis and Hawkins through a symbolic analysis, in which he argues that the Indian identity in Guatemala derives not from a core set of cultural characteristics, indicative of a pluralistic society, but from a symbolic opposition of "Indian" to Spanish characteristics that brought forth a single symbolic system. Wasserstrom (1983), in a related study, provides a history of ethnic relations between Indians and Ladinos in Chiapas, Mexico. He argues that many supposed cultural characteristics of Mayan people and communities are historical productions of the changing political economy of the region (also see Noveck 1988).

Still other studies look at relatively clearly established groups within complex societies and probe the nature of and basis for maintaining these identities over time. Both di Leonardo (1984) and Yanagisako (1985) look at particular ethnic groups in American culture. While di Leonardo looks at changing family forms, economic patterns, and gender relations as keys to Italian Americans' adaptation to northern California, Yanagisako looks at changing folk models of kinship among Japanese Americans in Seattle. Wylie's (1987) examination of the cultural and economic history of the Faroe Islanders, inhabitants of a remote Danish dependency, emphasizes not their family system as the symbol of a historically changing identity but their historical consciousness of themselves over a long period of time. While Wylie uses oral histories, as di Leonardo and Yanagisako do, he also examines governmental records, newspapers, and folklore, in legends and songs, to explore the strengthening of the Faroese identity. Both Spicer (1980) and Castile and Kushner (1981) analyze persistent ethnic identities as well (also see Rasnake 1988; Tonkin et al. 1989).

Beckett (1987) examines the ethnic identity and historical consciousness of the Torres Strait Islanders as they were incorporated as a colony, first of Britain, then of Australia. The evolution of "welfare colonialism" and its influence on Islanders' social practices are key themes. Both Holzberg (1987) and Friedman (1988) look at Jewish communities and the distinctive ways in which they have defined their cultural identities in larger societies. Holzberg examines Jews in Jamaica; Friedman, Algerian Jewish immigrants in France. The latter's novel question—how a people who defined themselves as European in a colonial society, but who were treated as different when they migrated to France, are adjusting culturally—leads to an interesting anthropological example of both "studying up" and stateethnic group relations.

The last group of historical ethnographies dealing with ethnicity examine the relationship between ethnic groups and the state. They include Katherine Verdery's (1983) wide-ranging examination of a community of Transylvanian peasants in modern-day Romania, from the eighteenth century to the present; Hickey's (1982a, 1982b) two-volume ethnopolitical history of highland groups in Vietnam; and Schryer's (1990) study of ethnic and class relations in Huejutla, Mexico. Heiberg (1989) and Handler (1988) examine the development of Basque and Quebec nationalism, respectively. Gonzalez (1988) illustrates the recent emergence of the Garifuna's ethnic identity as they begin to relate to a modern nation-state, Belize, and to transnational economic contexts. Many of these studies, but especially the latter three, also touch upon the historical consciousness of these various groups.

HISTORY AS A CULTURAL CATEGORY

A whole series of anthropological histories moves the question of defining historical consciousness in cultural terms to the fore. None of them surpasses the superb collection of oral historical texts, paired with exegesis based on painstaking archival research, by Price (1983). These texts have a profound set of cultural meanings in Saramaka culture, but they also demonstrate the impressive long-term memories held by the historians of this society. This book deals with the period 1685–1762; in an equally rewarding sequel, Price (1990) has brought this history forward in time.

Rosaldo (1980) investigates the cultural bases for and expressions of history in contemporary Ilongot culture. Parmentier (1987) exhibits a similar interest in his study of historical consciousness and changing political organization in Belau. But he asserts, contrary to Rosaldo, that "history [is] a universal cultural category differentially manifest in societies, in which the relationship between past, present and future states of a society is expressed by signs in various media which are organized by locally valorized schemes of classification" (ibid.: 4–5). Parmentier's definition is a useful starting point for comparative investigations of culturally and historically varying forms of historical consciousness (also see Lederman 1986; Foster 1988). Borofsky (1987), in his study of how Pukapukan leaders strove to change local forms of social organization in the light of their own knowledge of earlier forms, shows how local indigenous histories can be drawn on by particular groups in a society. Borofsky also looks at changing forms of anthropological knowledge, and this interest is paralleled in Sullivan's (1989) study of archaeologists working among the Maya. Rappaport's (1990) excellent study of the changing forms and uses of historical knowledge among the Páez of highland Colombia draws on careful observation of the changing political structure that the Páez respond to and resist. In a very recent book, Bowen (1991) looks at an Indonesian ethnic group's changing political and historical concepts through discursive and popular culture.

Another long-term study of changing notions of historical consciousness is found in Fowler's (1987) excellent ethnohistorical and ethnographic discussion of Montana's Fort Belknap reservation, home to both Gros Ventres and Assiniboine. Fowler argues that the groups' different versions of their history together are rooted in somewhat different contact and economic histories and in the different ways each group has developed for dealing with the federal government. Hill (1988) offers a collection of essays that discuss history as an explicit "mode of social consciousness" among Amazonian and Andean peoples. All these books, in one way or another, raise the question of how particular societies have understood the events and processes that helped shape their contemporary formations (also see Bowen 1989; Hanson 1989; Keesing 1990; Peel 1984). They also counter the notion that non-Western peoples had neither history nor historical consciousness before colonial contact (Dening 1980; also see Brown 1988).[12]

FAMILY AND KINSHIP

The most numerous studies in this category are those that deal with family life over time from demographic and structural perspectives. Many of these works deal with European family structure and show the influence not only of Goody's (1976, 1983, 1990) monumental set of historical, ethnographic, and comparative works on the family (also see Goody et al. 1976) but of several prominent historians, especially Laslett (1972), Wrigley (1969), and Stone (1977). Both Kertzer (1984; also see Kertzer and Hogan 1988, 1989) and Brettell (1986) have contributed well-executed studies, based primarily on parish and other kinds of quantitative historical data, of areas not examined at length by historians. Kertzer, on Italy, and Brettell, on Portugal, bring to bear theories and concepts based on anthropological studies. Plakans (1984) and Segalen (1986) synthetically apply anthropological concerns to historical data on family and kinship. Douglass (1984) and Viazzo (1989) use historical data and anthropological frameworks to explore emigration and geographic mobility in European peasant communities.[13]

Two ethnographic and historical works that examine family as an evolving symbol of elite identity are Lomnitz and Perez-Lizaur's (1987) study of an elite Mexican family and McDonough's (1986) of elite families in Barcelona. McDonough argues that any study of elites must examine the family both as a structure for holding and distributing power and as a key symbol of elite domination of political, economic, and cultural life. The volume edited by Medick and Sabean (1984) looks more at the subjective experiences of family life over time in different places and privileges emotion over interest or structure. Both anthropologists and historians contributed to this volume, and its introduction makes a compelling argument for the need to "see how, within moving contexts, emotions are constantly mapped onto new terrains, and with the changes of position, reorder and restructure experience and meaning" (ibid.: 4).

Many of the books on this topic also seek to illustrate subjective experience in a variety of temporally changing cultural contexts. Powers's (1986) rich study of Oglala women is based on extensive life history interviews she did in order to illuminate women's experiences and life cycles in pre- and post-reservation Oglala Sioux society. She argues that Oglala women were better able than men to adapt to the dominant white culture and are therefore the key to continuity and stability in contemporary reservation life. In her book about American farm women, Fink (1986) suggests that World War II and its aftermath had deleterious effects on women's productive work and experiences of community. The book draws not only on participant observation and oral histories but on a wide range of primary historical data as well, especially the records of agricultural extension agents and private family records, including photos and scrapbooks.

Lamphere's (1987) highly detailed study of Portuguese and other immigrant women offers vivid portraits about the changing economic contexts of women's work, along with their responses to it. She examines these questions within a political economy framework in order to trace "the transformation of the female labor force from one of working daughters to one dominated by working mothers" (ibid.: xiv). Lamphere's historical research, done with the help of assistants, encompasses large amounts of data on several different ethnic groups, and her ethnographic research, centered on her compelling account of her own experiences, shows the strategies of coping and resistance that women devised. Both Gailey (1987) and Silverblatt (1987) examine the changing nature of women's roles and authority relations in societies experiencing intensive colonial contact (also see Linnekin 1990). Stockard's (1989) study of "delayed transfer marriage" in South China makes use of a social structural and material approach. She emphasizes the place of this practice in the social structure of the area where it occurred in the nineteenth century and argues that it was strongly correlated with a specific form of silk production.[14]

COMMUNITY AND OTHER STUDIES

This final group of studies is organized around specific communities, regions, and ethnic or tribal groups. Behar's (1986) diachronic study of Santa María del Monte, Spain, emphasizes continuity over change. She argues that the past retains its power to shape current practices because both individual memories and collective traditions imbue a locally shaped history used by contemporary actors. Similarly, Olwig's (1985) long-term study of Afro-Caribbean culture on the island of St. John roots contemporary practices in a remembered and shared past which has shaped islanders' responses to tourism. Olwig places her diachronic discussion of family patterns in the larger context of cultural values that have shaped interpersonal relations. Her excellently researched book is unusual in its holistic approach to a Caribbean society. Another explicitly diachronic community study is Rosenberg's (1988) history and ethnography of Abreis in France. She uses a political economy framework and places the village in the historical context of an economically and politically modernizing France. Rosenberg argues that the peasants of Abreis have been long-term political actors, particularly in their use of courts and litigation.

Wallace (1978) has written a powerful synchronic description, based on anthropological concepts applied to a wide range of historical data, of the cotton-manufacturing town of Rockdale, in southeastern Pennsylvania. While he argues that his very detailed and particularistic study brings data to bear on "a general theory of paradigmatic processes in cultural change" (ibid.: xvi), the book speaks more to a historiographical question: why American workers did not engage in more radical forms of protest during the early to mid-nineteenth century. Wallace argues implicitly that the answer to this question lies in the story of individuals who, across class divides, shared a powerful hegemonic belief system that he calls "Christian industrialism." He also shows an interest in exploring written texts as a source for cultural anthropology (also see Bock 1984) and explicitly raises the issue of the utility of a narrative framework (Wallace 1978: xv–xvi).

Still other studies examine distinctive geocultural regions from an ethnographic and historical perspective. All of them are edited volumes that include chapters by both anthropologists and historians on a wide range of topics, held together principally by their common geographic focus. Kottak et al.'s (1986) collection of papers on Madagascar and Donham and James's (1986) volume on the hinterlands of Ethiopia deal with regions that are not anthropologically well known. Kopytoff (1987) examines a series of interstitial sub-Saharan societies in order to determine how social boundaries are manipulated and political identities constructed. These societies are seen as historical formations instead of macrodescent groups. Murra et al. (1986) include essays covering a wide array of anthropological and historical approaches to Andean ethnic and political groupings. MacLeod and Wasserstrom (1983) have treated southeastern Mesoamerica similarly. In a very geographically focused volume, Smith (1990) and her fellow authors discuss the history of Indian-state relations in Guatemala during the nineteenth and twentieth centuries.

The last studies in this category are histories of ethnic groups in which past events are used to explain patterns of internal stratification and/or external differentiation. Evans-Pritchard's (1971) path-breaking study of the Azande foreshadows several other studies that use history, conceptualized as short-term events or long-term processes, to explain current diversity. Eades (1980), drawing on ethnography and extensive readings of secondary sources, argues that Yoruba diversity must be seen as a historical product. Kottak (1980) uses history, especially of Merina and later French domination, as a context in which to place his ethnography of three Betsileo communities on the island of Madagascar. He argues that community differences relate more to differential access to strategic resources but uses historical evidence to delineate these differences over time. Walker (1986), updating Rivers's (1906) Toda ethnography, examines the impact of British colonialism on this South Asian tribal people.

Four tribal histories of native Americans that use explicitly chronological frameworks integrate information on distinctive practices, beliefs, or forms of sociopolitical organization that contextualize tribal actions and responses to historical events and processes imposed upon them. Knack and Stewart (1984) particularly stress the interethnic framework. Bailey and Bailey (1986), on the Navajo, and Bunte and Franklin (1987), on the Southern Paiute, emphasize changes within each society and their repercussions. Nelson (1988) emphasizes the changing responses of a little-studied tribe, the Hupa of California, to their contact history and relations with the federal government. These books, along with Officer's (1987) and Sheridan's (1986) studies of Hispanic Arizona, illustrate the interest of anthropological ethnohistorians in political histories richly informed by cultural concerns.[15]

Critical Issues in Historical Anthropology

In their discussions of rather traditional anthropological concerns (among them politics, economic organization, religion, and family), historical anthropologists have pursued a number of themes, including, as noted above, the transformation of peasant societies, the construction of ethnic identity and community, and changing legal and religious concepts and practices. I move now to a critical overview of the meaning of this outpouring of historical anthropology.

First, we need to consider historical practices. While anthropologists have shown a dramatically increased interest in diachronic and processual analysis, they have tended to remain uncritical in their use of historical sources, primary or secondary. While some books have introductions or appendixes that contain model discussions and evaluations of sources (e.g., Hansen 1989; Kumar 1988; Roseberry 1983), some otherwise excellent studies do not. The reader is often left with very specific questions about the sources: What does a document or book include, and what is left out? What was the social position of its author? Why was it written, that is, whom was its author trying to persuade, and how did that purpose shape the information in it? When anthropologists use secondary sources, most often written by historians, to create historical context, they generally ignore the historiographical debates addressed and historians' positions within those debates.[16]

Because anthropologists often work on societies that were not themselves literate and whose often sparse written historical records may begin with some type of colonial contact, these questions assume special importance. Even for places such as the Andes or central Mexico, for which colonial sources are not only abundant but often, as in the case of central Mexico, in native languages (Kellogg 1986), historical reconstructions are partially shaped by the conditions under which such texts were produced (Gillespie 1989). When anthropologists rely on the writings of European observers about colonized or soon-to-be-colonized peoples, they need to consider what kinds of attitudes shaped their observations, how great their linguistic abilities were, and how native responses may have shaped Europeans' perceptions.

While anthropologists do not always convey a critical perspective on their written sources, they often make rich use of oral histories and anthropologically unconventional written sources (also see Vansina 1965, 1985).

Price (1983) offers a model of critical scholarship by scrutinizing oral histories in the light of written historical documents, and vice versa. Similarly, Gewertz (1983) provides interpretive context for the oral accounts of Chambri informants through the unpublished fieldnotes of Margaret Mead and Reo Fortune and through colonial administrative and missionary reports (also see Gewertz and Schieffelin 1985). In addition to incorporating oral histories into their works, anthropologists have located unusual types of information in such sources as cookbooks (to illustrate the growing English working-class taste for sugar [Mintz 1985; also see Goody 1982; Appadurai 1988]), cemetery plans (to trace changes in social hierarchy in Barcelona [McDonough 1986]), and police station records (to describe festivals and popular culture in Banaras [Kumar 1988]).

Apart from influencing research practices by providing new methods and sources and new ways of thinking about culture and social action, history also gives anthropologists a chronological framework in which to order and present written material. In some cases, they rely heavily on a tripartite periodization, generally consisting of precolonial, colonial, and contemporary stages (e.g., Guyer 1984; Moore 1986; Warman 1980). In other cases, they have tended to emphasize an incremental chronological progression of events (e.g., Knack and Stewart 1984; Ortner 1989). In either case, however, history suggests useful textual strategies (also see Taussig 1989). Writers can also use history to make systematic comparisons over time instead of across cultures. As a textual strategy, it also offers a way of discussing the roles of specific individuals or groups in the process of social change.

This marked turn toward history bridges the great divide in anthropology between those who think of themselves as political economists and those who view themselves as culturalists (Fox 1985: 186–89; Roseberry 1989; Ortner 1989: 198; also see Comaroff 1982). Whatever their other differences, Marxists and interpretive anthropologists agree on the importance of historical process to anthropological understandings. The often pluralistic, agent-centered, politically contextualized approach of many recent ethnographies would not be possible without this grounding in historical events and processes. But this consensus about the importance of history masks certain underlying tensions having to do with concepts central to this body of literature: time, colonialism, and structure and agency.

One tension has to do with how to situate contemporary social processes in time, in other words, with how or whether to use the "ethnographic present." Ever since Fabian's (1983) critique of this concept as a trope that conceals more than it reveals, locating ethnography in time has become problematized (cf. Hastrup 1990; also see Moore 1987). Most writers opt to use it and state very carefully from what time period the material dates. At least one study (Carrier and Carrier 1989) situates its ethnography in time by using the "ethnographic past." Its authors argue that this device "lends an air of historical specificity, inevitably suggesting that what is described is rooted in a particular period and may have been different before that period or may become different afterwards" (ibid.: xiii). Their attempt to convey contingency is interesting but also troublesome: it implies to the reader that all of these practices will come to an end, when how they persist or change over time is precisely the issue of interest.

A second tension lies in the way colonialism as a structure is addressed in this literature. Colonialism and colonial governments are often reified, but some anthropologists have begun to study colonizers and colonial policies and structures in the way that they have addressed the colonized (Asad 1973; Dening 1980; Beidelman 1982; Cooper and Stoler 1989; Stoler 1989). What has not been done is to look at colonialism in a more comparative perspective across space and time. We need to ask broader analytical questions about types of colonial intervention, about the types of people and societies they were aimed at, and about the kinds of effects they produced. Thomas (1989a: 122) suggests that

> satisfactory analysis would depend on treating, for example, metropolitan intrusions into tribal territory as a structured process like that of the indigenous system, and it would be unwise to pretend that such analysis would be easy. However, this is an especially important area for investigation, because it bears more directly upon contemporary tribal and third-world problems than many issues which are currently more central to anthropological discussion.

Two recent books attempt to do this in greater detail. One, also by Nicholas Thomas (1991), examines theories of exchange, especially those of Mauss but also of many others writing on Melanesia and Polynesia. Assuming that patterns of exchange are both historically and culturally shaped, Thomas argues that colonialism and colonial relations provided a significant and novel context in which exchange occurred. The George Stocking edited volume, *Colonial Situations* (1991), emphasizes the colonial contexts of the production of anthropological knowledge from the late nineteenth century on. However, unless it is applied to comparative study, *no* analytical approach to colonialism will tell us much about it as a process.

A third tension opposes structure, on the one hand, to agency and event, on the other. From Sherry Ortner to Eric Wolf, a wide range of anthropologists place emphasis on the role of people as individual and collective actors who actively respond to social forces and as agents who shape the impact of those forces (Karp 1986; Asad 1987; Thomas 1989b). Yet anthropological histories overwhelmingly emphasize the role of structures, whether Sahlins's (1985: xiv, 125) "structure of the conjuncture" or Wolf's (1982: 77–100) "modes of production."

While Sahlins and Wolf diverge theoretically, because they disagree on what constitutes the shaping structures and how they operate, they hold in common notions of strong structures that overpower events or traditions. Anthropological histories take ironic attitudes toward agency and ambivalent attitudes toward events because they are almost always encapsulated in or explained by some deeper set of structures. Agency, however, is difficult to sustain as an analytical concept because of the power of global economic processes to reshape local economic organizations and political processes (Friedman 1989). Events continually creep back into these histories because there *are* events that do provoke fundamental changes (also see Fogelson 1989). Events are also useful for narrative or textual reasons. They bring change, and they illustrate structural forces at work (e.g., Sahlins 1981).

Moore (1986: 12) argues that "the hybrid historical/ethnographic perspective is a methodological advance. It serves as a means of overcoming the inevitable sociological and temporal myopia of the fieldworker or the villager, while simultaneously exploiting the detailed information about behavior and ideas to which only fieldwork can give access." It is impossible to read this body of work without being impressed by the seriousness with which anthropologists have gone about the task of situating their studies in time. The historicizing of anthropology may claim at least three significant achievements: it has deconstructed traditional anthropological categories, such as tribe, ethnic group, and kinship; it has demonstrated the importance of time in the formation of ethnographic categories; and it has shown far greater sensitivity toward the means by which indigenous peoples construct their own histories.

But this historical turn also reflects a general movement in anthropology away from theory and toward highly particularistic studies. One striking characteristic of recent historically informed anthropological scholarship is that scarcely a single book (Wolf 1982 notwithstanding) is comparative in any meaningful sense. This scholarship neglects to ask why all these historical understandings are important in theoretical terms, or whether it is possible to produce an authoritative history rather than simply a multiplicity of histories.

Notes

My greatest debt in writing this article is to my husband, Steven Mintz. We had many discussions and debates which helped me clarify certain points, but he holds no responsibility for those points on which I retain my own opinions. Elizabeth Brumfiel offered a detailed critique from which I greatly benefited even though I could not incorporate all her suggestions. Shepard Krech III kindly shared his then essay-in-progress which in several ways overlaps with mine. I both learned from and enjoyed our conversations about how to manage an unmanageable topic. I also thank my research assistant, Erika Forbes, for all her work and help. The financial support of the Bunting Institute and the NEH and the John Carter Brown Library made this work possible; special thanks go to the Bunting Institute and its director, Florence Ladd, for a grant to help pay for an assistant. The reference and circulation staffs at Tozzer and Widener Libraries (Harvard) and Rockefeller Library (Brown) were all helpful. The circulation staff at Rockefeller Library and the inter-library loan staff at the M.D. Anderson Library, University of Houston, deserve special thanks for tracking down materials in a short amount of time; their efforts are deeply appreciated.

   1   It is appropriate to delineate not only what I cover in this essay but what I do not cover. First, I concentrate on anthropological literature, primarily books in English. Over the last several years, the journal literature has become voluminous. Interested readers will find many relevant articles especially in the journals *American Ethnologist, Comparative Studies in Society and History, Critique of Anthropology, Dialectical Anthropology, Ethnohistory,* and *History and Anthropology.* I include works by anthropologists who would identify themselves as cultural anthropologists and ethnohistorians because both write historical anthropologies that are not necessarily fundamentally different. Because the literature of "historical anthropology" is so large, I do not include works of historical archaeology, although many of them respond to the shifts in anthropological thinking discussed in this article. Other topics that I do not address include the history *of* anthropology, modernization and development, and most historical work (i.e., work by historians) that uses anthropology. I aim for worldwide coverage, though some areas are covered sparsely or not at all. Whereas in the New World historical anthropology has often been written

by ethnohistorians, elsewhere cultural anthropologists have become increasingly interested in historical issues. I try in places to juxtapose literature on New World populations (many of them native in origin) with literature on other areas where similar themes are explored.

2 Standard statements on anthropology and history include Evans-Pritchard 1962; Fortes 1949; Kroeber 1935, 1963; Lévi-Strauss 1963; Lewis 1968; and Macfarlane 1970 (also see Macfarlane et al. 1977). Other writings that deal with this topic but are not cited as often include Cunnison 1951; Geertz 1965; Hultkranz 1967; Langness 1965; Lowie 1917; Obeyesekere 1967; Riley and Taylor 1967; Sapir 1949; Schapera 1962; Silverman 1979; Smith 1960, 1962; and Sturtevant 1966. An excellent survey of historical approaches in anthropology is Hudson 1973. Shepard Krech III (forthcoming) has also surveyed historical approaches in anthropology and ethnohistory.

3 Useful histories of the concept of cultural evolution and critiques of its applications include Bock 1956, Hodgen 1974, Nisbet 1969, and Stocking 1968. Also see Thomas 1989a for an insightful discussion of how evolutionary ideas continue to underlie some recent historical anthropological studies.

4 I have in mind some of Robert Redfield's (1930, 1953) writings. His ethnography of Tepoztlan is filled with discussions of customs that are pre-Hispanic and customs that are both European and "contemporary." This contrast between past and present also animates his *Primitive World and Its Transformations,* and a whole set of Mesoamerican ethnographies is organized by it (e.g., Parsons 1936; Madsen 1960).

5 Some examples of history as data bank would include Lévi-Strauss's (1973, 1975, 1978) work on myth, many of Jack Goody's (1968, 1976, 1983, 1986, 1987, 1990) writings on literacy and the family, and Victor Turner's (1969) later writings both on structure and antistructure and on pilgrimage (also see Turner and Turner 1978). Recent examples include Tedlock 1983 and Kertzer 1988.

6 Sherry Ortner (1984: 144–54, 158) has argued that "practice theory" was the resolution. A new book of essays by John L. and Jean Comaroff (1992) attempts to imagine concretely what a historical ethnography should look like, see especially the title essay, "Ethnography and the historical imagination."

7 Works such as Burke 1966; Derrida 1976, 1978; Jameson 1972, 1981; Rorty 1979; and Said 1979 suggested both that no culture could be reduced to a single voice and that no account could authoritatively reproduce that single voice.

8 Because social history took as its subjects previously neglected groups, including ethnic and racial minorities, workers, and women, it immediately resonated with anthropology's primary focus on non-Western peoples. Social history also focused on aspects of behavior previously neglected by historians: family life, sexuality, emotions, crime, and popular culture. Its concentration on the material bases of existence, demography, geography, and economics, for example, and on social structure and relations also was relevant for anthropology. Basic social history texts that influenced anthropologists include Thompson 1963, Stone 1977, and Gutman 1976a, 1976b.

9   Other studies that deal with changing economies include Brettell 1986; Bunker 1987; Fink 1986; Fox 1985; Kertzer 1984, 1989; Lamphere 1987; Smith 1984; Taussig 1980; Wasserstrom 1983; and Wolf 1982.

10   Also see Wilkinson 1987 for an interesting discussion of American Indian tribes and their changing legal relationships with the federal government.

11   Also see Sider 1986 and Hobsbawm and Ranger 1983 for a Marxist deconstruction of the whole category of "tradition."

12   There are several excellent recent studies of time as a cultural category. Apart from Fabian's (1983) brilliant critique of the use of the "ethnographic present" to suppress historical analyses in ethnographic writings, both Tedlock (1982) and Munn (1986) have written rich ethnographic studies of temporal concepts among indigenous peoples in Guatemala and Papua New Guinea.

13   For a discussion of these themes in a New World context, see Alvarez 1987. Other books that give analyses of changing domestic organization are Fink 1986, Guyer 1984, Lamphere 1987, Olwig 1985, Stockard 1989, and Stolcke 1988.

14   Other monographs that discuss gender in some detail include Brettell 1986, Guyer 1984, Gewertz 1983, Hansen 1989, Lomnitz and Perez-Lizaur 1987, Ong 1987, Sacks 1988, di Leonardo 1984, Stolcke 1988, Stoler 1985, and Yanagisako 1985.

15   There are also a great many ethnic histories of indigenous groups in Latin America, written primarily by anthropologically trained ethnohistorians. Among the best of them are Carmack 1981; Chance 1978, 1989; Hemming 1978, 1987; Jones 1989; Spores 1967, 1984; and Zuidema 1990.

16   Some useful discussions of historical methods include Axtell 1979, Breen 1989, Carmack 1972, Henige 1982, Pitt 1972, Sturtevant 1966, and Trigger 1982. On the topic of historical texts and histories as productions, see Clifford 1988 and Tompkins 1986.

References

Alvarez, R. (1987) *Familia: Migration and Adaptation in Baja and Alta California, 1800–1975.* Berkeley and Los Angeles: University of California Press.

Appadurai, A. (1981) *Worship and Conflict under Colonial Rule: A South Indian Case.* Cambridge: Cambridge University Press.

——— (1988) "How to make a national cuisine: Cookbooks in contemporary India." *Comparative Studies in Society and History* 30: 3–24.

Asad, T. (1973) *Anthropology and the Colonial Encounter.* New York: Humanities.

——— (1987) "Are there histories of peoples without Europe?" *Comparative Studies in Society and History* 29: 594–607.

Augé, M. (1982) *The Anthropological Circle: Symbol, Function, History,* translated by M. Thom. Cambridge: Cambridge University Press.

Axtell, J. (1979) "Ethnohistory: An historian's viewpoint." *Ethnohistory* 26: 1–13.

Babb, L. (1986) *Redemptive Encounters: Three Modern Styles in the Hindu Tradition.* Berkeley and Los Angeles: University of California Press.

Bailey, G., and R. Bailey (1986) *A History of the Navajos: The Reservation Years.* Seattle: University of Washington Press.

Barnes, J. A. (1951) "The perception of history in a plural society: A study of an Ngoni group in northern Rhodesia." *Human Relations* 4: 295–303.

Beckett, J. (1987) *Torres Strait Islanders: Custom and Colonialism.* Cambridge: Cambridge University Press.

Behar, R. (1986) *Santa María del Monte: The Presence of the Past in a Spanish Village.* Princeton, NJ: Princeton University Press.

Beidelman, T. (1982) *Colonial Evangelism: A Socio-Historical Study of an East African Mission at the Grassroots.* Bloomington: Indiana University Press.

Bloch, M. (1986) *From Blessing to Violence: History and Ideology in the Circumcision Ritual of the Merina of Madagascar.* Cambridge: Cambridge University Press.

——— (1989) *Ritual, History, and Power: Selected Papers in Anthropology.* London: Athlone.

Blu, K. (1980) *The Lumbee Problem: The Making of an American Indian People.* Cambridge: Cambridge University Press.

Bock, K. (1956) *The Acceptance of Histories: Toward a Perspective for Social Science.* Berkeley and Los Angeles: University of California Press.

Bock, P. (1984) *Shakespeare and Elizabethan Culture: An Anthropological View.* New York: Schocken.

Boehm, C. (1984) *Blood Revenge: The Anthropology of Feuding in Montenegro and Other Tribal Societies.* Lawrence: University Press of Kansas.

Borofsky, R. (1987) *Making History: Pukapukan and Anthropological Constructions of Knowledge.* Cambridge: Cambridge University Press.

Bowen, J. R. (1989) "Narrative form and political incorporation: Changing uses of history in Acch, Indonesia." *Comparative Studies in Society and History* 31: 671–93.

——— (1991) *Sumatran Politics and Poetics: Gayo History, 1900–1989.* New Haven, CT: Yale University Press.

Breen, T. H. (1989) *Imagining the Past: East Hampton Histories.* Reading, MA: Addison-Wesley.

Brettell, C. (1986) *Men Who Migrate, Women Who Wait: Population and History in a Portuguese Parish.* Princeton, NJ: Princeton University Press.

Bricker, V. (1981) *The Indian Christ, the Indian King: The Historical Substrate of Maya Myth and Ritual.* Austin: University of Texas Press.

Briggs, C. (1980) *The Wood Carvers of Córdova, New Mexico: Social Dimensions of an Artistic "Revival."* Knoxville: University of Tennessee Press.

Brown, D. (1988) *Hierarchy, History, and Human Nature: The Social Origins of Historical Consciousness.* Tucson: University of Arizona Press.

Bunker, S. (1987) *Peasants against the State: The Politics of Market Control in Bugisu, Uganda, 1900–1983.* Urbana: University of Illinois Press.

Bunte, P., and R. Franklin (1987) *From the Sands to the Mountain: Change and Persis-*

tence in a Southern Paiute Community. Lincoln: University of Nebraska Press.

Burke, K. (1966) *Language as Symbolic Action: Essays on Life, Literature, and Method.* Berkeley and Los Angeles: University of California Press.

Burkhart, L. (1989) *The Slippery Earth: Nahua-Christian Moral Dialogue in Sixteenth-Century Mexico.* Tucson: University of Arizona Press.

Carmack, R. (1972) "Ethnohistory: A review of its development, definitions, methods, and aims," in B. Siegel, A. Beals, and S. Tyler (eds.) *Annual Review of Anthropology,* no. 1. Palo Alto, CA: Annual Reviews: 227–46.

——— (1981) *The Quiché Mayas of Utatlán: The Evolution of a Highland Kingdom.* Norman: University of Oklahoma Press.

Carrier, J., and A. Carrier (1989) *Wage, Trade, and Exchange in Melanesia: A Manus Society in the Modern State.* Berkeley and Los Angeles: University of California Press.

Carrithers, M. (1983) *The Forest Monks of Sri Lanka: An Anthropological and Historical Study.* Delhi: Oxford University Press.

Castile, G., and G. Kushner, eds. (1981) *Persistent Peoples: Cultural Enclaves in Perspective.* Tucson: University of Arizona Press.

Chance, J. (1978) *Race and Class in Colonial Oaxaca.* Stanford, CA: Stanford University Press.

——— (1989) *Conquest of the Sierra: Spaniards and Indians in Colonial Oaxaca.* Norman: University of Oklahoma Press.

Clifford, J. (1988) "Identity in Mashpee," in *The Predicament of Culture: Twentieth-Century Ethnography, Literature, and Art, by J. Clifford.* Cambridge, MA: Harvard University Press: 277–346.

———, and G. Marcus, eds. (1986) *Writing Culture: The Poetics and Politics of Ethnography.* Berkeley and Los Angeles: University of California Press.

Cohn, B. (1980) "History and anthropology: The state of play." *Comparative Studies in Society and History* 22: 198–221.

——— (1987) *An Anthropologist among the Historians and Other Essays.* Delhi: Oxford University Press.

Collier, G. (1987) *Socialists of Rural Andalusia: Unacknowledged Revolutionaries of the Second Republic.* Stanford, CA: Stanford University Press.

Comaroff, J. (1985) *Body of Power, Spirit of Resistance: The Culture and History of a South African People.* Chicago: University of Chicago Press.

——— (1990) "Goodly beasts, beastly goods: Cattle and commodities in a South African context." *American Ethnologist* 17: 195–216.

———, and J. L. Comaroff (1986) "Christianity and colonialism in South Africa," *American Ethnologist* 13: 1–22.

Comaroff, J., and J. L. Comaroff (1991) *Of Revelation and Revolution: Christianity, Colonialism and Consciousness in South Africa.* Chicago: University of Chicago Press.

Comaroff, J. L. (1982) "Dialectical systems, history, and anthropology: Units of study and questions of theory." *Journal of Southern African Studies* 8: 143–72.

———, and J. Comaroff (1987) "The madman and the migrant: Work and labor in the historical consciousness of a South African people." *American Ethnologist* 14: 191–209.

————, and J. Comaroff (1992) *Ethnography and the Historical Imagination.* Boulder, CO: Westview Press.

Cooper, F., and A. L. Stoler (1989) "Tensions of empire" (special section). *American Ethnologist* 16: 609–765.

Cunnison, I. (1951) *History on the Luapula: An Essay on the Historical Notions of a Central African Tribe.* Cape Town: Rhodes-Livingston Institute; New York: Oxford University Press.

De Laguna, F. (1960) *The Story of a Tlingit Community: A Problem in the Relationship between Archaeological, Ethnological, and Historical Methods.* Bureau of American Ethnology Bulletin, no. 172. Washington, DC: U.S. Government Printing Office.

Dening, G. (1980) *Islands and Beaches: Discourse on a Silent Land, Marquesas, 1774–1880.* Honolulu: University of Hawaii Press.

Dennis, P. (1987) *Intervillage Conflict in Oaxaca.* New Brunswick, NJ: Rutgers University Press.

Derrida, J. (1976) *Of Grammatology,* translated by G. Spivak. Baltimore, MD: Johns Hopkins University Press.

———— (1978) *Writing and Difference,* translated by A. Bass. Chicago: University of Chicago Press.

di Leonardo, M. (1984) *The Varieties of Ethnic Experience: Kinship, Class, and Gender among California Italian-Americans.* Ithaca, NY: Cornell University Press.

Dillon, R. (1990) *Ranking and Resistance: A Precolonial Cameroonian Polity in Regional Perspective.* Stanford, CA: Stanford University Press.

Dirks, N. (1987) *The Hollow Crown: Ethnohistory of an Indian Kingdom.* Cambridge: Cambridge University Press.

Dominguez, V. (1986) *White by Definition: Social Classification in Creole Louisiana.* New Brunswick, NJ: Rutgers University Press.

Donham, D., and W. James, eds. (1986) *The Southern Marches of Imperial Ethiopia: Essays in History and Social Anthropology.* Cambridge: Cambridge University Press.

Douglass, W. (1984) *Emigration in a South Italian Town: An Anthropological History.* New Brunswick, NJ: Rutgers University Press.

Drake, S. C. J. (1987) *Black Folk Here and There: An Essay in History and Anthropology.* Los Angeles: Center for Afro-American Studies/University of California Press.

Eades, J. S. (1980) *The Yoruba Today.* Cambridge: Cambridge University Press.

Eggan, F. (1966) *The American Indian: Perspectives for the Study of Social Change.* Chicago: Aldine.

Evans-Pritchard, E. E. (1949) *The Sanusi of Cyrenaica.* Oxford: Clarendon.

———— (1962) "Anthropology and history," in *Essays in Social Anthropology,* by E. E. Evans-Pritchard. London: Faber and Faber: 46–65.

———— (1971) *The Azande: History and Political Institutions.* Oxford: Clarendon.

Fabian, J. (1983) *Time and the Other: How Anthropology Makes Its Object*. New York: Columbia University Press.

—— (1986) *Language and Colonial Power: The Appropriation of Swahili in the Former Belgian Congo, 1880–1938*. Cambridge: Cambridge University Press.

—— (1990) "Religious and secular colonization: Common ground." *History and Anthropology* 4: 339–55.

Fardon, R. (1988) *Raiders and Refugees: Trends in Chamba Political Development, 1750–1950*. Washington, DC: Smithsonian Institution Press.

Fenton, W. (1987) *The False Faces of the Iroquois*. Norman: University of Oklahoma Press.

Fink, D. (1986) *Open Country Iowa: Rural Women, Tradition, and Change*. Albany: State University of New York Press.

Fisher, L. (1985) *Colonial Madness: Mental Health in the Barbadian Social Order*. New Brunswick, NJ: Rutgers University Press.

Fitzpatrick, P. (1980) *Law and State in Papua New Guinea*. London: Academic.

Fogelson, R. (1989) "The ethnohistory of events and non-events." *Ethnohistory* 36: 133–47.

Fortes, M. (1949) "Time and social structure: An Ashanti case study," in M. Fortes (ed.) *Social Structure: Studies Presented to A. R. Radcliffe-Brown*. Oxford: Clarendon: 54–84.

Foster, S. (1988) *The Past Is Another Country: Representation, Historical Consciousness, and Resistance in the Blue Ridge*. Berkeley and Los Angeles: University of California Press.

Fowler, L. (1982) *Arapahoe Politics, 1851–1978: Symbols in Crises of Authority*. Lincoln: University of Nebraska Press.

—— (1987) *Shared Symbols, Contested Meanings: Gros Ventre Culture and History, 1778–1984*. Ithaca, NY: Cornell University Press.

Fox, R. (1985) *Lions of the Punjab: Culture in the Making*. Berkeley and Los Angeles: University of California Press.

Freedman, M. (1958) *Lineage Organization in Southeastern China*. London School of Economics, Monographs on Social Anthropology, no. 18. London: Athlone.

Friedlander, J. (1975) *Being Indian in Hueyapan: A Study of Forced Identity in Contemporary Mexico*. New York: St. Martin's.

Friedman, E. (1988) *Colonialism and After: An Algerian Jewish Community*. South Hadley, MA: Bergin and Garvey.

Friedman, J. (1989) "No history is an island: A review essay." *Critique of Anthropology* 8: 7–39.

Friedrich, P. (1970) *Agrarian Revolt in a Mexican Village*. Englewood Cliffs, NJ: Prentice-Hall.

—— (1986) *The Princes of Naranja: An Essay in Anthrohistorical Methods*. Austin: University of Texas Press.

Frykman, J., and O. Lofgren (1987) *Culture Builders: A Historical Anthropology of Middle-Class Life,* translated by A. Crozier. New Brunswick, NJ: Rutgers University Press.

Gailey, C. (1987) *Kinship to Kingship: Gender Hierarchy and State Formation in the Tongan Islands*. Austin: University of Texas Press.

Geertz, C. (1965) *The Social History of an Indonesian Town*. Cambridge, MA: MIT Press.

―――― (1980) *Negara: The Theatre State in Nineteenth-Century Bali*. Princeton, NJ: Princeton University Press.

Geschiere, P. (1982) *Village Communities and the State: Changing Relations among the Maka of Southeastern Cameroon since the Colonial Conquest*. London: Kegan Paul.

Gewertz, D. (1983) *Sepik River Societies: A Historical Ethnography of the Chambri and Their Neighbors*. New Haven, CT: Yale University Press.

―――― , and E. Schieffelin, eds. (1985) *History and Ethnohistory in Papua New Guinea*. Sydney: University of Sydney Press.

Gillespie, S. (1989) *The Aztec Kings: The Construction of Rulership in Mexica History*. Tucson: University of Arizona Press.

Gonzalez, N. (1988) *Sojourners of the Caribbean: Ethnogenesis and Ethnohistory of the Garifuna*. Urbana: University of Illinois Press.

Goody, J. (1976) *Production and Reproduction: A Comparative Study of the Domestic Domain*. Cambridge: Cambridge University Press.

―――― (1982) *Cooking, Cuisine, and Class: A Study in Comparative Sociology*. Cambridge: Cambridge University Press.

―――― (1983) *The Development of the Family and Marriage in Europe*. Cambridge: Cambridge University Press.

―――― (1986) *The Logic of Writing and the Organization of the State*. Cambridge: Cambridge University Press.

―――― (1987) *The Interface between the Written and the Oral*. Cambridge: Cambridge University Press.

―――― (1990) *The Oriental, the Ancient, and the Primitive: Systems of Marriage and the Family in the Preindustrial Societies of Eurasia*. London: Cambridge University Press.

―――― , ed. (1958) *The Developmental Cycle in Domestic Groups*. Cambridge Papers in Social Anthropology, no. 1. Cambridge: Cambridge University Press.

―――― , ed. (1968) *Literacy in Traditional Societies*. Cambridge: Cambridge University Press.

―――― , J. Thirsk, and E. P. Thompson, eds. (1976) *Family and Inheritance: Rural Society in Western Europe, 1200–1800*. Cambridge: Cambridge University Press.

Gordon, R., and M. J. Meggitt (1985) *Law and Order in the New Guinea Highlands: Encounters with Enga*. Hanover, NH: University Press of New England.

Greenberg, J. B. (1989) *Blood Ties: Life and Violence in Rural Mexico*. Tucson: University of Arizona Press.

Gunn, G. C. (1990) *Rebellion in Laos: Peasant and Politics in a Colonial Backwater*. Boulder, CO: Westview.

Gutman, H. (1976a) *The Black Family in Slavery and Freedom, 1750–1925*. New York: Pantheon.

—— (1976b) *Work, Culture, and Society in Industrializing America: Essays in American Working-Class and Social History.* New York: Knopf.

Guyer, J. (1984) *Family and Farm in Southern Cameroon.* Boston: Boston University Press/African Studies Center.

——, ed. (1987) *Feeding African Cities: Studies in Regional Social History.* Bloomington: Indiana University Press; London: International African Institute.

Handler, R. (1988) *Nationalism and the Politics of Culture in Quebec.* Madison: University of Wisconsin Press.

Hansen, K. (1989) *Distant Companions: Servants and Employers in Zambia, 1900–1985.* Ithaca, NY: Cornell University Press.

Hanson, A. (1989) "The making of the Maori: Cultural invention and its logic." *American Anthropologist* 91: 890–902.

Hastrup, K. (1990) "The ethnographic present: A reinvention." *Cultural Anthropology* 5: 45–61.

Hawkins, J. (1984) *Inverse Images: The Meaning of Culture, Ethnicity, and Family in Post-Colonial Guatemala.* Albuquerque: University of New Mexico Press.

Hefner, R. (1990) *The Political Economy of Mountain Java: An Interpretive History.* Berkeley and Los Angeles: University of California Press.

Heiberg, M. (1989) *The Making of the Basque Nation.* Cambridge: Cambridge University Press.

Hemming, J. (1978) *Red Gold: The Conquest of the Brazilian Indians.* Cambridge, MA: Harvard University Press.

—— (1987) *Amazon Frontier: The Defeat of the Brazilian Indians.* Cambridge, MA: Harvard University Press.

Henige, D. (1982) *Oral Historiography.* London: Longman.

Hickey, G. (1982a) *Sons of the Mountains: Ethnohistory of the Vietnamese Central Highlands to 1954.* New Haven, CT: Yale University Press.

—— (1982b) *Free in the Forest: Ethnohistory of the Vietnamese Central Highlands, 1954–1976.* New Haven, CT: Yale University Press.

Hill, J., ed. (1988) *Rethinking History and Myth: Indigenous South American Perspectives on the Past.* Urbana: University of Illinois Press.

Hobsbawm, E., and T. Ranger, eds. (1983) *The Invention of Tradition.* Cambridge: Cambridge University Press.

Hodgen, M. (1974) *Anthropology, History, and Cultural Change.* Tucson: University of Arizona Press.

Holmes, D. (1989) *Cultural Disenchantments: Worker Peasantries in Northeast Italy.* Princeton, NJ: Princeton University Press.

Holzberg, C. (1987) *Minorities and Power in a Black Society: The Jewish Community of Jamaica.* Lanham, MD: North-South.

Hoskins, J. (1989) "On losing and getting a head: Warfare, exchange, and alliance in a changing Sumba, 1888–1988." *American Ethnologist* 16: 419–40.

Howard, J. (1981) *Shawnee! The Ceremonialism of a Native Indian Tribe and Its Cultural Background.* Athens: Ohio University Press.

Huber, M. T. (1988) *The Bishops' Progress: A Historical Ethnography of the Catholic Missionary Experience on the Sepik Frontier*. Washington, DC: Smithsonian Institution Press.

Hudson, C. (1973) "The historical approach in anthropology," in J. Honigmann (ed.) *Handbook of Social and Cultural Anthropology*. Chicago: Rand-McNally: 111–42.

Hultkranz, A. (1967) "Historical approaches in American ethnology: A research survey." *Ethnologia Europaea* 1: 96–116.

James, W. (1988) *The Listening Ebony: Moral Knowledge, Religion, and Power among the Uduk of Sudan*. Oxford: Clarendon; New York: Oxford University Press.

Jameson, F. (1972) *The Prison-House of Language: A Critical Account of Structuralism and Russian Formalism*. Princeton, NJ: Princeton University Press.

——— (1981) *The Political Unconscious: Narrative as a Socially Symbolic Act*. Ithaca, NY: Cornell University Press.

Jones, G. (1989) *Maya Resistance to Spanish Rule: Time and History on a Colonial Frontier*. Albuquerque: University of New Mexico Press.

Kahn, J. (1980) *Minangkabu Social Formations: Indonesian Peasants and World-Economy*. Cambridge: Cambridge University Press.

Karp, I. (1986) "Agency and social theory: A review of Anthony Giddens." *American Ethnologist* 13: 131–37.

Keesing, R. (1990) "Colonial history as contested ground: The Bell massacre in the Solomons." *History and Anthropology* 4: 279–301.

Kellogg, S. (1986) "Kinship and social organization in early colonial Tenochtitlan," in R. Spores (ed.) *Ethnohistory: Supplement to the Handbook of Middle American Indians*, vol. 4. Austin: University of Texas Press: 103–21.

Kelly, J., and M. Kaplan (1990) "History, Structure, and Ritual," in B. Siegel, A. Beals, and S. Tyler, (eds.), *Annual Review of Anthropology*, vol. 19. Palo Alto, CA: Annual Reviews: 119–50.

Kelly, R. (1985) *The Nuer Conquest: The Structure and Development of an Expansionist System*. Ann Arbor: University of Michigan Press.

Kertzer, D. (1980) *Comrades and Christians: Religion and Political Struggle in Communist Italy*. Cambridge: Cambridge University Press.

——— (1984) *Family Life in Central Italy, 1880–1910: Sharecropping, Wage Labor, and Coresidence*. New Brunswick, NJ: Rutgers University Press.

——— (1988) *Ritual, Politics, and Power*. New Haven, CT: Yale University Press.

——— (1989) *Family, Political Economy, and Demographic Change: The Transformation of Life in Casalecchio, Italy, 1861–1921*. Madison: University of Wisconsin Press.

———, and D. Hogan (1988) *Social Dimensions of Demographic Change: The Transformation of Life in Casalecchio, Italy, 1861–1921*. Madison: University of Wisconsin Press.

Kipp, R. (1990) *The Early Years of a Dutch Colonial Mission: The Karo Field.* Ann Arbor: University of Michigan Press.

Knack, M., and O. Stewart (1984) *As Long as the River Shall Run: An Ethnohistory of the Pyramid Lake Indian Reservation*. Berkeley and Los Angeles: University of California Press.

Kopytoff, I., ed. (1987) *The African Frontier: The Reproduction of Traditional African Societies*. Bloomington: Indiana University Press.

Kottak, C. (1980) *The Past in the Present: History, Ecology, and Cultural Variation in Highland Madagascar*. Ann Arbor: University of Michigan Press.

——— , J. Rakotoarisa, A. Southall, and P. Vérin, eds. (1986) *Madagascar: Society and History*. Durham, NC: Carolina Academic.

Krech, S., III (1991) "The state of ethnohistory," in B. Siegel, A. Beals, and S. Tyler, eds., *Annual Review of Anthropology*, vol. 20. Palo Alto, CA: Annual Reviews: 345–75.

Kroeber, A. (1935) "History and science in anthropology." *American Anthropologist* 37: 539–69.

——— (1963) *An Anthropologist Looks at History*. Berkeley and Los Angeles: University of California Press.

Kumar, N. (1988) *The Artisans of Banaras: Popular Culture and Identity, 1880–1986*. Princeton, NJ: Princeton University Press.

Laguerre, M. (1987) *Afro-Caribbean Folk Medicine*. South Hadley, MA: Bergin and Garvey.

Lamphere, L. (1987) *From Working Daughters to Working Mothers: Immigrant Women in a New England Industrial Community*. Ithaca, NY: Cornell University Press.

Langness, L. L. (1965) *The Life History in Anthropological Science*. New York: Holt, Rinehart and Winston.

Laslett, P., ed. (1972) *Household and Family in Past Time*. Cambridge: Cambridge University Press.

Leacock, E., and R. Lee, eds. (1982) *Politics and History in Band Societies*. Cambridge: Cambridge University Press.

Lederman, R. (1986) *What Gifts Engender: Social Relations and Politics in Mendi, Highland Papua New Guinea*. Cambridge: Cambridge University Press.

Lévi-Strauss, C. (1963) "Introduction: History and anthropology," in *Structural Anthropology*, translated by C. Jacobson and B. Grundfest Schoepf. New York: Basic: 1–27.

——— (1973) *From Honey to Ashes*, translated by J. Weightman and D. Weightman. New York: Harper and Row.

——— (1975) *The Raw and the Cooked*, translated by J. Weightman and D. Weightman. New York: Harper and Row.

——— (1978) *The Origin of Table Manners*, translated by J. Weightman and D. Weightman. New York: Harper and Row.

Lewis, I. M. (1968) *History and Social Anthropology*. London: Tavistock.

Linnekin, J. (1990) *Sacred Queens and Women of Consequence: Rank, Gender, and Colonialism in the Hawaiian Islands*. Ann Arbor: University of Michigan Press.

Lomnitz, L., and M. Perez-Lizaur (1987) *A Mexican Elite Family, 1820–1980: Kinship, Class, and Culture*. Princeton, NJ: Princeton University Press.

Low, S. (1988) "The medicalization of healing cults in Latin America." *American Ethnologist* 15: 136–54.

Lowie, R. (1917) "Oral tradition and history." *Journal of American Folklore* 30: 161–67.

McDonough, G. (1986) *Good Families of Barcelona: A Social History of Power in the Industrial Era*. Princeton, NJ: Princeton University Press.

Macfarlane, A. (1970) *The Family Life of Ralph Josselin, a Seventeenth-Century Clergyman: An Essay in Historical Anthropology*. Cambridge: Cambridge University Press.

——, S. Harrison, and C. Jardine (1977) *Reconstructing Historical Communities*. London: Cambridge University Press.

MacLeod, M., and R. Wasserstrom, eds. (1983) *Spaniards and Indians in Southeastern Mesoamerica: Essays on the History of Ethnic Relations*. Lincoln: University of Nebraska Press.

Madsen, W. (1960) *The Virgin's Children: Life in an Aztec Village Today*. Austin: University of Texas Press.

Mandelbaum, J. (1989) *The Missionary as a Cultural Interpreter*. New York: Peter Lang.

Marcus, G., and M. Fischer (1986) *Anthropology as Cultural Critique: An Experimental Moment in the Human Sciences*. Chicago: University of Chicago Press.

Medick, H. (1987) "'Missionaries in the row boat'? Ethnological ways of knowing as a challenge to social history." *Comparative Studies in Society and History* 29: 76–105.

——, and D. Sabean, eds. (1984) *Interest and Emotion: Essays on the Study of Family and Kinship*. Cambridge: Cambridge University Press; Paris: Editions de la Maison des Sciences de l'Homme.

Mintz, J. (1982) *The Anarchists of Casas Viejas*. Chicago: University of Chicago Press.

Mintz, S. (1985) *Sweetness and Power: The Place of Sugar in Modern History*. New York: Viking.

Moore, S. F. (1986) *Social Facts and Fabrications: "Customary" Law on Kilamanjaro, 1880–1980*. Cambridge: Cambridge University Press.

—— (1987) "Exploring the present: The theoretical dilemmas in processual ethnography." *American Ethnologist* 14: 727–36.

Munn, N. (1986) *The Fame of Gawa: A Symbolic Study of Value Transformation in a Massim (Papua New Guinea) Society*. Cambridge: Cambridge University Press.

Murra, J., N. Wachtel, and J. Revel, eds. (1986) *Anthropological History of Andean Polities*. Cambridge: Cambridge University Press; Paris: Editions de la Maison des Sciences de l'Homme.

Nash, J. (1979) *We Eat the Mines and the Mines Eat Us: Dependency and Exploitation in Bolivian Tin Mines*. New York: Columbia University Press.

—— (1981) "Ethnographic aspects of the world capitalist system," in B. Siegel, A. Beals, and S. Tyler (eds.) *Annual Review of Anthropology*, vol. 10. Palo Alto, CA: Annual Reviews: 393–423.

———— (1989) *From Tank Town to High Tech: The Clash of Community and Industrial Cycles*. Albany: State University of New York Press.

Nelson, B. (1988) *Our Home Forever: The Hupa Indians of Northern California*, edited by L. Bayer. Salt Lake City, UT: Howe Brothers.

Nisbet, R. (1969) *Social Change and History: Aspects of the Western Theory of Development*. New York: Oxford University Press.

Noveck, D. (1988) "Class, culture, and the Miskito Indians: A historical perspective." *Dialectical Anthropology* 13: 17–30.

Nutini, H. (1984) *Ritual Kinship: Ideological and Structural Integration of the Compadrazgo System in Rural Tlaxcala*, vol. 2. Princeton, NJ: Princeton University Press.

———— (1988) *Todos Santos in Rural Tlaxcala: A Syncretic, Expressive, and Symbolic Analysis of the Cult of the Dead*. Princeton, NJ: Princeton University Press.

————, and B. Bell (1980) *Ritual Kinship: The Structure and Historical Development of the Compadrazgo System in Rural Tlaxcala*, vol. 1. Princeton, NJ: Princeton University Press.

Obeyesekere, G. (1967) *Land Tenure in Village Ceylon: A Sociological and Historical Study*. Cambridge: Cambridge University Press.

O'Brien, J., and W. Roseberry, eds. (1991) *Golden Ages, Dark Ages: Imagining the Past in Anthropology and History*. Berkeley and Los Angeles: University of California Press.

Officer, J. (1987) *Hispanic Arizona, 1536–1856*. Tucson: University of Arizona Press.

Ohnuki-Tierney, E. (1987) *The Monkey as Mirror: Symbolic Transformations in Japanese History and Ritual*. Princeton, NJ: Princeton University Press.

————, ed. (1990) *Culture through Time: Anthropological Approaches*. Stanford: Stanford University Press.

Olwig, K. (1985) *Cultural Adaptation and Resistance on St. John: Three Centuries of Afro-Caribbean Life*. Gainesville: University Presses of Florida.

O'Neill, B. (1987) *Social Inequality in a Portuguese Hamlet: Land, Late Marriage, and Bastardy, 1870–1978*. Cambridge: Cambridge University Press.

Ong, A. (1987) *Spirits of Resistance and Capitalist Discourse: Factory Women in Malaysia*. Albany: State University of New York Press.

Ortner, S. (1984) "Theory in anthropology since the sixties." *Comparative Studies in Society and History* 26: 126–66.

———— (1989) *High Religion: A Cultural and Political History of Sherpa Buddhism*. Princeton, NJ: Princeton University Press.

Parmentier, R. (1987) *The Sacred Remains: Myth, History, and Polity in Belau*. Chicago: University of Chicago Press.

Parsons, E. C. (1936) *Mitla, Town of the Souls, and Other Zapoteco-speaking Pueblos of Oaxaca, Mexico*. Chicago: University of Chicago Press.

Peel, J. D. Y. (1984) "Making history: The past in the Ijesha present." *Man* 19: 111–32.

Peña, G. (1981) *A Legacy of Promises: Agriculture, Politics, and Ritual in the Morelos Highlands of Mexico*. Austin: University of Texas Press.

Pitt, D. (1972) *Using Historical Sources in Anthropology and Sociology*. New York: Holt, Rinehart and Winston.

Plakans, A. (1984) *Kinship in the Past: An Anthropology of European Family Life, 1500–1900*. New York: Basil Blackwell.

Pomeroy, C. (1988) "The salt of highland Ecuador: Precious production of a female domain." *Ethnohistory* 35: 131–60.

Powers, M. (1986) *Oglala Women: Myth, Ritual, and Reality*. Chicago: University of Chicago Press.

Price, R. (1983) *First-Time: The Historical Vision of an Afro-American People*. Baltimore, MD: Johns Hopkins University Press.

——— (1990) *Alabi's World*. Baltimore, MD: Johns Hopkins University Press.

Rappaport, J. (1990) *The Politics of Memory: Native Historical Interpretation in the Colombian Andes*. Cambridge: Cambridge University Press.

Rasnake, R. (1988) *Domination and Cultural Resistance: Authority and Power among an Andean People*. Durham, NC: Duke University Press.

Rebel, H. (1989) "Cultural hegemony and class experience: A critical reading of recent ethnological-historical approaches." *American Ethnologist* 16: 117–36, 350–65.

Redfield, R. (1930) *Tepoztlan, a Mexican Village: A Study of Folk Life*. Chicago: University of Chicago Press.

——— (1953) *The Primitive World and Its Transformations*. Ithaca, NY: Cornell University Press.

Riley, C., and W. Taylor, eds. (1967) *American Historical Anthropology: Essays in Honor of Leslie Spier*. Carbondale: Southern Illinois University Press.

Rivers, W. H. R. (1906) *The Todas*. London: Macmillan.

Rodman, M. (1987) *Masters of Tradition: Consequences of Customary Land Tenure in Longana, Vanuatu*. Vancouver: University of British Columbia Press.

Rorty, R. (1979) *Philosophy and the Mirror of Nature*. Princeton, NJ: Princeton University Press.

Rosaldo, R. (1980) *Ilongot Headhunting, 1883–1974: A Study in Society and History*. Stanford, CA: Stanford University Press.

Roseberry, W. (1983) *Coffee and Capitalism in the Venezuelan Andes*. Austin: University of Texas Press.

——— (1988) "Political economy," in B. Siegel, A. Beals, and S. Tyler (eds.) *Annual Review of Anthropology*, vol. 17. Palo Alto, CA: Annual Reviews: 161–85.

——— (1989) *Anthropologies and Histories: Essays in Culture, History, and Political Economy*. New Brunswick, NJ: Rutgers University Press.

Rosenberg, H. (1988) *A Negotiated World: Three Centuries of Change in a French Alpine Community*. Toronto: University of Toronto Press.

Sacks, K. (1988) *Caring by the Hour: Women, Work, and Organizing at Duke University Medical Center*. Urbana: University of Illinois Press.

Sahlins, M. (1981) *Historical Metaphors and Mythical Realities: Structure in the Early History of the Sandwich Islands Kingdom*. Ann Arbor: University of Michigan Press.

———— (1985) *Islands of History*. Chicago: University of Chicago Press.

Said, E. (1979) *Orientalism*. New York: Vintage.

Sallnow, M. (1987) *Pilgrims of the Andes: Regional Cultures in Cusco*. Washington, DC: Smithsonian Institution Press.

Salomon, F. (1986) *Native Lords of Quito in the Age of the Incas: The Political Economy of North Andean Chiefdoms*. Cambridge: Cambridge University Press.

Sangren, P. S. (1987) *History and Magical Power in a Chinese Community*. Stanford, CA: Stanford University Press.

Sapir, E. (1949) "Time perspective in aboriginal American culture: A study in method," in D. Mandelbaum (ed.) *Selected Writings of Edward Sapir*. Berkeley: University of California Press: 389–462.

Schapera, I. (1962) "Should anthropologists be historians?" *Journal of the Royal Anthropological Institute* 92: 143–56.

Schryer, F. (1980) *The Rancheros of Pisaflores: The History of a Peasant Bourgeoisie in Twentieth-Century Mexico*. Toronto: University of Toronto Press.

———— (1990) *Ethnicity and Class Conflict in Rural Mexico*. Princeton, NJ: Princeton University Press.

Segalen, M. (1986) *Historical Anthropology of the Family*, translated by J. C. White-house and S. Matthews. Cambridge: Cambridge University Press.

Seligmann, L. (1987) "The chicken in Andean history and myth: The Quechua concept of *wallpa*." *Ethnohistory* 34: 138–70.

Sheridan, T. (1986) *Los Tucsonenses: The Mexican Community in Tucson, 1854–1941*. Tucson: University of Arizona Press.

———— (1988a) "How to tell the story of a people without history: Narrative vs. ethnohistorical approaches to the study of the Yaqui Indians through time." *Journal of the Southwest* 30: 168–89.

———— (1988b) *Where the Dove Calls: The Political Ecology of a Peasant Corporate Community in Northwestern Mexico*. Tucson: University of Arizona Press.

Shokeid, M. (1971) *The Dual Heritage: Immigrants from the Atlas Mountains in an Israeli Village*. Manchester: Manchester University Press.

Sider, G. (1986) *Culture and Class in Anthropology and History: A Newfoundland Illustration*. Cambridge: Cambridge University Press.

Silverblatt, I. (1987) *Moon, Sun, and Witches: Gender Ideologies and Class in Inca and Colonial Peru*. Princeton, NJ: Princeton University Press.

Silverman, S. (1979) "On the uses of history in anthropology: The *palio* of Siena." *American Ethnologist* 6: 413–36.

Singer, M. (1959) *Traditional India: Structure and Change*. Philadelphia: American Folklore Society.

Smith, C. (1984) "Local history in global context: Society and economic transitions in western Guatemala." *Comparative Studies in Society and History* 25: 109–33.

————, ed. (1990) *Guatemalan Indians and the State: 1540 to 1988*. Austin: University of Texas Press.

Smith, G. (1989) *Livelihood and Resistance: Peasants and the Politics of Land in Peru*. Berkeley and Los Angeles: University of California Press.

Smith, M. G. (1960) *Government in Zazzau, 1800–1950*. New York: Oxford University Press; London: International African Institute.

——— (1962) "History and social anthropology." *Journal of the Royal Anthropological Institute* 92: 72–85.

Snyder, F. (1981) *Capitalism and Legal Change: An African Transformation*. New York: Academic.

So, A. (1986) *The South China Silk District: Local Historical Transformation and World-System Theory*. Albany: State University of New York Press.

Spicer, E. (1962) *Cycles of Conquest: The Impact of Spain, Mexico, and the United States on the Indians of the Southwest, 1533–1960*. Tucson: University of Arizona Press.

——— (1980) *The Yaquis: A Culture History*. Tucson: University of Arizona Press.

Spores, R. (1967) *The Mixtec Kings and Their People*. Norman: University of Oklahoma Press.

——— (1984) *The Mixtecs in Ancient and Colonial Times*. Norman: University of Oklahoma Press.

Starr, J., and J. Collier, eds. (1989) *History and Power in the Study of Law: New Directions in Legal Anthropology*. Ithaca, NY: Cornell University Press.

Stewart, O. (1987) *Peyote Religion: A History*. Norman: University of Oklahoma Press.

Stockard, J. (1989) *Daughters of the Canton Delta: Marriage Patterns and Economic Strategies in South China, 1860–1930*. Stanford, CA: Stanford University Press.

Stocking, G. (1968) *Race, Culture, and Evolution: Essays in the History of Anthropology*. New York: Free.

———, ed. (1991) *Colonial Situations: Essays On the Contextualization of Ethnographic Knowledge*. History of Anthropology, vol. 7. Madison: University of Wisconsin Press.

Stolcke, V. (1988) *Coffee Planters, Workers, and Wives: Class Conflict and Gender Relations on São Paulo Plantations, 1850–1980*. New York: St. Martin's.

Stoler, A. L. (1985) *Capitalism and Confrontation in Sumatra's Plantation Belt, 1870–1979*. New Haven, CT: Yale University Press.

——— (1989) "Rethinking colonial categories: European communities and the boundaries of rule." *Comparative Studies in Society and History* 31: 134–61.

Stone, L. (1977) *The Family, Sex, and Marriage in England, 1500–1800*. New York: Harper and Row.

Sturtevant, W. (1966) "Anthropology, history, and ethnohistory." *Ethnohistory* 13: 1–51.

Sullivan, P. (1989) *Unfinished Conversations: Mayas and Foreigners between Two Wars*. New York: Knopf.

Tambiah, S. (1970) *Buddhism and the Spirit Cults in Northeast Thailand*. Cambridge: Cambridge University Press.

——— (1976) *World Conqueror and World Renouncer: A Study of Buddhism and Polity in Thailand against a Historical Background*. Cambridge: Cambridge University Press.

——— (1984) *The Buddhist Saints of the Forest and the Cult of Amulets: A Study* in *Charisma, Hagiography, Sectarianism, and Millennial Buddhism*. Cambridge: Cambridge University Press.

———— (1987) "At the confluence of anthropology, history, and indology." *Contributions to Indian Sociology* 21: 187–216.

Taussig, M. (1980) *The Devil and Commodity Fetishism in South America*. Chapel Hill: University of North Carolina Press.

———— (1987) *Shamanism, Colonialism, and the Wild Man: A Study in Terror and Healing*. Chicago: University of Chicago Press.

———— (1989) "History as commodity in some recent American (anthropological) literature." *Critique of Anthropology* 9: 7–23.

Taylor, J. (1979) *Eva Perón: The Myths of a Woman*. Chicago: University of Chicago Press.

Tedlock, B. (1982) *Time and the Highland Maya*. Albuquerque: University of New Mexico Press.

Tedlock, D. (1983) *The Spoken Word and the Work of Interpretation*. Philadelphia: University of Pennsylvania Press.

Thomas, N. (1989a) *Out of Time: History and Evolution in Anthropological Discourse*. Cambridge: Cambridge University Press.

———— (1989b) "Taking people seriously: Cultural autonomy and the global system." *Critique of Anthropology* 9: 59–69.

———— (1990) *Marquesan Societies: Inequality and Political Transformation in Eastern Polynesia*. Oxford: Clarendon; New York: Oxford University Press.

———— (1991) *Entangled Objects: Exchange, Material Culture, and Colonialism in the Pacific*. Cambridge, MA: Harvard University Press.

Thompson, E. P. (1963) *The Making of the English Working Class*. New York: Vintage.

Tompkins, J. (1986) " 'Indians': Textualism, Morality, and the Problem of History," in H. L. Gates (ed.) *"Race," Writing, and Difference*. Chicago: University of Chicago Press: 59–77.

Tonkin, E., M. McDonald, and M. Chapman, eds. (1989) *History and Ethnicity*. London: Routledge.

Trigger, B. (1982) "Ethnohistory: Problems and prospects." *Ethnohistory* 29: 1–19.

Trouillot, M. R. (1988) *Peasants and Capital: Dominica in the World Economy*. Baltimore, MD: Johns Hopkins University Press.

Turner, V. (1969) *The Ritual Process: Structure and Anti-Structure*. Chicago: Aldine.

————, and E. Turner (1978) *Image and Pilgrimage in Christian Culture: Anthropological Perspectives*. New York: Columbia University Press.

Valeri, V. (1985) *Kingship and Sacrifice: Ritual and Society in Ancient Hawaii*, translated by P. Wissing. Chicago: University of Chicago Press.

Vansina, J. (1965) *Oral Tradition: A Study in Historical Methodology*, translated by H. M. Wright. Chicago: Aldine.

———— (1985) *Oral Tradition as History*. Madison: University of Wisconsin Press.

Verdery, K. (1983) *Transylvanian Villagers: Three Centuries of Political, Economic, and Ethnic Change, 1700–1980*. Berkeley and Los Angeles: University of California Press.

Viazzo, P. (1989) *Upland Communities: Environment, Population, and Social Structure in the Alps since the Sixteenth Century.* Cambridge: Cambridge University Press.

Vincent, J. (1982) *Teso in Transformation: The Political Economy of Peasant and Class in Eastern Africa.* Berkeley and Los Angeles: University of California Press.

Walker, A. (1986) *The Toda of South India: A New Look.* Delhi: Hindustan.

Wallace, A. (1970) *Death and Rebirth of the Seneca.* New York: Knopf.

———— (1978) *Rockdale: The Growth of an American Village in the Early Industrial Revolution.* New York: Knopf.

———— (1987) *St. Clair: A Nineteenth-Century Coal Town's Experience with a Disaster-Prone Industry.* New York: Knopf.

———— (1989) " 'Plot' and the concept of culture in historiography," in M. Freilich, (ed.), *The Relevance of Culture,* pp. 31–38. NY: Bergin and Garvey.

Warman, A. (1980) *"We Come to Object": The Peasants of Morelos and the National State,* translated by S. Ault. Baltimore, MD: Johns Hopkins University Press.

Wasserstrom, R. (1983) *Class and Society in Central Chiapas.* Berkeley and Los Angeles: University of California Press.

Waterman, C. (1990) *Jùjú: A Social History and Ethnography of an African Popular Music.* Chicago: University of Chicago Press.

Weiner, A., and J. Schneider, eds. (1989) *Cloth and Human Experience.* Washington, DC: Smithsonian Institution Press.

Weller, R. (1985) "Bandits, beggars, and ghosts: The failure of state control over religious interpretation in Taiwan." *American Ethnologist* 12: 46–61.

Whiteley, P. (1988) *Deliberate Acts: Changing Hopi Culture through the Oraibi Split.* Tucson: University of Arizona Press.

Wilkinson, C. (1987) *American Indians, Time, and the Law: Native Societies in a Modern Constitutional Democracy.* New Haven, CT: Yale University Press.

Wilmsen, E. (1989) *Land Filled with Flies: A Political Economy of the Kalahari.* Chicago: University of Chicago Press.

Wolf, E. (1982) *Europe and the People without History.* Berkeley and Los Angeles: University of California Press.

Wrigley, E. A. (1969) *Population and History.* London: Weidenfeld and Nicholson.

Wylie, J. (1987) *The Faroe Islands: Interpretations of History.* Lexington: University Press of Kentucky.

Yanagisako, S. (1985) *Transforming the Past: Tradition and Kinship among Japanese Americans.* Stanford, CA: Stanford University Press.

Zuidema, R. T. (1990) *Inca Civilization in Cuzco,* translated by J. Decoster. Austin: University of Texas Press.

HISTORY AND ECONOMICS

Hugh Rockoff

Introduction

In a well-known paper published some years ago Donald McCloskey (1976) addressed his fellow economists on the importance of history to their discipline. He argued that greater emphasis on economic history would make for better economics and for better economists. It cannot be said that McCloskey's arguments were taken completely to heart. Economists continue to expend a major part of their effort on (and award their honors for) the refinement of mathematical models and statistical techniques. This emphasis has led many scholars in related disciplines, social science historians in particular, to believe that economists are uninterested in history and unreceptive to arguments based on historical evidence.

But economists, as I will try to show below, are surprisingly open to historical arguments, perhaps more than many economists themselves realize. Recent developments in econometrics (I have in mind the growing literature on cointegration of time series and related developments), moreover, far from enabling economists to rely more heavily on current data, have in fact served to show how difficult it is to draw valid inferences from short runs of time-series data. The result, I believe, will be a greater emphasis by economists on economic history. In at least one area, financial and monetary history, there is already a minor boom in historical studies as attested to by the many papers on these issues in the journals and by the formation within the National Bureau of Economic Research (a major focal point for empirical research) of groups specializing in macroeconomic and financial history.

Below I will try to document the important role of history in economics and try to identify the channels through which history influences economics, relying for examples primarily on papers in the three most prestigious mainstream journals, the *Quarterly Journal of Economics,* the *Journal of Political Economy,* and the *American Economic Review* (the official organ of the American Economic Association). There are, of course, other prestigious journals, particularly in the specialized areas of econometrics and mathematical economics. And the articles that appear in these three are influenced by the eccentricities of individual editors. Nevertheless, I believe that the papers that appear in these journals were chosen because they were expected to interest and influence the profession as a whole. If other types of historical papers were demanded by these journals, economic historians would bend to the task of producing them.[1] My concern then is not with history's imports from economics, a subject of much distinguished writing, but rather with the somewhat neglected issue of history's exports to economics.

The picture of the way history influences economics that emerges from this survey will be surprising, I believe, to scholars outside the economics profession, and perhaps to many within. I don't want to give away the whole story yet, but consider this: as a first guess one might assume that economists are interested in the history of the major institutions they normally deal with. One might expect to find papers in the major journals on, say, the evolution of Federal Reserve policies, the market for skilled labor, or the industrial structure of major industries. But few such papers are to be found in the economic journals. One does find papers, however, on the Dutch Tulipmania of the seventeenth century, medieval grain storage, unemployment in the disintegrating Hapsburg empire, and similarly esoteric subjects. My purpose, in short, is to explain this apparent preference for the irrelevant.

Before surveying the current scene, it will be useful to briefly look at the role of history in the development of economics. The reliance of economists on history, and on a particular sort of esoteric historical illustration, it turns out, is nothing new.

The Founding Fathers

A look at Adam Smith's *The Wealth of Nations* (1937 [1776]), the starting point of modern economics, reveals a document replete with historical essays on a remarkable range of topics—the Royal African Company, Smith's famous "Digression Concerning the Variations in the Value of Silver during the Course of the Last Four Centuries," the poor laws, even religious education—to select a few.

Most modern economists skip these sections, if they read Smith at all, considering them digressions (following Smith's misleading use of the term) rather than as central building blocks of his argument. But the reader who skips these sections misses more than some delightful reading, he also misses the point. Smith was an empiricist, and his conclusions are suggested and supported by his historical raw material. The history of the Royal African Company reveals the dangers inherent in granting commercial monopolies, the digression on the price of silver serves (among other purposes) to show that the long-run decline in the nominal price of grain was not the result of subsidies paid to producers, the history of the poor laws reveals how these laws undermined the mobility of labor, and the history of religious education reveals that competition works better than monopoly even in an activity that at first appears to be far removed from the marketplace.

Smith could have confined himself to more prosaic examples such as his detailed study of the Herring Bounty—a subsidy paid in Smith's day to ships engaged in fishing for herring off Scotland.[2] Typically, however, as we have seen, he went much farther afield. This choice was dictated by more than the desire to catch the reader's attention, although this motive undoubtedly played a role. Smith realized that his far flung examples were crucial for demonstrating the usefulness of his theory. The idea is that if economic theory works in these unlikely times and places, then surely it must work when applied to modern-day markets. This is the approach to the use of history that has continued to characterize the best scholarship in economics.

A similar reliance on history is to be found in the work of most of the major figures who followed Smith: John Stuart Mill, Karl Marx, William Stanley Jevons, Alfred Marshall, and so on.[3] Not all the founding fathers, of course, relied heavily on history. David Ricardo, for example, stands out as an economist who relied primarily on abstract models and his knowledge of current affairs. But there was a strong emphasis on history in the work of most of the influential nineteenth-century writers.

This tradition did not die out as economics moved into the twentieth century. Irving Fisher used numerous historical examples to illustrate his monetary theories. And John Maynard Keynes used historical examples to make his arguments in *The Treatise on Money* and in *The General Theory*. Keynes's illustrations went far afield. He pointed (1964 [1936]: 131), for example, to pyramid building in ancient Egypt and church building in the Middle Ages as successful, if unconscious, applications of his policy of public works to maintain full employment.[4]

The most influential book in macroeconomics in the postwar period, undoubtedly, has been Milton Friedman and Anna Jacobson Schwartz's *A Monetary History of the United States* (1963). This book, a crucial building block in the revival of monetarism, traces the stock of money and monetary policy from 1867 to 1963. If one goes down the list of economists who have won the Nobel prize one finds, of course, many who made their mark through theoretical or statistical studies. But one will also find a number, including Friedman, Simon Kuznets, Friedrich Hayek, Arthur Lewis, and Gunnar Myrdal with strong interests in economic history.

Not a few economists today are likely to argue that history is no longer important, even though historical studies may have been important to economists in the past. After all, economic history, as more than one economist has told me, is simply economics with bad data. With governments collecting abundant data, and econometricians refining powerful statistical techniques for dealing with it, it is no longer necessary to ransack the past for examples with which to test theories. This attitude is likely to discourage historians who wish to connect their work with economics. But a review of the current economic literature reveals that historical studies continue to play their traditional Smithian role of testing and defining the limits of economic analysis.

The historical studies that I survey below almost all test economic ideas in unlikely settings. They can be further classified according to the purpose served by the historical setting. These are not mutually exclusive; a well chosen historical example may have several desirable properties. I begin with the category that produces the most esoteric sounding papers, the testing of the mythology of economics.

Very little of the modern corpus of economics is established on a rigorous basis of statistical tests of current data. Some skeptics would say none. Inevitably, economists rely on bits and pieces of history, what might be called the mythology of economics, to form a coherent view of the limits of their discipline, although they may be only partly conscious of the role played by economic mythology in their own thinking.[5] One of the main functions of the economic historian is to examine the substance of these myths. This is not, I want to emphasize, a mere sideshow. Some extremely influential recent work falls in this category.

Perhaps the classic example of an economic myth is the story of the Tulipmania. It may surprise scholars in other disciplines to learn that economists are interested in the strange happenings in the market for tulip bulbs in seventeenth-century Holland. In fact most economists, especially those working in the area of monetary and financial economics, are familiar with the story. The account generally referred to is in MacKay's (1852) *Extraordinary Popular Delusions and the Madness of Crowds,* an old work of popular history. The story serves as a reminder that asset markets can get carried away, that prices can take off, leaving the fundamental determinants of prices behind. The story often motivates theoretical studies of asset markets. Thus, Peter Garber's (1989, 1990) reexamination of this story, which argues that bulb prices, for the most part, were determined by fundamentals (expected future production), will influence the economist's attitude toward other alleged cases of asset market "bubbles."

The Mississippi Bubble and the South Sea Bubble, eighteenth-century stock market booms also described by MacKay, have received similar treatments (Neal, 1990). Not all myths, of course, deserve debunking, even if this is the most fun. Recent work by Eugene White (1990) and by Peter Rappoport and White (1990) has argued that there was indeed a bubble in the stock market in the late 1920s.

Economic myths derive much of their influence from the strong emotional response produced by the initial events (it helps us remember the lesson) and from the inherent authority of ideas that we imbibe before our critical faculties are fully formed. Economists, moreover, tend to keep one eye on public opinion. Bits of history that influence public perceptions of economic policy must be dealt with if economists are to remain influential. Nowhere are these factors more important than with respect to the

Great Depression. The Depression was not a good natural experiment in the sense I will discuss below. Too many things were happening at once. But this experience made such a powerful impression on generations of Americans that no theory in macroeconomics is considered viable that does not account in some way for the Depression.

A decade ago much of debate centered on the role of money in the Great Depression.[6] Friedman and Schwartz (1963: 299–492) initiated the debate by attacking a myth: that the Federal Reserve had tried everything in its power to expand the money supply and stop the banking crisis but was unable to do so. Their argument, that the Federal Reserve failed because it did not try, was supported by both quantitative evidence (new estimates of the money supply) and qualitative evidence (internal documents of the Federal Reserve and a diary kept by one of the participants).

The lines of research that followed are not easily summarized. Some work extended the Friedman and Schwartz interpretation. For example, Alexander J. Field (1984) showed that the Federal Reserve responded inappropriately to the increase in the demand for money caused by the stock market boom of the late 1920s. But a major counterattack was launched by Peter Temin (1976) who argued that the behavior of certain variables was inconsistent with the monetarist interpretation. The nominal (not adjusted for deflation) interest rate declined, for example, and this he thought was inconsistent with a shortage of money. Much of this literature is surveyed in Michael Bordo (1989).

Recent work on the Great Depression often can still be classed as monetarist or Keynesian, but the trend has been to posit supplementary causes for the depth and persistence of the Depression. Anthony P. O'Brien (1989) has pointed to social pressures to maintain nominal wages in the early months of the Great Depression as a factor making for rigid real wages and high unemployment. Christina Romer (1990) has pointed to the stock market crash as a factor reducing consumer confidence and spending on consumer durables.

Perhaps the most influential work since Temin's has been a paper by Ben S. Bernanke (1983)—extended to other countries in Bernanke and Harold James (1991)—that argued that disturbances to the credit market were crucial in producing and prolonging the Depression. Bernanke's work, and related developments in financial economics, stimulated studies by Charles W. Calomiris and R. Glenn Hubbard (1989) of the crises in the period 1894–1909 which drew a detailed response by Bordo, Rappoport, and Schwartz (1992), who cover the national banking era, and by Joseph G. Haubrich (1990) of the Depression in Canada. It also helped stimulate studies by Kathryn M. Dominguez, Ray C. Fair, and Mathew D. Shapiro (1988), Stephen G. Cecchetti (1992), and James D. Hamilton (1992) of the degree to which declines in income and prices were anticipated. This literature has been thoughtfully surveyed recently by Calomiris (1992).

Most of the recent work on the Depression stresses factors that economists believe might be important, if on a lesser scale, in determining current fluctuations in the economy. Romer's paper contains an explicit comparison between the stock market crash of 1929 and the crash of 1987. But even when such comparisons are absent, macroeconomists would have little trouble drawing lessons from the other papers for current discussions of macroeconomic theory.

The myth of the gold standard plays a conspicuous part in almost any discussion of whether we should return to a regime of fixed exchange rates. In these discussions one will inevitably find references to how well or (less often) how badly the world economy functioned under the classical gold standard, 1879–1914. The research conducted on this period by economists and economic historians is immense. The crucial issues are laid out in Bordo (1981) and in an NBER (National Bureau of Economic Research) conference volume by Bordo and Schwartz (1984). The continuing interest in the period is shown by a recent paper by Francis X. Diebold, Steven Husted, and Mark Rush (1991) which examined data from six countries for roughly a century before 1913 to test whether exchange rates and prices adjusted in the long run to equate the purchasing power of currencies under the gold standard. There has even been some interest in the bimetallic standard (silver and gold): Friedman (1990a, 1990b) and Hugh Rockoff (1990).

Another myth is that an unregulated banking system would not work. Most monetary economists long believed that an unregulated banking system would produce high rates of bank failure, reduced service, and inflation. Even Adam Smith was sympathetic to part of this indictment, based on his interpretation of the Scottish experience with free banking. One of the supporting elements of this belief was the view that so called "wildcat banking" had developed during the free banking era in the United States (1838–1860). This view has been attacked in a number of papers by Rockoff (1974) and by Arthur Rolnick and Warren Weber (1983, 1984, 1988). The 1983 paper was published in the *American Economic Review*, indicating that the analysis, although about a minor episode that happened long ago, was thought to be of general interest to the profession. There were comments by James Kahn (1985) and Rockoff (1985). The lesson here is that no matter how esoteric the episode on which an historian is working, it is conceivable that a market for it exists among economists.

Microeconomics has its own set of historical myths. One of the classic examples of a public good is the lighthouse. A ship passing silently through the night cannot easily be charged for the light it receives from the lighthouse. The lighthouse, then, in the hands of John Stuart Mill and other economists, became a standard metaphor for a public good, one that must be provided by government. In a justly famous paper Ronald Coase (1974) reexamined the history of lighthouse finance. He showed that the conventional view was mistaken by drawing attention to numerous ways that the charges for constructing and using lighthouses had been brought home to the ships that benefited. His clarification of the history of lighthouses encouraged economists to think more creatively about the nature and finance of alleged public goods and to become more cautious about declaring a particular good a public good. His research, moreover, stimulated a series of related studies of classic public goods.

The development of economics was strongly influenced by the debate over the removal of British taxes on imported grain in the 1840s, the "Corn Laws." It was in this policy debate that Ricardo constructed his theory of comparative advantage. Economists at the time realized that the net effect of the removal of the Corn Laws depended on several factors and that in theory the benefits might have been small or even negative. But the consensus was that the improvement in the internal allocation of resources in Britain outweighed all other considerations. This view strongly influenced the commitment of the professional economist to free trade, a commitment that continued unbroken (although of course with many individual exceptions) to our own day. It is not surprising, then, that the Corn Laws have continued to interest economic historians such as McCloskey (1980) and Jeffrey Williamson (1990) and that Douglas A. Irwin's (1988) reconsideration of the effects of the removal of the Corn Laws warranted publication in an important general-interest journal.

Natural Experiments

A common claim made by economists when they present an historical example is that it is a natural experiment. The idea is that we may be able to untangle economic relationships that normally defy resolution if we can find an episode in which government policy, or some other variable, changed while other aspects of the economy were relatively undisturbed.

Friedman and Schwartz (1963) make repeated use of this tool in their reinterpretation of American monetary history. Economists would have forgotten the Federal Reserve's decision to double bank reserve requirements between August 1936 and March 1937 if Friedman and Schwartz had not drawn attention to the episode. The Federal Reserve had intended to impound the excess reserves then held by banks by raising the required reserve ratio, a decision it viewed as a purely technical adjustment. But banks, according to Friedman and Schwartz (1963: 520–32), reacted by building up their excess reserves once more. The result was a decline in the stock of money and a more intense recession than would otherwise have occurred. The Federal Reserve had inadvertently performed an experiment that gives economists unique evidence on the effects of changes in the stock of money. A number of studies of this episode have followed, and a recent survey of the literature by Bordo (1989: 47) concluded that a "deeper look" at the episode would be worthwhile.

The opposite of Depression is hyperinflation, a phenomenon that fascinates the economist and exercises an important influence on the public mind in those countries that have experienced it. In some ways, moreover, these episodes are natural experiments because changes in the stock of money are so much larger than any other economic changes thought to be taking place in these economies. The modern study of hyperinflations was inaugurated by Phillip Cagan (1956) who studied the demand for money in a large sample of hyperinflations. The German hyperinflation, perhaps the most famous, lasted some sixteen months. Today the bibliography of books and articles on the German hyperinflation is a substantial multiple of that number, and considerable research has been done on many other hyperinflations. As with the Depression, any macroeconomic theory that seeks to gain wide acceptance must deal in some manner with hyperinflation.

Natural experiments in microeconomics are equally illuminating. Theodore Schultz (1964: 63–70), in an example cited by McCloskey (1976: 446), examined data on agricultural output and population in India during the influenza epidemic of 1918–19 to test the proposition that there was surplus labor in Indian agriculture. Friedman and George Stigler (1972) studied vacancy rates after the San Francisco earthquake to test the ability of an unregulated housing market to allocate a reduced supply of housing. A study of current housing markets, where any increase in demand relative to supply would naturally be of a smaller order of magnitude, would not illustrate the point nearly as well.

A few additional examples will illustrate the range of natural experiments uncovered by economists in recent years. The oil price shocks of the 1970s prompted Alan Olmstead and Paul Rhode (1985) to examine the neglected case of the West Coast gas shortage of 1920. In the early 1980s farm foreclosures were high, and legislatures were considering limiting foreclosures. Lee Alston (1984) and Randal R. Rucker and Alston (1987) investigated government policies aimed at limiting farm foreclosures in the 1930s. Paul Evans (1982) investigated price controls during World War II, at a time when there was some interest in imposing controls to reduce inflation.

Economic theory is far from a settled matter, and some natural experiments are important because they clarify emerging theories. Thus, Rashid Salim (1988) argued that it would be hard to maintain quality in markets characterized by many producers and ease of entry and exit. As examples he cited the British woolen industry in the seventeenth century, Chinese raw silk production in the nineteenth century, and milk production in Baltimore in the 1920s, among others. His examples illuminated certain aspects of the emerging theory of contestable markets. Similarly, Bruce Greenwald and Robert R. Glasspiegel (1983) examined the market for slaves in New Orleans in 1830–60 for the purpose of clarifying the problem of adverse selection—the tendency of owners to withhold units of the highest quality from the resale market. Robert A. Margo (1991) showed at the turn of the century the freedom of blacks to leave the South limited (partially) the ability of Southern whites to underfund black schools, thus illuminating an important issue in the theory of public finance while shedding additional light on the origin of current social prolems. And Irwin (1991) used the Anglo-Dutch rivalry for the East India trade in the seventeenth century to illustrate aspects of the emerging theory of government intervention in international markets characterized by oligopoly.

Monetary theorists are in the forefront of those using historical evidence to shape emerging theories. Elmus Wicker (1986) asked whether certain conclusions about the unemployment to be expected from ending inflation, drawn from the emerging theory of rational expectations, held in the dismembered Hapsburg Empire after World War I. Robert P. Barsky and J. Bradford Delong (1991) asked why interest rates did not adjust to inflation from 1896 to 1914. Their answer, that market participants, although well informed, were uncertain about the appropriate macroeconomic model, served to reveal the limits of the techniques that economists normally use to model expectations. Bruce Smith (1985) tested theories about the effect on the price level to be expected from a change in the stock of money using data from Colonial America. This paper inspired a number of attempts to look at other colonial experiences. Recently, Bennett T. McCallum (1992) offered a new attempt to resolve the issue, relying on data from ten disputed colonial episodes. And Bernanke and Martin L. Parkinson (1991) have used depression era data to explore the increase in labor productivity that accompanies economic expansions in the postwar period.

History seldom performs its experiments as cleanly as we might wish. In the case of the 1937–1938 recession cited above, taxes were changed, a factor stressed by Keynesian economists, as well as monetary policy, the factor stressed by Friedman and Schwartz. So the ability to distinguish between the two approaches on the basis of this episode is less than ideal.

Political or social trends sometimes complicate the experiment. Elizabeth M. Landes (1980) investigated the effect of Progressive Era legislation limiting the hours women could work. She argued that this legislation was effective and may have been inspired by white male workers trying to limit competition from immigrant women. But Claudia Goldin (1988), on the basis of additional evidence, argued that the legislation was not very effective and may have been part of a broader effort by labor to limit hours of work. Labor may have pushed this limitation simply because legislatures and courts were more sympathetic to legislation intended to protect women. As the last example makes clear, social science historians can contribute to the economic historian's understanding of natural experiments by drawing attention to noneconomic disturbances that may be influencing the outcome of the proposed natural experiment.

Creating and Exploring Long Time Series

Economists, typically, are interested in variables they can measure—wages, interest rates, unemployment, and so on—and determining the relationships among them. Frequently, modern data simply do not exhibit enough variance to allow the impact of one variable on another to be determined. By pushing data back in time, it is sometimes possible to include periods with more variance and so to increase the chance of identifying correctly the underlying relationships through statistical techniques. This is one additional reason for the intense attention paid to the Great Depression. At least during this period all of the time series were not dominated by smooth upward trends. Even earlier periods may be relevant. Michael Edelstein's (1977) study of British savings rates illuminated current debates with data going back into the nineteenth century.

Even when it can be shown, moreover, that a "statistically significant" correlation exists between variables, it may still be difficult to show that a fundamental causative relationship exists. The correlation may be simply the result of a particular set of institutional arrangements.

A good example, again, is the relationship between money and economic activity. Suppose there exists a correlation between changes in the stock of money and changes in nominal GNP in the current data. How do we know that money, as many economists assert, is a causative agent in producing movements in GNP? How do we know that we are not simply observing the Federal Reserve passively accommodating the increase in the demand for money that occurs when economic activity expands in nominal terms? While it is true that econometricians have developed sophisticated techniques for addressing this problem, difficulties persist. The most influential attack on the problem using historical methods was by Friedman and Schwartz (1963) who carried their study of the relationship between money and economic activity back to 1867. Their contention that the basic relationship held under a variety of institutional arrangements (for example, before the Federal Reserve was founded in 1913) made a deep impression on the economics profession.

In the 1970s, to give a second example, the contention by the rational expectations school that anticipated monetary or fiscal policies were ineffective was tested in a host of studies based on current data. Robert J. Gordon (1982) made an important contribution to the debate by creating a new time series and testing these ideas over a long (1890–1980) time frame.

While these may be the chief motives at work when economists extend standard economic series backward, it would be inappropriate to draw a sharp line between this effort and the studies of isolated episodes considered above. For example, Christina Romer (1986a, 1986b, 1989) and Nathan Balke and Gordon (1989) have reworked the estimates of GNP, the GNP deflator (price index), and related series for the prewar period. And Romer has refined and explored the industrial production series and its components. The motivation for this work is partly to provide better inputs for econometric studies, but it is partly also to be found in the "stylized fact" that real economic activity fluctuated more violently in the pre-Depression era than it has since World War II. This myth has important consequences for how economists model the economy and the policies they recommend, because the stylized fact of greater postwar stability was associated by many economists with greater government intervention.

The use of long runs of data increases the value of the historian's knowledge of the social context in which the numbers are generated. Consider, for example, the evidence developed by Peter Lindert (1986) that wealth in Britain was far less equally distributed in the past than it is today. This finding is important to economists because, for one thing, it contributes to his general faith in the equalizing effects of capitalist development (or depending on the economist, to his faith in the value of increasing government intervention in market economies). But the producers of such statistics cannot rely on their intuitive understanding of what the numbers mean. They must turn to the historical literature (as good scholars such as Lindert do) to understand what a particular wealth or income differential meant in terms of social position, living standards, self-esteem, and so on.

The Invisible Hand

Many of the examples cited above are variations on a theme. The central myth of economics is that the market works—that people are rational profit maximizing agents and that economic activity can be explained through the operation of market forces. The Tulipmania challenges the central myth because it claims that people did not act rationally in buying and selling tulip bulbs. The Great Depression challenges the central myth because it seems to show that the labor market failed to equate the supply and demand for labor. Economists are often criticized for their excessive faith in economics, for trying to apply economic theory to issues where social and political motives are dominant. Even the most convinced economists sometimes have doubts on this score. Consequently, evidence provided by historians and other social scientists that economic principles can be applied to institutions far removed in time and place from America in the 1990s reinforces the confidence of economists in the usefulness of their tools, in their faith, if you will, in the central myth. Thus, David Galenson's (1981) elegant demonstration that the theory of human capital can be used to explain the institution of indentured servitude in colonial America reinforces the confidence of economists applying human capital theory in modern circumstances. If it worked then, surely it must work now. Other cases in point are McCloskey and John Nash (1984) on medieval grain storage and William Hausman (1980) on the London coal trade in the eighteenth century. The institutions have disappeared, the technologies are obsolete, but if people are rational maximizers of their material well-being, economic theory should still work. Barry Eichengreen's (1984) finding that differences in mortgage interest rates among states in 1890 can be explained primarily by differences in risk and usury limits is of great interest to historians of the Populist movement. But this finding is significant to economists because it confirms the power of the market, even in circumstances in which there was a loud cry at the time, that is echoed in some historical studies, that the market was not working, a particularly satisfying environment (for economists) in which to illustrate the power of economic analysis. Presumably this is why the editors of the *American Economic Review* thought that it would be of general interest to the profession.

Eichengreen's paper is one in a long line of work on the capital market in the nineteenth century started by Lance Davis (1965). Davis argued that the capital market had been slow to integrate (interest rates had been slow to equalize across regions) and that institutional innovations had been important in promoting integration. His finding touched a raw nerve, and an impressive list of papers and books followed including contributions by Richard Sylla (1969), Richard Keehn (1975), Gene Smiley (1975), John James (1976a, 1976b), and David Good on Austria (1977), to select a few that have been particularly influential in my own thinking about the issue. The conclusion that emerged from these studies was that the market had been somewhat slow to integrate, although a considerable amount of blame could be laid at the door of government regulation of the capital market. A recent study by Howard Bodenhorn and Rockoff (1992) illustrates that the issue can still draw the interest of economic historians. My point here is simply that although the problem of interregional barriers to capital mobility was solved before World War I, the demonstration that the market had been slow to work its magic was enough to generate a considerable amount of scholarly interest.

As Davis's study, and a number that it stimulated, illustrate, not all studies by economic historians confirm the central myth. This is true of those studies that appear in the leading professional journals as well as in the journals devoted to economic history or other specialized journals. The study by Olmstead and Rhode (1985), cited above, showed that gas rationing has been produced in unregulated private markets. The assumption before their paper was that gas rationing was always the consequence of price controls imposed by government. Gary Libecap and Steven Wiggins (1985) identified limits to private contracting (and to regulation) as means of achieving an efficient market structure for exploiting oil fields. Gavin Wright (1981) argued that wages in southern textiles rose during World War I and then remained too high for a long time afterward to equate the supply of and demand for labor. William Lazonick (1981) disputed the alleged rationality of entrepreneurs in the British textile industry before World War I.

But there is a bias. Papers showing that markets failed, or even simply that noneconomic factors must be given some weight, are less likely to receive a sympathetic hearing in economics journals than papers showing that markets functioned successfully. To some extent this is a function of the ideological perspective of the journal. More papers outlining failures of the market are to be found in the liberal *Quarterly Journal of Economics,* or the middle of the road *American Economic Review,* than in the free market oriented *Journal of Political Economy.* But most economists have at least a modicum of pride and confidence in their tools, and so a paper demonstrating the irrelevance of economic analysis will have an uphill battle at any mainstream journal.

Ultimately, the test that economists apply is a simple one: has the scholar who champions an explanation based on market failure or nonmarket determinants of economic behavior exhausted every plausible economic argument. A model response to this test is provided by Goldin's (1990) *Understanding the Gender Gap.* Goldin places considerable weight on societal norms and legislative enactments in her interpretation of the changing roles of women in the labor force. Her book has already become influential among economists precisely because purely economic explanations are given every chance to succeed. Wage equations are carefully specified with the full complement of economic variables; possible biases in econometric estimations are analyzed and tested. Economic historians may develop market-based explanations for some of the phenomena that she attributes to societal norms, but her argument persuades economists because it makes its first task explanation through economic variables. Her recent study with Margo (1992) of the narrowing of wage differentials between skilled and unskilled workers during World War II adopts a similar methodology.

Economic journals are filled with comments and replies so one might assume that whenever an economist attempted to apply economic theory to an event or institution long past, an historian would rise to the challenge to criticize the work. But I cannot offer examples from the major journals I surveyed. There are many possible explanations. One may be simply that the illustrations that interest economists because they test economic ideas in a particularly challenging environment may be of only passing interest to historians. Perhaps if historians develop a greater appreciation of the significance of these exercises to economists, they will make more of an effort to challenge the economists who tread upon their domain.

Persuading the Public

So far we have been examining professional debates among economists. History plays an even larger role when the economist becomes an advocate. Neither policymakers nor the general public are likely to understand nor be persuaded by the sort of mathematical-theoretical arguments and statistical proofs that are the normal fare of the professional journals. The economist is forced back upon the historical illustration to make his point. One could provide almost limitless examples of historical illustrations, some well chosen, some in need of considerable research, that economists have trotted out to promote policies they advocate. Fixed exchange rates are defended by a reference to how well they worked under the gold standard, price controls are defended by reference to how well they worked in World War II, tax cuts are defended by how well they worked in the 1920s, and so on. Advocacy, it should be noted, is not a separate compartment of economics. There is an ongoing dialogue between the economist as advocate and the economist as social scientist. Today's policy problem begets historical example, begets empirical research, and (hopefully) begets new policy recommendations.

Economic History for Its Own Sake

Many economic historians study the past for its own sake, rather than provide exotic tests of economic ideas. This is as it should be; progress ultimately depends on letting scholars go where they want. And it is conceivable that economic history done for its own sake will not be of interest to economists. It may be a fascinating period, the scholarship may be first rate, the writing may be elegant, but the end product may not test the limits of economics in a way that is important for economists. But it is often the case that studies that appear to be solely about the past have strong lessons for current policy below the surface. In many cases, I believe, both history and economics would be better served if implicit lessons were made explicit. A few examples will make these generalizations clearer.

One of the most vigorous debates in economic history in the 1960s was on the contribution of the railroad to American economic growth. Major contributions were made by Robert Fogel (1964) and Albert Fishlow (1965). The railroads, of course, have long since ceased to play a dominant role in the transportation system. The argument would seem to be without relevance to modern policy debates. But below the surface was the question of whether government should intervene to create social overhead capital. Fishlow explicitly examined whether the railroads in the Middle West had been built ahead of demand with the help of government subsidies, a claim (that his research rejected) that reinforced the belief that government has a crucial role to play in the development process. The studies of the railroads, in other words, while they did not contribute direct answers to current problems helped to limit and refine the economist's overall view of the appropriate role of government. Fogel (1966) took on the relationship with current problems explicitly by comparing the railroads with the space program. There should be more studies in this mode.

The controversy over the economics of slavery in the 1960s and 1970s was even more animated. Much of this literature was stimulated by the classic paper by Alfred Conrad and John R. Meyer (1958). The controversy reached its peak after the publication of Fogel and Stanley Engerman's *Time on the Cross* (1974). In 1977 the controversy spilled on to the pages of the *American Economic Review* when Fogel and Engerman (1977) published new productivity estimates which took previous criticisms of their work into account and showed that slave agriculture was even more productive than they had claimed in *Time on the Cross*. This paper led to one of the longest debates in the *American Economic Review* in the last two decades, with critical comments by Paul David and Peter Temin (1979), Thomas Haskell (1979), Donald Schaefer and Mark D. Schmitz (1979), and Gavin Wright (1979). Fogel and Engerman (1980) replied, and the issue was "revisited" by Elizabeth Field (1988).

This was no ordinary controversy among specialists; the participants and the editor of the *Review* felt that they were playing for high stakes. The source of much of the heat generated by the debate, of course, was the belief that the depiction of slavery offered by economic historians, rightly or wrongly, would influence the attitude of economists and the public toward the problems of black America. One of the most salutary consequences of this debate was the spur to further empirical research. One need only cite the work by Richard Steckel on slave nutrition and mortality to make the point (Steckel 1986). The debate also served to focus attention on the position of blacks in the economy after the Civil War, with important books by Stephen Decanio (1974), Robert Higgs (1977), Roger Ransom and Richard Sutch (1977), and Gavin Wright (1978).

But the slavery debate was important to economists for still another reason. The antebellum South is a prime example in the minds of most Americans of a "noneconomic" society. The mythology of *Gone with the Wind* claims its share of the economist's imagination. Thus, the evidence that economic explanations work in the antebellum South provides a convincing test of the economist's tools. Fogel and Engerman offered explanations of slave prices, hire rates, the allocation of labor, the organization of the slave family, the treatment of slaves, and many other aspects of the antebellum South—a convincing demonstration, if they were right, of the power of economic analysis. In recognizing the ability of slavery to test the limits of economic analysis, economists were merely following the lead of Adam Smith (1937 [1776]: 365–66) who discussed the profitability of slavery in the ancient world and in the British colonies in his own day.

The passage of time has led to a cooling of passions, if not to a resolution of the debate, but the antebellum economy remains a fertile testing ground for economic analysis. A more recent example is Claudia Goldin and Kenneth Sokoloff's (1984) examination of why the North industrialized more rapidly than the South in the period 1820–50. Their explanation stresses the relatively high wages of women and children relative to adult males in the South, a phenomenon they attribute to the crop mix in the South. The high relative wage made it uneconomic to start factories dependent on the labor of women or children. The issue is important to historians of the period. But it is also of general interest to economists because it provides an economic explanation of relative rates of industrialization in an environment that might at first seem particularly ripe for a cultural explanation.

The Historical Mode of Explanation

Traditional historians, of course, often use a different mode of analysis than economists or economic historians trained as economists. A particular event or institution is seen to be the result of a long sequence of contingent events where the balance at any moment in time might easily have swung one way or the other. The explanation of the final outcome resides in laying out the actual sequence of contingencies, and the possibly minor forces and chance events that determined each outcome. An economist who wanted to explain the development of Akron, Ohio, as the center of the American tire industry could look at a series of underlying economic forces: the location of markets, the availability of labor, the availability of water, economies of scale, etc. But such factors could take the explanation only so far. To explain why the industry located in Akron, Ohio, and not, say, in Dayton, one would also have to look at events that were influenced by chance such as the decision by Benjamin Franklin Goodrich to relocate his firm in Akron.

Some economic historians have always understood the role of historical narrative in the explanation of the evolution of the economy. Jonathan Hughes, an able practitioner of the model-building form of analysis, adopted the traditional historical mode in his study of entrepreneurship, *The Vital Few* (1973). The title catches the essence of the contingent nature of history.

Recently, however, there has been a new wave of interest in such modes of explanation that is more methodologically self-conscious. A well-known paper by David (1985) showed how a series of historical "accidents" led to the universal adoption of the wrong (less easy to learn and use) typewriter keyboard known as the QWERTY board for the letters on the upper left. His paper helped popularize the term "path dependence" to describe this mode of analysis. What is at issue, obviously, is not the minor problem of whether the keys on the typewriter are arranged in the most efficient order. Indeed, the esoteric nature of the illustration helped to draw attention to the real issues, the appropriate mode of analysis, and the ability of market forces to produce optimal results. If outcomes are path dependent, and the choice among alternative paths are sometimes made on the basis of limited short-run concerns, the final outcome may not be the most efficient. The road not taken may be the right one. Warren Whatley's (1985) revitalization of the argument that the organization of southern agriculture inhibited the invention and spread of mechanized production is a good example of how focusing on path dependence can illuminate economic history.

There is no guarantee, as the public choice school reminds us, that relying on political forces to choose the paths along which the economy moves will lead to better solutions than allowing market forces to dominate. The same path dependence that characterizes some forms of market evolution also characterizes the political process. Robert Higgs (1987) demonstrates that a path dependent analysis can be applied to the growth of government, and his analysis suggests that government may grow to a larger than optimal size.

One of the most ambitious recent undertakings in combined political and economic explanation is Fogel's (1989: 320–87) attempt to explain the sequence of events that led to the formation of the Republican party and Lincoln's nomination and election in 1860. In Fogel's view, hundreds of separate events, some of them conditioned on fundamental economic forces, but others conditioned on chance events and political realignments, must be considered in the final explanation of events which in retrospect may seem inevitable. Path dependence is the centerpiece in this analysis: "The overarching role of contingent circumstances in their ultimate victory needs to be emphasized. There never was a moment between 1854 and 1860 in which the triumph of the antislavery coalition was assured" (1989: 320).

James M. McPherson's (1988) brilliant account of the Civil War argues that the traditional narrative form of history is best adapted to investigating path dependent processes. The total defeat of the South and immediate emancipation now seem inevitable. His narration of events, however, shows that had chance intervened differently at numerous points along the way, the outcome might have been very different. Most social science historians, I believe, would agree. But in a recent paper Fogel (1990) has sketched a possible way in which a complex path dependent process—in this case the political realignment of the 1850s—could be modeled mathematically. This may be the beginning of an alternative approach to path dependent processes. But as McCloskey (1990: 300) has recently reminded us, there need be no final choice between traditional narrative and social sciences methods. Some problems may be best attacked by traditional methods, some by social science methods, and most, perhaps, by a combination.

Conclusions

Economics has always had, and continues to have, a strong relationship with history. Only by testing economic ideas in challenging environments can the true scope and limits of economic ideas be determined. The original meaning of the phrase "the exception proves the rule," which presumably was "the exception tests the rule," conveys the point. This has meant, traditionally, that the principal interest of economists has been in historical settings that are far removed in time and place from the problems economists normally address. Hence, the willingness of economists to listen to stories about the medieval grain trade, the Dutch Tulipmania, and so on.

Indeed, the economist's view of the world is shaped by many partly examined "lessons" derived from history—the lesson, first of all, that most of the time people seek to maximize profits and that markets work, the lesson that financial markets can explode in speculative bubbles, the lesson that free trade produces greater benefits than costs, and so on. Thus, historical studies by debunking or sustaining old myths, and creating new ones, shape the culture in which economists do their work. Some economists may not be fully aware of their debt to history, but the willingness of the economic journals, including the most prestigious, to publish historical studies suggests that more than a few economists appreciate the potent force of the well-chosen historical illustration. In one area, monetary and financial economics, a strong boom in historical studies has developed.

The conclusion that economists value history primarily as a device for illustrating the power of their theories can be either reassuring or discouraging to other social scientists seeking to open trade with economists. On the one hand, it suggests that a topic that at first glance seems far distant from the current concerns might in fact be of great interest to a large group of economists. Medievalists can take heart. On the other hand, it suggests that economists will be less interested in what other social scientists have to say about current policy issues.

There are signs, however, of change. Recent discussions of path dependent processes both by economic historians and by theorists specializing in international trade have drawn attention to the potential role of historical analysis in understanding current economic problems. An outstanding recent example is Wright's (1990) discussion of the role of America's endowment of nonreproducible resources in her industrial success. And works by economic historians that establish a role for noneconomic variables after taking economic explanations to their limit—as done for example in Goldin's (1989) *Understanding the Gender Gap*—may encourage economists to listen more attentively to other social scientists. But it is far too early to claim that the traditional role of history in economics has been enlarged.

The increasing sophistication of economic theory and economic statistics, and related developments in history and kindred disciplines, makes it increasingly difficult for an individual scholar to master the skills of both the historian and the economist. The only solution is relying on the discussion of ideas among scholars from a wide range of disciplines, and in many cases, joint work. But it can be done. I believe that if social science historians once realize how important history is to the way economists persuade each other and the public, imports of history into economics will grow at a rapid pace.

Notes

1 Below I cite many of the historical papers that appeared in these journals during 1980–92. I have omitted some, however, either because the basic point I wanted to make could be illustrated by other examples that I was more familiar with or because for technical reasons they were difficult to summarize for non-economists. Omission of a paper does not imply that for some reason I thought it was less important than those mentioned in the text.

2 Smith (1937 [1776]: 486) found that ships were sometimes outfitted "for the sole purpose of catching, not the fish, but the bounty."

3 Although an assiduous student of economic history, Marshall's views were

often eccentric. Among the factors that formed the superior character of the English, Marshall (1961 [1920]: 740) noted that England's "climate is better adapted to sustain energy than any other in the northern hemisphere."

4 The reliance on history is more evident in *A Treatise on Money*. It contains (1930: vol. 2, 148–210) a section on "Historical Illustrations." Some were recent illustrations, but he included detailed examinations of the effect of Spain's extraction of precious metals from the new world and the depression of the 1890s.

5 The term myth is not entirely satisfactory since it suggests something that is misleading or untrue. In fact, I believe most of the myths of economics. But I have not found a more neutral term that conveys equally well what I have in mind. Economists often use the term "stylized facts," although most frequently this is used to refer to simplified characterizations of numerical data, as in "the savings rate is approximately constant."

6 Even earlier E. C. Brown (1956) had attacked a myth that was damaging to the Keynesian view of the Depression: that Keynesian policies had been tried by the Roosevelt administration but had failed to bring relief. Also see the revision of Brown's work by L. Peppers (1973).

References

Alston, L. J. (1984) "Farm foreclosure moratorium legislation: A lesson from the past." *American Economic Review* 74: 445–57.

Balke, N. S., and R. J. Gordon (1989) "The estimation of prewar gross national product: Methodology and new evidence." *Journal of Political Economy* 97: 38–92.

Barsky, R. P., and J. B. DeLong (1991) "Forecasting pre–World War I inflation: The Fisher Effect and the gold standard." *Quarterly Journal of Economics* 106: 815–36.

Bernanke, B. S. (1983) "Nonmonetary effects of the financial crises in the propagation of the Great Depression." *American Economic Review* 73: 257–76.

———— (1991) "Procyclical labor productivity and competing theories of the business cycle: Some evidence from interwar U.S. manufacturing industries." *Journal of Political Economy* 99: 439–59.

————, and H. James (1991) "The gold standard, deflation, and financial crisis in the Great Depression: An international comparison," in G. R. Hubbard (ed.) *Financial Markets and Financial Crises*. Chicago: University of Chicago Press.

Bodenhorn, H., and H. Rockoff (1992) "Regional interest rates in antebellum America," in C. Goldin and H. Rockoff (eds.) *Strategic Factors in Nineteenth Century American Economic History: A Volume to Honor Robert W. Fogel*. Chicago: University of Chicago Press.

Bordo, M. D. (1981) "The classical gold standard: Some lessons for today." Federal Reserve Bank of St. Louis, *Review* 63: 1–17.

————— (1989) "The contribution of *A Monetary History of the United States, 1867–1960* to monetary history," in Michael D. Bordo (ed.) *Money, History, and International Finance: Essays in Honor of Anna J. Schwartz.* Chicago: University of Chicago Press: 15–70.

—————, and A. J. Schwartz (1984) *A Retrospective on the Classical Gold Standard.* Chicago: University of Chicago Press.

—————, P. Rappoport, and A. J. Schwartz (1992) "Money versus credit rationing: Evidence for the national banking era, 1880–1914," in C. Goldin and H. Rockoff (eds.) *Strategic Factors in Nineteenth Century American Economic History: A Volume to Honor Robert W. Fogel.* Chicago: University of Chicago Press.

Boyer, G. R. (1989) "Malthus was right after all: Poor relief and birth rates in southeastern England." *Journal of Political Economy* 97: 93–114.

Brown, E. C. (1956) "Fiscal policy in the thirties: A reappraisal." *American Economic Review* 46: 857–79.

Cagan, P. (1956) "The Monetary Dynamics of Hyperinflation," in Milton Friedman (ed.) *Studies in the Quantity Theory of Money.* Chicago: University of Chicago Press.

Calomiris, C. W. (forthcoming, 1992) "Financial factors in the Great Depression." *Journal of Economic Perspectives.*

—————, and G. Hubbard (1989) "Price flexibility, credit availability, and economic fluctuations: Evidence from the United States, 1894–1909." *Quarterly Journal of Economics* 104: 429–52.

Coase, R. H. (1974) "The lighthouse in economics." *Journal of Law and Economics* 17: 357–76.

Conrad, A. H., and J. R. Meyer (1958) "The economics of slavery in the Ante Bellum South." *Journal of Political Economy* 66: 95–130. Reprinted in their book *The Economics of Slavery and Other Studies in Econometric History.* Chicago: Aldine, 1964: 43–92.

David, P. A. (1985) "Clio and the economics of QWERTY." *American Economic Review, Papers and Proceedings* 75: 332–37.

—————, and P. Temin (1979) "Explaining the relative efficiency of slave agriculture in the Antebellum South: A comment." *American Economic Review* 69: 213–18.

Davis, L. (1965) "The investment market, 1870–1914: Evolution of a national market." *Journal of Economic History* 25: 355–99.

DeCanio, S. J. (1974) *Agriculture in the Postbellum South: The Economics of Production and Supply.* Cambridge: MIT Press.

Diebold, F. X., S. Husted, and M. Rush (1991) "Real exchange rates under the gold standard." *Journal of Political Economy* 99: 1252–71.

Edelstein, M. (1977) "U.K. savings in the age of high imperialism and after." *American Economic Review, Papers and Proceedings* 67: 282–87.

Eichengreen, B. (1984) "Mortgage interest rates in the populist era." *American Economic Review* 74: 995–1015.

Evans, P. (1982) "The effects of general price controls in the United States during World War II." *Journal of Political Economy* 90: 944–66.

Field, E. B. (1988) "The relative efficiency of slavery revisited: A translog production function approach." *American Economic Review* 78: 543–49.

Fishlow, A. (1965) *American Railroads and the Transformation of the Antebellum Economy*. Cambridge: Harvard University Press.

Fogel, R. W. (1964) *Railroads and American Economic Growth: Essays in Econometric History*. Baltimore, MD: Johns Hopkins Press.

——— (1966) "Railroads as an analogy to the space effort." *Economic Journal* 76: 16–43.

——— (1989) *Without Consent or Contract: The Rise and Fall of American Slavery*. New York: W. W. Norton.

——— (1990) "Modelling complex dynamic interactions: The role of intergenerational, cohort, and period processes and of conditional events in the political realignment of the 1850s." National Bureau of Economic Research, Working Paper Series on Historical Factors in Long Run Growth, no. 12.

Fogel, R. W., and S. L. Engerman (1974) *Time on the Cross: The Economics of American Negro Slavery*. Boston: Little Brown.

——— (1977) "Explaining the relative efficiency of slave agriculture in the Antebellum South." *American Economic Review* 67: 275–96.

——— (1980) "Explaining the relative efficiency of slave agriculture in the Antebellum South: Reply." *American Economic Review* 70: 672–90.

——— (1990a) "Bimetallism revisited." *Journal of Economic Perspectives* 4: 85–104.

Friedman, M. (1990b) "The crime of 1873." *Journal of Political Economy* 98: 1159–94.

———, and A. J. Schwartz (1963) *A Monetary History of the United States, 1867–1960*. Princeton: Princeton University Press, for the NBER.

———, and G. Stigler (1972) "Roofs or ceilings? The current housing problem," in *Verdict on Rent Control*. Sussex, United Kingdom: Cormorant Press, for the Institute of Economic Affairs.

Galenson, D. W. (1981) "The market evaluation of human capital: The case of indentured servitude." *Journal of Political Economy* 89: 446–67.

Garber, P. M. (1989) "Tulipmania." *Journal of Political Economy* 97: 535–60.

——— (1990) "Who put the mania in the tulipmania," in E. N. White (ed.) *Crashes and Panics*. Homewood, IL: Dow Jones-Irwin: 3–32.

Goldin, C. (1988) "Maximum hours legislation and female employment: A reassessment." *Journal of Political Economy* 97: 535–60.

——— (1990) *Understanding the Gender Gap: An Economic History of American Women*. New York and Oxford: Oxford University Press.

Goldin, C., and R. A. Margo (1992) "The great compression: The wage structure in the United States at mid-century." *Quarterly Journal of Economics* 107: 1–35.

———, and K. Sokoloff (1984) "The Relative Productivity Hypothesis of Industrialization: The American Case, 1820–1850." *Quarterly Journal of Economics* 99: 461–88.

Good, D. F. (1977) "Financial integration in late nineteenth-century Austria." *Journal of Economic History* 37: 890–910.

Gordon, R. J. (1982) "Price inertia and policy ineffectiveness in the United States, 1890–1980." *Journal of Political Economy* 90: 1087–1117.

Greenwald, B. C., and R. R. Glasspiegel (1983) "Adverse selection in the market for slaves: New Orleans 1830–1860." *Quarterly Journal of Economics* 98: 479–500.

Haskell, T. L. (1979) "Explaining the relative efficiency of slave agriculture in the antebellum South: A reply to Fogel and Engerman." *American Economic Review* 69: 206–07.

Hausman, W. J. (1980) "A model of the London coal trade in the eighteenth century." *Quarterly Journal of Economics* 94: 1–14.

Higgs, R. (1977) *Competition and Coercion: Blacks in the American Economy, 1865–1914*. New York: Cambridge University Press.

———— (1987) *Crisis and Leviathan: Critical Episodes in the Growth of American Government*. New York: Oxford University Press.

———— (1982) "Accumulation of property by southern blacks before World War I." *American Economic Review* 72: 725–35.

Hughes, J. *The Vital Few: American Economic History and its Protagonists*. New York: Oxford University Press.

Irwin, D. A. (1988) "Welfare effects of free trade: Debate and evidence from the 1840s." *Journal of Political Economy* 96: 1142–64.

———— (1991) "Mercantilism as strategic trade policy: The anglo-dutch rivalry for the East India Trade." *Journal of Political Economy* 99: 1296–1314.

James, J. (1976a) "Banking market structure, risk, and the pattern of local interest rates in the United States, 1893–1911." *Review of Economics and Statistics* 1976: 453–62.

———— (1976b) "The development of the national money market." *Journal of Economic History* 36: 878–97.

Kahn, J. A. (1985) "Another look at free banking in the United States." *American Economic Review* 75: 881–85.

Keehn, R. (1975) "Market power and bank lending: Some evidence from Wisconsin, 1870–1900." *Journal of Economic History* 35: 591–620.

Keynes, J. M. (1930) *A Treatise on Money*. London: Macmillan.

———— (1964 [1936]) *The General Theory of Employment, Interest, and Money*. New York: Harbinger, Harcourt, Brace & World.

Landes, E. M. (1980) "The effect of state maximum-hour laws on the employment of women in 1920." *Journal of Political Economy* 88: 476–94.

Lazonick, W. (1981) "Factor costs and the diffusion of ring spinning in Britain prior to World War I." *Quarterly Journal of Economics* 96: 89–110.

Lewis, F. D. (1983) "Fertility and savings in the United States: 1830–1900." *Journal of Political Economy* 91: 825–40.

Libecap, G. D., and S. N. Wiggins. "The influence of private contractual failure on regulation: The case of oil field unitization." *Journal of Political Economy* 93: 690–714.

Lindert, P. H. (1986) "Unequal English wealth since 1670." *Journal of Political Economy* 94: 1127–62.

MacKay, C. (1852) *Extraordinary Popular Delusions and the Madness of Crowds*. London: Office of the National Illustrated Library, vol. 1 (2d ed.).

McCallum, B. T. (1992) "Money and prices in colonial America: A new test of competing theories." *Journal of Political Economy* 100: 143–61.

McCloskey, D. N. (1976) "Does the past have useful economics." *Journal of Economic Literature* 14: 434–61.

—— (1980) "Magnanimous Albion: Free trade and British national income, 1841–1881." *Explorations in Economic History* 17: 303–20.

—— (1990) "Ancients and moderns." *Social Science History* 14: 289–304.

McCloskey, D. N., and J. Nash. (1984) "Corn at interest: The extent and cost of grain storage in medieval England." *American Economic Review* 74: 174–82.

Margo, R. A. (1991) "Segregated schools and the mobility hypothesis: A model of local government discrimination." *Quarterly Journal of Economics* 106: 61–74.

Marshall, A. (1961 [1920]) *Principles of Economics*. London: Macmillan. Annotated by C. W. Guillebaud.

Neal, L. D. (1990) "How the South Sea bubble was blown up and burst: A new look at old data," in Eugene N. White (ed.) *Crashes and Panics*. Homewood, IL: Dow Jones-Irwin: 33–46.

North, D. C. (1978) "Structure and performance: The task of economic history." *Journal of Economic Literature* 16: 963–78.

O'Brien, A. P. (1989) "A Behavioral explanation for nominal wage rigidity during the Great Depression." *Quarterly Journal of Economics* 109: 719–36.

Olmstead, A. L., and P. Rhode (1985) "Rationing without government: The West Coast gas famine of 1920." *American Economic Review* 75: 1044–55.

Peppers, L. C. (1973) "Full-employment surplus analysis and structural change: The 1930s." *Explorations in Economic History* 10: 197–210.

Ransom, R., and R. Sutch (1977) *One Kind of Freedom: The Economic Consequences of Emancipation*. New York: Cambridge University Press.

Rappoport, P., and E. White (1990) "Was there a bubble in the 1929 stock market?" Unpublished, Rutgers University.

Rashid, S. (1988) "Quality in contestable markets: A historical problem?" *Quarterly Journal of Economic* 103: 245–50.

Rockoff, H. (1974) "The free banking era: A re-examination." *Journal of Money, Credit and Banking* 6: 141–73.

—— (1985) "New evidence on free banking in the United States." *American Economic Review* 75: 886–89.

—— (1990) "The 'Wizard of Oz' as a monetary allegory." *Journal of Political Economy* 98: 739–60.

Rolnick, A. J., and W. E. Weber (1983) "New evidence on the free banking era." *American Economic Review* 73: 1080–91.

—— (1984) "The causes of free bank failures: A detailed examination of the evidence." *Journal of Monetary Economics* 14: 267–91.

————— (1988) "Explaining the demand for free bank notes." *Journal of Monetary Economics* 21: 47–71.

Romer, C. D. (1986a) "Spurious volatility in historical unemployment data." *Journal of Political Economy* 94: 1–37.

————— (1986b) "Is the stabilization of the postwar economy a figment of the data." *American Economic Review* 76: 314–34.

————— (1989) "The prewar business cycle reconsidered: New estimates of gross national product, 1869–1908." *Journal of Political Economy* 97: 1–37.

————— (1990) "The great crash and the onset of the Great Depression." *Quarterly Journal of Economics* 105: 597–624.

————— (1991) "The cyclical behavior of individual production series, 1889–1984." *Quarterly Journal of Economics* 106: 1–32.

Rucker, R. R., and L. J. Alston (1987) "Farm failures and government intervention: A case study of the 1930s." *American Economic Review* 77: 724–30.

Schaefer, D., and M. D. Schmitz (1979) "The relative efficiency of slave agriculture: A comment." *American Economic Review* 69: 208–12.

Schultz, T. (1964) *Transforming Traditional Agriculture.* New Haven, CT: Yale University Press.

Smiley, G. (1975) "Interest rate movements in the United States, 1888–1913." *Journal of Economic History* 35: 591–620.

Smith, A. (1937 [1776]) *The Wealth of Nations.* Edited by Edwin Cannan. New York: Modern Library Edition.

Smith, B. (1985) "Some colonial evidence on two theories of money: Maryland and the Carolinas." *Journal of Political Economy* 93: 1178–1211.

Steckel, R. (1986) "A peculiar population: The nutrition, health, and mortality of American slaves from childhood to maturity." *Journal of Economic History* 46: 721–42.

Sylla, R. (1969) "Federal policy, banking market structure, and capital mobilization in the United States, 1863–1913." *Journal of Economic History* 29: 657–86.

Temin, P. (1976) *Did Monetary Forces Cause the Great Depression?* New York: W. W. Norton.

Whatley, W. C. (1985) "A history of mechanization in the cotton South: The institutional hypothesis." *Quarterly Journal of Economics* 100: 1191–1216.

White, E. N. (1990) "When the ticker ran late: The stock market boom and Crash of 1929," in Eugene N. White (ed.) *Crashes and Panics.* Homewood, IL: Dow Jones-Irwin: 143–87.

Wicker, E. (1986) "Terminating Hyperinflation in the Dismembered Habsburg Monarchy." *American Economic Review* 76: 350–64.

Williamson, J. G. (1990) "The impact of the Corn Laws just prior to repeal." *Explorations in Economic History* 27: 123–56.

Wright, G. (1978) *The Political Economy of the Cotton South.* New York: Norton.

————— (1979) "The efficiency of slavery: Another interpretation." *American Economic Review* 69: 219–26.

———— (1981) "Cheap labor and southern textiles." *Quarterly Journal of Economics* 96: 605–30.

———— (1990) "The origins of American industrial success, 1879–1940." *American Economic Review* 80: 631–68.

The Lost Synthesis

Andrew Abbott

One might have predicted that "as sociology meets history" (Tilly 1981), there would arise a demand for synthesis, for a history-as-social-science that would combine the best of both disciplines. A few voices, chief among them the late Philip Abrams (1982), issued that call. But the synthesis has not arrived. Today the relation between history and sociology is that of parents from differing backgrounds whose adolescent children have contracted a friendship at school. There is a pleasant but empty cordiality between the elders. Although the adolescents have an acrimonious rivalry, they close ranks against parental orthodoxies of either sort. One hopes that the young people will cooperatively transform the social attitudes of their parents, but unthinking loyalties ultimately prevent this transformation. So the synthesis of history and sociology, or more broadly of history and social science, has not arrived. Today, the most synthetic call we hear is for each (sub)discipline to keep the other honest (e.g., Roy 1987b).

I begin this article by tracing the various rebellions that drove some historians toward the social sciences and some sociologists toward history. I then detail the institutional structure of historical work in sociology, a structure that arose in the 1970s and 1980s in response to these earlier rebellions. This structural analysis leads into a detailed discussion of position statements by historical sociologists, statements that, I shall argue, misconstrue the relation of history and social science. I close by urging, once again, the synthetic revolution that Abrams and others wished to see—the merging of determinate and contingent explanations in a fully historicized social science.

My just-so story about parents and children should warn the reader why I am not talking much about history and sociology generally. The relation between these parents has been conducted largely through their children. And the children are a diverse lot. In each case there is one group with an official interdisciplinary label: social science history on the one side and historical sociology on the other. But there are also many other relevant groups. In history, there are the various new social histories (of labor, cities, and so on), as well as broader groups like Marxist and feminist history. In sociology many people do historical work in various subdisciplines without the name of historical sociologists.

I start with an institutional analysis partly because I am an institutionalist myself and partly because, to my knowledge, no one else has. Concept-based studies of historical sociology, most of them more or less prescriptive, are by contrast quite common (e.g., Skocpol 1984a; Tilly 1981, 1984; Sztompka 1986; Hamilton and Walton 1988). But more importantly, an institutional analysis shows why historians and sociologists together have produced so little beyond what they produced apart. The synthetic project has not been intellectually defeated. Quite the contrary. It has never been tried.

The Rebellions in Sociology and History

Most of the border groups between history and sociology emerged as oblique attacks on orthodoxies in their disciplines. They were generational ideologies aimed at that overthrow of the elders perpetually necessary in every profession. Like most such overthrows, they usually involved an alliance between a small out-group in the dominant generation and a larger segment of the rising one. And they drew some of their force from the radical politics that animated the generation of the 1960s. But as Skocpol (1987) has pointed out, the differing orthodoxies faced by these groups called for fundamentally differing attacks.

In sociology, 1960s orthodoxy was Parsonian functionalism. Despite its commendable interdisciplinarity and theoretical consistency, functionalism never generated an empirical research program. Moreover, it shared with its predecessors in English social anthropology an extreme disattention to social change. Opposition to functionalism was dominated by the Chicago school and its descendants, who concentrated on the study of deviance and community and whose customary methodologies were field observation and case study. These topics and methodologies had their own disattention to macro change, even though Park, Thomas, and the other Chicago progenitors originally constructed interactionism in order to study the effects of macro change.[1]

The empirical vacuum left by functionalism was only partly filled by the case study and observation literature. The third and soon-to-be-dominant strand of sociology was quantitative empiricism. Ogburn had pioneered this area with his "social trends," simple sums of individual indicators that could hardly be considered historical. Lazarsfeld and others developed survey research methods from the 1930s onward, and these received a mathematical push when path analysis was borrowed from biology in the mid-1960s by Blalock and Duncan. Suddenly dominant in sociology, the general linear model drove the discipline rapidly away from grand theory (some would say away from theory altogether) and established, in the Wisconsin status attainment model, a basic paradigm and method for investigating social affairs. The Wisconsin model was micro in focus and historical in only the loosest sense. Real actors were replaced by variables, narrative causality by the reified causality of variables, real time by the order of the variables. So dominant was this view that its rhetoric pervades even those historical sociologists who most actively seek its overthrow.[2]

Historical sociology emerged in the 1970s to attack these theoretical and methodological orthodoxies. While its leaders included contemporaries of the Parsonians (Charles Tilly, for example), the rank and file were students from the radical years. Theoretically, they saw historical sociology as a way to attack the Parsonian framework on its weakest front—its approach to social change—and as a way to bring Marx into sociology. Methodologically, historical sociology directly impugned the status attainment model with its micro focus, its antihistorical and antistructural character, its reifications, and its scientism. As for the Chicago interactionists, already deep in their own critique of established society via the labeling theory of deviance, historical sociology simply bypassed them.

The keystone of historical sociology was its invocation of the ponderous respectability of History. History's unimpeachable if obscure methodology and its immense factual mastery justified rejection of the Wisconsin view of the world. And while History's comprehensive scope matched that of Parsonian orthodoxy, its focus on events and macro change justified rejection of Parsons. Above all, History's inherent respectability justified the radical politics of the historical sociologists. Even as an evolutionist, Marx was more historical than Parsons, and the Marx of the *18th Brumaire* was a downright storyteller. In summary, many sociologists of the 1970s, particularly the younger ones, turned to historical sociology because it enabled a criticism of both the conservatism of Parsonian theory and the misplaced concreteness of the linear modelers.

John Hall (1989) notes the somewhat different emergence of historical sociology in England. There, the preceding sociological tradition of Marshall, Lockwood, Dore, and others never accepted Parsonian theory and never lost touch with historical workers like E. P. Thompson and Raymond Williams. This older tradition had been receptive to the earlier historical sociology of Americans like Bendix, Lipset, and Moore. So the younger generation, while strongly influenced by structural Marxism, extended rather than attacked earlier work. England, moreover, had a long-standing empirical tradition in historical sociology—the Cambridge historical demography group—whose contributions to both history and sociology were of undoubted greatness.[3]

Historical sociology in the sense used so far denotes a certain body of work and a certain group of people who do it. It is this group (outlined in detail in the next section) that possesses, in the eyes of the discipline as a whole, the legitimate claim to the label of "historical sociologists." There are, however, other ways of thinking about historical sociology, defining it as sociological work that (a) involves data over time, (b) theorizes about social processes, or (c) self-consciously examines past social groups. Each of these bears some comment.

Work involving data over time is becoming common in sociology, since methodological change has finally slowed to the point that old data sets can support current techniques. But one can hardly consider as "historical sociology" the standard article on "blacks in the labor force, 1972–1982." Such an article merely does cross-sectional analysis with time as an index variable. Work involving data over time often boils down to "trends and counts," with little sensitivity to historical context or contingency, and less to qualitative temporal fluctuations in the social categories or attributes analyzed. However, there are those in the methodological community who are convinced that techniques designed for such analyses effectively merge history and social science.[4]

Similarly, many sociologists have theorized about social processes —in interactions and organizations, for example—without particularly worrying about "historical change." Sociologists who focus directly on contingency (a central aspect of history) are usually microtheorists like interactionists and ethnomethodologists whose common assumption of an unchanging "social a priori" is hardly historical in the usual sense. Nonetheless, such process theorists have clearly understood history's long-standing emphasis on contingency, accident, and process, even if they ignore the limits it places on the extent of generalization.[5]

There remains a third view, that historical sociology comprises those who self-consciously study past social groups or cultures. Like my initial definition, this too labels a body of work and the people who do it. Although it clearly includes the historical sociologists discussed earlier—the "official" historical sociologists, as we might call them—it covers many others as well, scattered throughout sociology. (Historical demographers are the most conspicuous example.) I shall examine these "unofficial" historical sociologists in the next section.

The history that the official historical sociologists embraced was in many respects an orthodoxy that their contemporaries in history departments sought to escape. Historical orthodoxy in the 1950s and 1960s was above all an orthodoxy of genre and style. As the old New History (e.g., Robinson and Beard) had subsided under the pressure of the war and the postwar "American high" (O'Neill 1986), the discipline had reoriented around "consensus history," as John Higham labeled it in 1959 (see Hofstadter 1968: chap. 12). Although aware of the ever-increasing power of the Annales school, American historians showed little desire to emulate its distinctive (and to the American taste peculiar) mixture of history and the social sciences. The political tenor of American history was even and conservative, with broad acceptance of the liberal theory of Louis Hartz (1955). To the retrospective eye, there were clear signs of change, but even by 1980, signs of transformation in history were "muted" at best (Kammen 1980: 29).

Quantitative history, a direct borrowing of social science methods, was one revolt against this orthodoxy. Its political version arose at the University of Iowa in the 1950s, where William Aydelotte, Allan Bogue, and Samuel Hays developed a program for "behavioral" history and adapted Guttman scalogram analysis to carry it out methodologically. With the blessings of Paul Lazarsfeld, Lee Benson published in 1957 a manifesto on quantitative political history. Benson, the Iowa group, and others helped found the historical archives at the Inter-university Consortium for Political and Social Research (ICPSR) in the mid-1960s, and Michigan rapidly became a center for quantitative history, a development reinforced by Tilly's arrival in 1969. The 1960s and 1970s brought a methodological swing away from scaling (regarded as purely descriptive) toward regression (perceived as "causal"; see Alter 1981).[6]

The economic strand of quantitative history also had strong local roots, at Purdue. This economic strand produced the most visible products of quantitative history: Robert Fogel's counterfactual demonstration that railroads had not been necessary for American economic growth, and his and Stanley Engerman's controversial revision of the historiography of slavery. Throughout the 1960s and 1970s debates over counterfactual analysis kept cliometrics, as it was called, in the disciplinary eye (Gerschenkron 1967; McClelland 1975). The application of quantitative techniques in social history was more diffused. They had long been central in demographic history, but Stephan Thernstrom's 1964 attack on anthropologist Lloyd Warner's analysis of Newburyport, Massachusetts, was the first highly visible quantitative study in social history more generally. The effort required to generate usable data from manuscript censuses and biographical databases clearly slowed the application of quantitative techniques in this area, although the ultimate results have been considerable.

Institutionally, quantitative history took on the name of "social science" history. In fact, the social science involved was rather restricted, based on quantitative methods in general and on standard linear models in particular. The serial history characteristic of the Annales school (Bourdelais 1984) never caught on in America. Microeconomics proper, though highly (social) scientific and in its own way highly quantitative, affected only the economic wing of social science history, and that wing has in any case relied on linear models for empirical analysis like everyone else. Anthropological theory, although equally social scientific, seems until the advent of postmodernism to have bypassed social science history entirely. In the long run, some have judged social science history a success, while others have judged it a failure. Quantitative training has found its way into about half the graduate curricula in the country (Kousser 1990), but Floud (1984) argues that the decline in controversy over quantitative history reflects more a conviction that it can be safely ignored than a fear that its practitioners need be answered seriously.

McDonald (1990a, 1990b) has argued that history's reaching out toward social science was less methodological than theoretical. He traces this borrowing not only through institutions—showing the central importance of the SSRC reports on historical and social science methodologies—but also through an elegant analysis of social-scientific citations in the urban history literature of 1940–85. To some extent McDonald's methods overstate the case; authors almost always provide citations for common theories while not doing so for common methods. But other writers have also argued for separating "theoretical" history and "quantitative" history as departures from traditional practices. In Germany, for example, the two represented quite different traditions (Kocka 1984). In England, too, theoretical borrowing seems to have been more powerful than methodological borrowing, at least outside the demographic group (Stedman Jones 1976).

McDonald's argument about theory underscores the importance of the other "new histories" (beyond the quantitative ones) in joining history and social science. When the *Journal of Interdisciplinary History* first appeared in 1970, psychohistory filled many of its pages, which also featured climatic history and similar refugees from dominant journals. (Kousser [1980: 887] called it a "crazyquilt.") But in the 1970s the central alternative to the quantitative connection between history and social science came through the various radical histories, loosely connected under the labels of New Left or Marxist history.

Unlike the turn to history in sociology, the turn to social science in history had predated the arrival of radicalism.[7] Thernstrom's book, like Fogel and Engerman's, lacks the overt advocacy that would mark much later social (and social science) history. But if the historical generation of the 1950s and early 1960s had found quantitative history an effective tool in generational overthrow, it was for many of their students one of several ways to make the "peoples without history" legitimate targets of inquiry. This new interest in the little people arose from the revival of Marxist scholarship.

In the United States, the new Marxist (or New Left) scholarship began with William Appleman Williams's students, who started *Studies on the Left* in 1959 and helped set forth the "corporate liberalism" interpretation of American history since the Civil War. At a more micro level, Herbert Gutman, David Montgomery, and their students produced detailed studies of working-class groups in city after city. Eugene Genovese produced a brilliant analysis of slavery whose cultural emphasis owed much to E. P. Thompson. Thompson had produced in 1963 the most visible single work of what became an extensive Marxist historical movement in England. The stronghold of historical Marxism in England was the History Workshop, whose origins as a seminar for the adult students at labor's Ruskin College dictated its emphasis on personal experience and working-class history (Samuel 1980). The History Workshop drew relatively little on social science history, in fact being anti-quantitative; its emphasis tended to be cultural, following Thompson, with Gramsci as its theoretical lodestar (Hall 1978; Floud 1984).[8]

The Left historical community was divided by a number of issues, most of which were also central to debates between history and sociology more generally. Johnson (1978), Selbourne (1980), and others condemned the History Workshop, Thompson, and even Genovese for their emphasis on experience, for distrust of theory, for unwillingness to make large interpretive statements, and indeed for romanticism about the past. Others saw the same problems in the incipient professionalism of American Marxists. As radical social historians marched with considerable success into professorial positions, some thought their work forsook theoretical focus for the study of minutiae. This tendency was angrily protested by Judt (1979) and others (see sources cited in Novick 1988: 443), who saw the study of detail as "ignoring politics." The Marxists were thus to some extent divided over empiricism versus theory and to some extent divided over micro versus macro. Indeed the two distinctions were often run together, a conflation that recurred in historical sociology, where these debates have proved equally important.

The Marxist historians pushed into many of the same areas as did the social science historians. Indeed, the two met on the turf of labor history, where some commentators (Floud 1984) wondered why there wasn't more collaboration between the two (others expected none, e.g., Berkhofer 1983). To say, however, that Marxist history resembled social science history in lying between history and sociology is to mispeak. Rather, Marxist history moved toward a radical scholarship that was as removed from standard sociology as from standard history. As we shall see, this radical pole attracted historical sociologists as well. Yet it did not strongly link the historians and the sociologists.

Another "new" history important in relation to sociology was women's history. Women's history emerged in the early 1970s, taking organizational form in the Berkshire Conferences (from 1973). Articles on women and women's issues in leading journals ballooned from 1 percent of the total in the late 1960s to well over ten percent by 1980. Like Marxist history, early women's history was closely tied to activism, and, as in Marxist history, more recent years have seen some conflict between the professionalized and activist wings. The gradual institutionalization of women's history also saw an intellectual shift from an early focus on domination, through an emphasis on a separate women's sphere in the early 1980s, to a renewed focus on conflict and differences in the late 1980s.[9]

Quantitative history, Marxist history, and feminist history were the three most clearly distinguishable branches of history moving toward social science or paralleling major movements in the social sciences. All three eventually developed connections with various parts of historical sociology. But these connections reflected the divergent histories just discussed. The historians and the sociologists had turned toward each other for quite different reasons. The sociologists were mainly younger people who saw history, radical or otherwise, as a way of attacking functionalism, which they disliked on both intellectual and political grounds. To them history meant comparative studies of particular great events or systems, and their heroes were less Charles Tilly with his numbers and variables than Barrington Moore and Perry Anderson with their comparative cases and congenial politics.[10] Quantification as then dominant in sociology was a nightmare from which they wished to awaken, and hence they defined historical sociology as a theoretically impregnated analysis that was qualitative but not quite narrative.

On the historical side, the quantitative historians were led by an earlier generation attacking a historical orthodoxy on largely intellectual grounds. They and their students had little love for functionalism—*Poverty and Progress* was, after all, an attack on functionalism—but they had equally little love for grand narratives, however theoretical. Theory meant microeconomic theory for Fogel and North, as it meant behaviorism—what would today be called rational choice—for Benson and others. The Marxist historians, meanwhile, had split. An older group, less active as the 1970s wore on, worked with general theoretical and explanatory schemes aimed at political and economic systems. The other, which increasingly dominated academic Marxism, focused at the micro level and tended toward culturalism and the study of lived experience. This last would be the central connection for feminist history as it developed the concept of separate spheres in the late 1970s.

The stage was thus set for actors on the two sides of the disciplinary divide to misunderstand each other profoundly. The social science historians had rejected history's intentional narration for social science's theoretical causality. They had also exchanged history's grand and often political stories for social science's breadth of interest in the economic and the social, the micro and the unstudied. They understood causality in social science terms but accepted history's insistence on factual mastery and on the limitation of explanation in place and time. Among Marxist historians, it was by contrast the group emphasizing large-scale studies that endorsed theory and causality (as well as, in some cases, transhistorical generalizations), while the radical social historians studied "the way things really were" in people's lived, micro experience and usually gave only limited interpretations. Women's historians were split in similar ways, although their common claim that feminist theory grew out of lived experience rang yet another change on these dichotomies.

Unlike the social science historians, the historical sociologists accepted from history the positive value of limiting generalizations and mastering details but reinterpreted social science's belief in causality in *qualitative* terms. Moreover, as we shall see below, they accepted, with the traditional and the large-scale Marxist historians, a belief in the centrality of politics and political economy. Generalizing and particularizing, quantitative and qualitative, radical and nonradical, political and social, macro and micro: each of the various groups in history and sociology represented some unique combination of choices among these dichotomies. There is little reason to be surprised at their failure to come together.

The Institutional Structure of Historical Sociology

In some ways, the consequences of these differences are easy enough to demonstrate, at least on the sociological side. One can look through the American Sociological Association's (ASA) teaching materials on historical sociology (Roy 1987a), for example, and not find any substantive references—among twenty-six syllabuses and eleven bibliographies (including bibliographies on capitalism, development, and economic history; political sociology; and race and ethnicity)—to the work of Robert Fogel, William Aydelotte, or Lee Benson. The social science historians are safely quarantined in the general bibliography on methods, and in fact none of the six syllabuses on historical sociological methods teaches any of them, or any quantitative techniques to speak of. The Marxists are somewhat better represented—Thompson was one of the "great men" of the historical sociologists—but the micro work of the Gutman and History Workshop type is far less evident than one might expect.

No doubt the ignorance was probably as great in the other direction. The Social Science History Association (SSHA), for example, did not prove hospitable to the theory-laden papers characteristic of the comparative-historical sociologists and has no network providing easy access for such papers to the program. But it did prove hospitable to another large group of sociologists who thought of themselves as historical. These were students of past social groups—families, occupations, and the like—who for various methodological or substantive reasons were not part of the "historical sociology" movement just outlined. These people make up a second large group of "historical sociologists" (hereinafter HS2) who augment the initial group discussed above (HS1). As it has happened, it is HS2 that provides the main link in sociology to the social science historians. By contrast, Marxist history has connected into sociology partly through the Marxist sociologists of present societies, partly through HS2, and partly through HS1, while feminist history had its predominant (but surprisingly weak) effect through sociologists of gender who happened to be historical in orientation.

To see how history is understood in sociology today, then, it is necessary to sketch the institutional distinctions between HS1 and HS2. (I shall consider the Marxist and feminist links once this first distinction is clear.) An easy procedure is to study the organizations with which the two groups are most closely associated, the SSHA for HS2 and the American Sociological Association Section on Comparative Historical Sociology (ASACHS) for HS1.

The SSHA was founded as part of the institutionalization of quantitative history in the 1970s. The 1960s had brought the ICPSR historical archives and, in 1967, *Historical Methods Newsletter*. In 1970 the substantive *Journal of Interdisciplinary History* commenced publication, and Allan Bogue, with Jerome Clubb, began to agitate for a quantitative history association. The SSHA and its journal began official life in 1976 (Bogue 1983). The association is organizationally structured around "networks" of common interest: Methods, Family, Demography, Labor, Urban, Rural, Economic, and so on. Networks plan future programs on a panel-by-panel basis, making the SSHA largely member-driven. Some SSHA networks had strong ties to sociology from the outset; the linkage to HS2 therefore began with the organization. For example, among the SSHA's numerous international connections was one to the British historical demographers, a connection that built a strong link to sociological demography. (For an overview of international quantitative history, see Jarausch 1984.)

The other institutional setting for historical sociology is the quite different ASA. A much larger organization, the ASA has fragmented since 1970 into nearly thirty sections, with varying degrees of overlapping membership (see Ad Hoc Committee 1989). The new sections are usually smaller, specialized groups that institutionalize political splits (Marxist Sociology) or methodological cum intellectual ones (Culture, Political Economy of the World System [PEWS]). Cappell and Guterbock have used joint section membership data to demonstrate that the ASACHS is one of seven sections (World Conflict, Collective Behavior, Theory, Marxist, PEWS, Political Sociology, and CHS) tied tightly together by joint memberships and relatively isolated from other sections (Cappell and Guterbock 1986; Guterbock and Cappell 1990). The members of this group are, in general, radical, theory-oriented, and anti-quantitative when compared to the rest of the discipline.

The importance of the ASA sections lies in their control of about one-third of ASA program space. Most of the ASA program is in the hands of the president, who appoints a Program Committee that loosely controls the thematic and general sessions via personal networks. Since there are no panel submissions (only individual papers), the only way for outsiders to present intellectually coherent panels is through the sections, which get the remaining program space in proportion to their membership. Since control of an ASA section is thus the only effective means to intellectual visibility in institutionalized sociology, most new sections bespeak new paradigms craving legitimacy.[11] It turns out that HS1 has dominated the program of the ASACHS for nearly a decade. HS2 has by contrast played little role in it.

I have surveyed the ASA programs from 1983 to 1989 for all people who have either held office in the ASACHS, organized the section sessions, or presented papers in section sessions including roundtable sessions. In order to make a conservative test, I have also included organizers and speakers at the general ASA sessions on historical sociology, even though these are more likely to be controlled by the Program Committee. (I have since acquired the full CHS Section Council lists, but they add no real information.) People who appear two or more times in those various capacities are listed in Table 1. I have also surveyed the programs of the SSHA from 1981 to 1989 for paper presenters identified as sociologists. (Since the SSHA lists affiliation by current department, not Ph.D. discipline, these identities are occasion-

Table 1   Frequency of Participation in ASA and SSHA Conferences

Appearances Conferees

I. ASA

9	B. Laslett
8	J. Quadagno
7	C. Calhoun
6	W. Brustein, R. Glassman, J. Goldstone, S. Rose
5	G. Hamilton, A. Orloff, T. Skocpol
4	E. Amenta, S. Arjomand, L. Hochberg, M. Kimmel, R. Lachmann, J. Marcus, E. Morawska, F. O. Ramirez, D. Rueschemeyer
3	R. Antonio, D. Champagne, J. Goodwin, M. Gould, L. J. Griffin, P. McMichael, J. Markoff, J. Nagel, W. Roy, C. Tilly, M. Traugott, R. Wuthnow
2	R. Aminzade, V. Bonnell, B. Carruthers, M. A. Clawson, A. Darnell, F. Dobbin, S. R. Duncan-Baretta, M. Emirbayer, M. A. Font, B. Fuller, M. A. Garnier, T. F. Gieryn, J. R. Hall, T. D. Hall, J. Haydu, S. Kalberg, H. Kimeldorf, R. F. Levine, D. R. Meyer, C. Ragin, G. Shafir, M. Somers, G. Steinmetz, J. D. Stephens, P. B. Walters, D. Zaret, V. Zelizer

II. SSHA

8	B. Laslett, S. Watkins
7	A. Abbott, T. Skocpol
6	A. Baron, R. Liebman, C. Turbin
5	K. Blee, L. Cornell, G. Elder, C. Tilly, S. E. Tolnay
4	R. Aminzade, D. Billings, M. C. Brown, C. Conell, G. Darroch, D. Hogan, P. Kivisto, A. Orloff, S. Rose, M. Schwartz
3	S. Cohn, C. Fischer, C. Loftin, P. McMichael, K. O. Mason, E. Morawska, M. Myers, S. Pedraza-Bailey, J. Salaff, K. Voss, S. K. Ward, V. Zelizer

---

ally wrong. I have corrected them as my knowledge permits.) Table 1 lists those observed three or more times as presenters at the SSHA. (I used three appearances here because the observation period was slightly longer.)[12]

The central point about the table is at once clear. The two groups of "historical sociologists" are virtually disjunct. Only four people make four or more appearances on each list: B. Laslett, S. Rose, A. Orloff, and T. Skocpol. By contrast, eighteen appear four or more times at the SSHA but not four or more times in these particular sessions of the ASA (most of these people have of course appeared four or more times at the ASA if one counts their ASA appearances outside the historical sociology sessions): A. Abbott, S. Watkins, A. Baron, R. Liebman, C. Turbin, L. Cornell, G. Elder, K. Blee, S. E. Tolnay, D. Hogan, P. Kivisto, R. Aminzade, D. Billings, C. Tilly, C. Conell, G. Darroch, M. C. Brown, and M. Schwartz. And fourteen appear four or more times in these ASA sessions without appearing at least four times at the SSHA: J. Quadagno, C. Calhoun, W. Brustein, R. Glassman, J. Goldstone, G. Hamilton, E. Amenta, S. Arjomand, L. Hochberg, M. Kimmel, R. Lachmann, J. Marcus, F. O. Ramirez, and D. Rueschemeyer.

It is fairly clear who is on which list. The SSHA list includes Tilly and his students (Liebman, Conell, Aminzade), historical demographers (Watkins, Cornell, Tolnay, Hogan), a group studying family and gender (Baron, Turbin, Elder, Blee), and some diverse others (Abbott, Kivisto, Darroch, Brown, Schwartz). The ASA list includes holdovers from the section's early days as a Max Weber study group (Glassman, Marcus), macrosociological students of whole societies (Brustein, Goldstone, Hamilton, Arjomand, Rueschemeyer), and people who have written about Western European or American capitalism and their general effects (Amenta, Calhoun, Kimmel, Hochberg, Ramirez, Quadagno). The people on both lists are two macrosociologists (Theda Skocpol and one of her collaborators, Orloff) and two historical sociologists of gender/family (Laslett, Rose).[13] This simple listing to some extent conceals how absolute the disjunction is; most of the four-or-more-participations ASA people have appeared at the SSHA only once or twice, most of the SSHA people once or never at the ASACHS. There is good reason, then, to think that HS1 and HS2 are somewhat separate groups.

This difference continues in the actual topics considered in the two venues. These topics show rather clearly the organizations' respective histories. The ASACHS was founded by Ronald Glassman and others as a Weber club, reserving the term *comparative historical sociology* for work resembling Weber's empirical work and sponsoring sessions on Weber and his theoretical relatives. The early council members were all hagiographical theorists (writers about other theorists): R. Glassman, J. Marcus, R. Antonio, E. Kurzweil, and Z. Tar. At a bitter business meeting in Detroit in 1983, the Weber group was ousted. The section concentrated thereafter on macropolitical sociology of the nation-state. There was little representation of micro areas in historical sociology (demography, family, labor, urban, etc.)

other than a few sessions on types of inequality.[14] In the last seven years, the section has sponsored (by my rough count) seven general sessions (e.g., "The Resurgence of Historical Sociology"), six methodological sessions (e.g., "Concepts and Methods in Historical Sociology"), four sessions on national or international macrosociological issues (e.g., "State and Economy"), six sessions on various types of inequality and social problems (e.g., "Comparative Historical Research and Contemporary Social Issues"), and three sessions on topics related to culture (e.g., "Comparative Historical Studies of Cultural Change"). (I am ignoring undifferentiated "comparative historical sociology" sessions, roundtables, and the last of the Weber-related sessions.) Methodologically, the section emphasized comparative work of a strongly theoretical and quasi-narrative bent, paying little attention to quantitative work either of the traditional sort (demography) or of the newer sort (e.g., time series, event history). L. J. Griffin is the only predominantly quantitative scholar on the ASA list.[15]

Much of sociology disappears in this list of topics. Some areas are missing because they have their own societies; the historical sociologies of science, medicine, and religion have their chief venues outside the ASA. But strikingly, the major fields represented in the SSHA are missing as well. These include historical demography and studies of the family and migration; labor, urban, and rural history; and even the historical sociologies of education, criminality, and deviance.[16]

The SSHA history is just as clearly inscribed in the sociological work dominant there. There is no macrohistorical or macropolitical network, and so relatively little of that kind of work is presented. ("Political analysis" at the SSHA has traditionally meant voting studies.) Two of the existing networks, demography/family and women, provide the principal component of the sociologists presenting at the SSHA. The SSHA sociologists' obvious connection to Tilly reflects his (and more generally Michigan's) role in starting and maintaining the organization. The work appearing at the SSHA has been relatively quantitative and more closely tied to primary data than that presented at the ASACHS sessions.

If one considers the lists from Table 1 in terms of date and location of Ph.D., one finds further confirmation of the relatively orthogonal nature of HS1 and HS2. Among SSHA-active sociologists, the dominant universities are Chicago and Michigan, then North Carolina and Harvard. West Coast universities are conspicuously absent, a factor no doubt reflecting the SSHA's distinctly regional character. (I have Ph.D. locations only for those teaching in graduate departments, who are about 90 percent of both groups.)

Chicago—Laslett 1969, Mason 1970, Pedraza-Bailey 1980, Abbott 1981
Michigan—Aminzade 1978, Conell 1980, Cohn 1981, Liebman 1981
Harvard—Tilly 1958, Fischer 1972, Skocpol 1975
North Carolina—Elder 1961, Loftin 1971, Billings 1976
Cornell—Brown 1976, Cornell 1981
Wisconsin—Hogan 1976, Blee 1982
Princeton—Watkins 1980, Orloff 1985
Columbia—Schwartz 1965, Zelizer 1977

With the exception of the Michigan group of Tilly Ph.D.s, there is no consistent logic. The major population programs tend to contribute at least one person (Chicago, Princeton, Wisconsin), but some do not (Michigan, Pennsylvania), although represented by current staff.

The ASA listing tells quite a different story.

Harvard—Tilly 1958, Skocpol 1975, Bonnell 1975, Goldstone 1981, Lachmann 1982, Champagne 1982, Somers 1986, Goodwin (student), Emirbayer (student)
Chicago—Laslett 1969, Meyer 1970, Arjomand 1980, Darnell 1989, Amenta 1989, Carruthers (student)
Berkeley—Wuthnow 1975, Traugott 1976, Shafir 1980, Kimmel 1981, Haydu 1984
Washington—Hamilton 1975, J. R. Hall 1975, Brustein 1981, T. D. Hall 1981
Michigan—Roy 1977, Aminzade 1978, Font 1983
Johns Hopkins—Markoff 1972, Griffin 1976, Walters 1983
Stanford—Ramirez 1974, Nagel 1977, Dobbin 1987
Oxford—Zaret 1977, Calhoun 1979
Columbia—Zelizer 1977, Gieryn 1979
UCLA—Garnier 1969, Kimeldorf 1985

The first clear fact is the obvious dominance of Harvard and Chicago, traceable to the influence of Theda Skocpol, a graduate school (or faculty) contemporary or advisor of all but one of the Harvard products and of three of those from Chicago. (Tilly's students are by comparison a smaller fraction than in the SSHA.) Second, the representation of the major West Coast departments better reflects their general status in the discipline; in the SSHA list their only representatives are Voss (Stanford 1986), Salaff (Berkeley

1972), and Tolnay (Washington 1981). And virtually absent from the ASA list are the quantitative powerhouses: Wisconsin (Steinmetz 1987 is its lone representative), North Carolina (Ragin 76), and Indiana (no one). Except for the common prominence of Chicago—and only one of Chicago's nine is on both lists—the two lists have little in common either in pattern or in detail.

Some final corroborating evidence about the distinction of HS1 and HS2 comes from yet another source, the ASA Teaching Resources Center collection of teaching materials for historical sociology, edited by William Roy (1987a). Of the twenty-six syllabuses contained in the document, half cover general topics: three for historical sociology generally, four for "masters" (the heritage of the ASACHS's veneration for Weber et al.), and six for "historical comparative methods." (I have noted above how anti-quantitative the methods syllabuses are.) Of the thirteen specialized syllabuses, seven concern class, capitalism, development, and related historical aspects of political sociology. Ideas, demography/family, urban, and even gender rate only one apiece. Although the editor is a Tilly Ph.D.—and hence, one would predict, more likely HS2 than HS1—the emphasis is still clearly on the macrosociology and politics of capitalism.

Of course, the disjunction is not absolute. Many personal relations cross these boundaries. Sociology graduate students interested in history often came together whether quantitative or qualitative. SSHA-active sociologists are often active at the ASA in other ASA sections: Family, Gender, and so on. And there are other ASA sections that often put on historical sessions, not only among the group of seven mentioned earlier (PEWS and Political Sociology, for example) but also among the mainstream sections like Population. But it remains the case that while the ASACHS has historically controlled the label of "historical sociology" as far as the general ASA audience is concerned, much if not most work that is *conceptually* historical sociology is presented beyond the confines of, and seemingly beyond the interests of, that section.

One common pattern does emerge across the lists: the explosion of historical sociology Ph.D.s around 1975. Only eight of the SSHA group precede this date, while 1976 produces four by itself. Among the ASA group, only seven Ph.D.s predate 1974, while 1975 and 1976 produce five apiece. The generational interpretation of the field thus clearly rests on secure foundations.

We can summarize this evidence fairly simply. Historical sociology had its major expansion in the mid-1970s, about a decade after the major expansion of both quantitative history and Marxist history and roughly contemporaneous with women's history. It was strongly colored by its generational and political origins. Work appearing under the auspices of the ASACHS has since 1983 come largely from a fairly well-defined group, HS1. It has emphasized comparative macrosociology, usually of nations and usually focused on political systems, and has mostly ignored the quantitative orthodoxy of sociology. In a broader sense, however, much or most "historical sociology" appearing at the ASA has appeared outside the CHS and explicitly "historical sociology" sessions, usually at the sessions of other sections: Population, Gender, Criminology, and so on. It is the people appearing at these other sessions—HS2—who provide the major links of historical sociology to substantive areas other than macrosociology of modern states: occupations, gender, organization, population, family, and so on. And it is these people, too, who provide the principal link between historical sociology and the quantitative communities in both sociology and history. It appears that Chirot (1976: 235) was quite correct in his prediction that "the conflict [over the utility of quantitative approaches to historical sociology] is so fundamental that it is unlikely to be resolved."

Although the link between HS2 and the social science historians has been a relatively clear one, it is presently changing. Apparent at recent SSHA meetings is the increasing role of gender studies in the linkage between the two disciplines. The gender connection has historically gone through more general institutional channels, through journals like *Signs* that publish both historical and social-scientific work, through interdisciplinary conferences, and the like. But gender studies is clearly becoming more important within the SSHA. Indeed, the 1990 panel on the current state of social science history (and some other unobtrusive indicators, like the size of network meetings) seemed to indicate that the quantitative emphasis of the SSHA was weakening even further and that the organization was headed for new interdisciplinary waters in which women's studies, with its diverse but seldom quantitative methods and approaches, would play an even more important part.

Surprisingly, however, the net effect of history on sociology in the gender area seems slight. In the first three years of sociology's new (1987) gender journal, *Gender and Society,* only about 20 percent (10 of 51) of the articles had any temporal component at all. Of these, several were standard quantitative "trends and counts" articles covering recent periods, a familiar form of sociological article owing nothing to history in general or to women's history in particular. The real figure is probably closer to 10 percent, about the level of historical material in sociological journals generally (McDonald 1990a). Gender, then, may not have been as important an avenue for historical influence in sociology as one might have expected, especially given the appearance of two gender sociologists on the list joining HS1 and HS2 and the strong representation of gender scholars in HS2 generally.

The links between Marxist history and sociology, like those in the gender area, lie partly within and partly without historical sociology per se. As with feminism, there are interdisciplinary Marxist scholars' conferences, as well as Marxist journals. But there are also direct ties within substantive areas. For example, there are historical sociologists of work who relate directly to the new labor history (Haydu and Kimeldorf on the ASACHS/HS1 list and Voss, Liebman, Cohn, and others on the SSHA/HS2 list). Yet even so, there are complaints that Marxist historians and sociologists of labor have not transformed each other's practice (Kimeldorf forthcoming).

Such substantive connections do, however, illustrate a more general point. Links between history and sociology have tended to travel along particular substantive lines rather than along general theoretical ones. Many sociologists working on contemporary crime know of the work of Roger Lane and Eric H. Monkkonen, although few other sociologists do. This tendency may well have been the central difficulty with historicizing sociology as a whole; the relations between the two disciplines have been largely on a subject-by-subject (or method-by-method) basis.

I have said little about the historical counterparts of HS1. HS2 links up with the social science historians; Marxist and feminist sociologists link up with Marxist and feminist historians. Whom, then, does HS1 link up with? To a certain extent, no one at all. McDonald (1990a) has done a citation analysis of forty-eight selected position papers in historical sociology (broadly defined) since 1957. The twenty-five most-cited authors include only four historians (Stedman Jones, Bloch, Thompson, and Carr). The top figures are themselves historical (or sometimes theoretical) sociologists: Tilly, Skocpol, Giddens, Stinchcombe, Collins, and Smelser.

One possible reason for this self-referentiality is the lack of likely candidates on the historical side. The obvious candidates were ruled out by differences outlined in the last section. The social science historians were too quantitative and often too micro. The dominant strands of Marxism— the new labor history and the History Workshop school—were emphatically micro in their approaches and fell on the experiential and factual side of the theory/facts dispute.[17] Like the social science historians, too, the new Marxists were less tied to global political analysis than HS1 has generally been. The older, large-scale Marxist historians of the Weinstein, Kolko, or even Montgomery type were perhaps a more likely match, but they were fewer in number and less dominant among the new generation of Marxists. HS1's institutional heritage of Weberianism may also have hindered a connection between the two sides.

The chief institutional affiliations of HS1 seem to have been to other historically minded and more or less Left scholars in sociology and related social sciences. Within sociology, this has meant a strong connection with the seven sections mentioned above that make up the young (now middle-aged) Turk group of the ASA. Another clear group of reference for HS1 were their English counterparts, a diverse group extending across several disciplines and now countries: Perry Anderson, Gianfranco Poggi, Derek Sayer, Michael Mann, John Urry, Scott Lash, and others. These English scholars have generally had very wide interdisciplinary connections (Hall 1989). Beyond sociology, HS1 has linked up with like-minded members of other social science disciplines, particularly political science. Surprisingly, however, links between all these communities and history proper seem weak.

One can see this institutional structure by scanning the editorial boards of the major journals representing these communities, *Theory and Society* and *Politics and Society*. HS1 is strongly represented on the editorial staff of *Theory and Society*. The ASA-active group in Table 1 includes nine people who have been editors or corresponding editors of *Theory and Society* since 1980, while the SSHA group includes only three, all of whom are also on the ASA list. Although in its early years quite interdisciplinary, *Theory and Society* has steadily moved toward sociological dominance on its editorial boards, which include many sociologists not in HS1 but active in the theory/ history/politics area: J. Alexander, M. S. Larson, E. Kurzweil, T. Gitlin, W. Goldfrank, M. Burawoy, N. Chodorow, J. Rule, M. Schudson, and I. Szelenyi. *Politics and Society* is by contrast more interdisciplinary, but as with *Theory and Society*, there is minimal representation of historians on the editorial board. Of the current senior editors, sociologists F. Block, P. Evans, M. S. Larson, T. Skocpol, and E. O. Wright have all been on the masthead since the early 1980s, as have been political scientists I. Katznelson and

M. Levi. There is no historian with equivalent tenure, although nearly every article is thoroughly informed by a sense of history.[18]

At present, then, it seems that most of the links between history and sociology come within limited areas—either within particular analytical approaches like Marxism and feminism or within particular substantive areas like demography, studies of the family, labor history, criminology, and so on. As for the visibly defined "historical sociology" of HS1, although it has clear admiration for certain great historians, it seems to lack a direct connection to any particular group within history. And in summarizing, we should not forget the sociological methodologists, not a few of whom are convinced that time and temporality are basically to be treated as clocks for variables (see Tuma and Hannan 1984 for the best technical review of this school).

Central Themes of the Unfinished Revolution

That the links between sociology and history have generally been within particular areas has meant that the central issue—whether the two disciplines are really about the same thing or something different—has never seen sustained theoretical investigation.[19] The group with the best chance to conduct this investigation was clearly HS1. They had the name, the incentive, and the energy to theorize the links between the fields; indeed, their progenitor Weber ably bestrode the two himself. Yet they have failed to theorize the history-sociology linkage because they recreated within themselves the same history/sociology dichotomy that created the disciplinary division in the first place. The contrast of the two original disciplines proves to be a fractal one (Abbott 1990a). We can see this easily by watching how the words *history* and *sociology* are used to divide intellectual turf by the spokesmen of the historical sociologists.[20]

In reflecting on the relation of historical sociology and social (science) history in 1987, William Roy (1987b) saw "history" as meaning that generalizations had to be time- and place-specific. In her remarks at the same symposium, Skocpol (1987) took much the same position. The social historians had to learn theory (and a willingness to see "the big picture") from the historical sociologists; they had to become more "causal," less "descriptive."[21] For their part, Skocpol argued, the historical sociologists had to make theory more time- and place-specific, to eschew reification, to become less Western-centric. Thus, history limits generalization by emphasizing changing causal universes, while sociology provides the causal arguments (see Knapp 1983 for the "metatheoretical" version of this argument).[22]

The subsequent analysis of Gary Hamilton and John Walton (1988: 189) makes this division of the turf yet more clear.

> First, historical sociology includes a variety of analytical styles that, when taken together, do not exhaust all forms of valid or useful sociological inquiry. Sociology is not "intrinsically" historical in any concise sense. Second, by implication there are legitimate forms of ahistorical sociology. These forms, such as the situational analysis developed by Goffman, are not necessarily incompatible with historical work, simply distinct.

Not only does this passage take it for granted that historical sociology is simply the same old sociology but about past times and data. The authors explicitly reject the argument of Giddens (1979), Abrams (1982), and others that all sociology (more broadly, all social science) is inherently historical, although they provide little justification for this judgment other than differences in disciplinary practices. That Goffman's work is about the "histories" of interactions has escaped them, because they use the history/sociology distinction in a completely relative manner. They imply that one can move the distinction to whatever level and unit of analysis one wishes and then use "sociology" to denote the causal study of things that change meaningfully within that level and unit and "history" to denote the larger parameters whose constancy defines that level and unit. Since their own main concerns are with macrosociology, and since Goffman studies interaction in a much shorter time frame, Hamilton and Walton see him as legitimately ahistorical.

But Goffman's work is deeply "historical" in one of the senses mentioned earlier in this article: it concerns process. It regards all identity as negotiated over time. It sees nothing as fully fixed. Moreover, pace Hamilton and Walton, one can narrow one's temporal focus to such a point that every Goffmanian interaction has *within it* its fixed structures, its changing conjunctures, and its trivial events. And the apparently fixed structures themselves change in conjunctural or even "evenemential" ways if we again lengthen our epoch of interest, as does Norbert Elias, for example. The notion, then, that social history should be setting limits within which historical sociology can write causal explanations simply replicates at some new level the same old history/sociology dichotomy. And it breaks down because its argument applies to itself. Each "time- and space-specific" generalization is shown to generalize ahistorically when we move to a shorter time scale.

Of course, one cannot rule out analyses that proceed in Hamilton-Walton manner. Sometimes it is useful to define zones of temporal constancy and to do "pure sociology" within them; that is what the Annales distinction of structure, conjuncture, and event is about. But usually such procedures are inappropriate. An example may show why. Suppose we want to know why 95 percent of American psychiatrists worked for mental hospitals in 1880 but only 50 percent did so in 1930 (for details, see Abbott 1982). We can analyze year-to-year mobility conditions—salaries, vacancies, markets—and see the proximate forces impelling doctors to move. We can also analyze the growth, over periods of five to fifteen years, of powerful local communities of psychiatrists in major cities, local communities whose structures and enticements drove the individual mobility and yet were simultaneously created by that mobility. And we can analyze the shift of psychiatric knowledge from an organic to a Freudian paradigm, a development also conditioning and conditioned by these micro and meso changes but taking place over an even longer time frame. Of similar duration was the change in the social control functions of psychiatry, driven in part by psychiatrists seeking jobs but also by large changes in the society. The move toward outpatient practice, in short, arises in a process whose several layers move at different speeds but nonetheless mutually condition each other.[23]

Isolating epochal periods within which "sociological" causal judgments hold cannot analyze such a process. Yet in fact most historical and indeed most sociological processes have precisely this shape. It is only by a trick that standard empiricism avoids the question, the trick of taking as a dependent variable an outcome at a particular point, a procedure that allows different independent variables to have causal "pasts" of widely varying depths. (A rare example of a quantitative study facing the multiple-levels question squarely is Padgett 1981.) Historical sociology cannot use this trick, since much of its work concerns lengthy processes. In such cases, the history/sociology distinction becomes impossible on the grounds just argued, and consequently "causal" analysis based on that distinction itself becomes impossible. One central intellectual challenge in the history/sociology relation is therefore dealing with the fact that the social process moves on many levels at once.

Other challenges in this relation have to do with the concept of causality itself. Among the various possible philosophies of history, the historical sociologists stand squarely under the Hempelian banner of causality. By "causes," they essentially mean "causal variables" (see, e.g., Skocpol 1984a: 379). Following the major recent traditions of sociology (Bernert 1983), they conceptually organize the world into largely independent cases with various properties and aim to account for the largest amount of social life with the shortest list of these (independent) properties. In such a model, relatively simple effects by single properties (main effects) are preferred, while complex (interactive) effects are grudgingly accepted because history is complex.

There are serious problems with this approach. As Wallerstein, Meyer, and many others argue, the cases typically analyzed by the historical sociologists are not independent. And as Charles Ragin's (1987) work shows, historical sociologists usually have so much information on their cases that finding simple causal arguments is virtually impossible; we must have recourse to formal means of grouping causes. Even that proves difficult, because in the typical historical data set most possible values of most interactions between variables do not occur; most possible types of revolutions or transitions to capitalism or whatever are never observed. If this is true, then we effectively cannot investigate the effects of independent causes (I have specified this argument in detail in Abbott 1990c).

Finally, regarding social causes as independent is more than a little disingenuous. Causality is nearly always joint (cf. Marini and Singer 1988). No social cause ever acts alone in a human system; gender never does anything without having other variables along for the ride. To be sure, Isaac Newton made history by ignoring everything about objects but their point-masses and velocities. But Newton was not interested in the details of physical objects in the ways in which we are interested in the details of social objects. That being the case, looking at the social world not in terms of simple variables but in terms of complexes of variables may be not only more important than we think, but may be all we are able to do.

The concept of causality in social science thus has its problems quite apart from its difficulties with temporal levels. Given those difficulties in addition, it becomes clear that we must directly theorize the multilevel social process, at the same time avoiding the dangers of simple-minded causality. The major alternative available for this task is familiar to every historian: thinking narratively. For Hempel's insistence on covering-law arguments in history called forth a long and distinguished literature defending "narrative knowledge." Founding our concept of generalization on narrative offers a way to allow for both multiple temporal levels and the real complexities of causality.

Moreover, theorizing the social process via narrative is a deep tradition in both history and sociology. If there is any one idea central to historical ways of thinking, it is that the order of things makes a difference, that reality occurs not as time-bounded snapshots within which "causes" affect one another (snapshots therefore subject to "sociology" in the fractal sense used above) but as stories, cascades of events. And events, in this sense, are not single properties, or simple things, but complex conjunctures in which complex actors encounter complex structures. On this argument, there is never any level at which things are standing still. All is historical. Furthermore, there are no independent causes. Since no cause ever acts except in complex conjuncture with others, it is chimerical to imagine the world in terms of independent causal properties acting in and through independent cases.

At the heart of much classical sociological theory lie exactly these same insights. The Chicago school focused on social change in the city and organized their textbook around social processes. Their students, the symbolic interactionists, fought the rising empiricists precisely over the meaninglessness of the idea of a variable (Blumer 1931, 1956). Weber himself insisted that the foundations of sociology lay in social action, in the interplay of agents within structures. His methodological writings place complex particulars ("ideal types," i.e., descriptions, not "causes") at the center, and he urged a search for ideal type narratives, not a reified "causal analysis."

A focus on action and event therefore means thinking about the social world narratively and means generalizing not in terms of "causes" but in terms of narratives. Yet the historical sociologists' own position on the traditions mentioned was both early and strong. Skocpol provided the clearest example. In the opening pages of *States and Social Revolutions* she explicitly separated her "comparative-historical" project from that of the "natural historians" best exemplified by Lyford Edwards (a Chicago sociology Ph.D. and student of Park). Comparative-historical sociology, she argued, was about causes, while natural history was about sequences of stages. Although the natural historians had talked about causes, "little attempt was made to use comparisons of historical cases to validate them" (Skocpol 1979: 38). Her aim was to "identify and validate causes, rather than descriptions, of revolutions" (ibid.). Skocpol (ibid.) argued that "analytically similar sets of causes can be operative across cases even if the nature and timing of conflicts during the revolutions are different and even if, for example, one case culminates in a conservative reaction whereas another does not (at all or in the same way)." Skocpol's focus was therefore quite traditional in empiricist sociological terms; the flow of events was not her central concern, any more than narratives of suicide were for Durkheim. In a sense description came *after* causal analysis rather than before, much as in Durkheim's celebrated *petitio principii* in the introductory chapters of *Suicide* (Lukes 1975: 201). For Skocpol, causal analysis *was* description.[24]

Of course, relative to much sociological work, that of Skocpol has been quite narrativistic. But her methodological language betrays the dream of somehow generating "causal explanations" that are abstracted from actors and stories, a dream that historical sociologists are doing something different from searching for Weber's typical narratives. In fact they aren't. But by using the familiar empiricist rhetoric of causes and explanations, they *are* forgetting the basic insights of process-oriented theorizing in social science. Such theorizing holds that the meaning of an event is determined by the story in which it appears and by the ensemble of contemporaneous events. There is therefore no abstracting "causes" out of their narrative environments; the notion of analytically similar causes producing different results, quoted above, is a mirage (not to mention a violation of classical definitions of causality). The search for typical narratives becomes the first and perhaps the only means for generalization.

In retrospect, it seems likely that the historical sociologists finessed the levels problem and stuck with traditional causality because of their practical environment. Locating islands of causal regularities within a sea of historical change was essential to justify historical sociology to a hostile discipline. To have asserted the validity of process or narrative conceptions of historical sociology, even by demonstrating their importance in classic writers, was probably not feasible in the Wisconsin-dominated sociology of the late 1970s.

Thus the historical sociologists have expended most of their methodological ammunition on comparison, not narrative (e.g., Bonnell 1980; Tilly 1984; McMichael 1990).[25] This comparative emphasis reflects their desire for higher-level generalizations (Bonnell 1980), despite the tendency some see in historical sociology toward a (quite traditional) methodology focused on particular historical problems (Goldstone 1986). Skocpol has addressed the topic several times (e.g., Skocpol 1984a). Her justificatory papers and chapters elaborating Mill's methods of analytical induction embody a clear focus on variables and detach social causality from its immediate narrative milieu (e.g., Skocpol 1979: chap. 1; Skocpol and Somers 1980).[26] The best recent work on comparison—Charles Ragin's (1987) attempt to address complexity with algebras combining causes—astonishes one by its complete disattention to process and narrative, even though Ragin's earlier work saw case-based comparative work as inherently "genetic" (i.e., narrative) in structure (Ragin and Zaret 1983). The same absence can be noted, beyond historical sociology per se, in the best recent work on the "philosophy" of social history, Lloyd's *Explanation in Social History* (1986). The comparative school has sometimes testified to the importance of narrative in its theoretical writing and has often done so in substantive practice. But it has never analyzed the historical process in formal terms.

Citation provides a useful indicator of historical sociologists' disattention to the problem of narrative. The 1960s and 1970s produced a half dozen classic analyses of narrative by literary theorists: Roland Barthes's *S/Z* (1974), Seymour Chatman's *Story and Discourse* (1978), Gerard Genette's monumental *Narrative Discourse* (1980), Vladimir Propp's *Morphology of the Folktale* (1975), Scholes and Kellogg's *Nature of Narrative* (1966), and Tzvetan Todorov's *Grammaire du Décaméron* (1969) and *Poetics of Prose* (1977). The 1980s brought Paul Ricoeur's three-volume *Time and Narrative*. If we search the social science citation indexes for 1987–89, we will not find any historical sociologists citing these works. There are linguists citing them, and psychoanalysts, and a rather surprising number of lawyers. Communication writers cite them, as do a variety of psychologists and a smattering of anthropologists and historians. (There are about fifty-five citations of these works in the fields just listed.) Of the ten citations in sociology journals, nearly all (like most of those in the other fields) invoke these writers as authorities who help us analyze cultural documents—films, ideologies, and the like. The majority are in English journals, and several are, in fact, by nonsociologists, despite the locus of publication. Only two of these articles see the great narrative theorists as helping us decide how to handle the central problems of causality, explanation, and the social process. Neither is by a historical sociologist.[27]

Conclusion

So the story of history and sociology is the story of the mutual enlightenment that never happened. Everyone involved had other agendas and other needs. Firm connections between history and sociology have tended to occur only within substantive areas or within general approaches like Marxism and feminism. Even there, while the links are cordial, they have not really transformed the practice of either side. Above all, everyone involved missed the conceptually and technically profound critique of causal social science implicit in the traditional narrative conceptions of history.

This seems a terrible loss. Conceptualization of social reality as processes of complex events is fundamental to the most effective theoretical traditions in both history and sociology. Only by following it can we address, much less solve, the problem of multiple temporal layers of change that lies at the heart of the history/sociology split. There is every hope that such a revolution can yet take place. Methods that can bring this narrative conception into positivist practice are clearly possible. Moreover, there are potential allies for a "narrative revolution." The same shift toward studying particular complexes that is embodied in narrative thinking is embodied cross-sectionally in the study of social networks pioneered by Harrison White. At least a few historians (e.g., Kammen 1980: 39) and historical sociologists (Lachmann 1989) have begun to recognize that the relating of processes happening at different levels is the central intellectual difficulty dividing their areas. I believe that a combination of narrative and network approaches will prove the only serious way to address that problem and thereby to carry out the actual unification of the two disciplines.[28]

In the meantime, however, the future will see the continuation of current trends. HS1 and its allies will continue to produce excellent general studies of large-scale social and political structures from a Weberian/Marxist point of view. The various constituents of HS2 will continue to exchange work across the disciplinary divide, although the historical side of that exchange—the quantifiers and social science historians—seems to be in fairly serious retreat. Marxism proper will also continue its exchange, although, as I have argued, it has been surprisingly weak. One might expect a serious historical transformation of gender studies in sociology, but that too has not yet materialized, although prospects for it are probably good.

The major short-run changes on the history/sociology interface will reflect the steady turn of the younger generation of historians toward skeptical epistemology, literary theory, and a curious mixture of elegant cultural analyses with simple-minded sociopolitical ones. The epistemological stance may bring these historians closer to a variety of micro traditions in sociology—interactionism, ethnomethodology—although most young historians to whom I have talked (as well as young English professors passing as historians under the rubric of "cultural studies") dismiss that body of sociological work out of hand; what they are doing is utterly new. At best, the various strong culturalist traditions in historical analysis—discourse analysis (Schottler 1989), the study of mentalités, the Marxist culturalism of Thompson and the History Workshop—will pull together with the various strands of sociological work on identities to produce a rich historical sociology of culture. How these long-standing traditions will withstand the onslaught of the literati remains to be seen. But in any case a swing away from quantification and toward qualitative and often cultural analysis is certain to continue on the history/sociology interface for some time.

Notes

1   Schwartz (1987) sees the Chicago school as more openly anti-historical than I do, while Hamilton and Walton (1988) agree more with my judgment.

2   See Abbott 1988 for my full analysis of this approach and Bernert 1983 for a useful history of it.

3   Writing a decade before Hall, Stedman Jones (1976) saw considerably less receptivity to historical ideas among English sociologists, although much borrowing of sociological ideas by historians. Perhaps Stedman Jones described the general attitudes of the discipline, while Hall described a particular line of scholarship that never lost sight of history.

4   Chief among these are the proponents of event history analysis, an approach that construes history as a matter of waiting times till given events happen. The methods are of profound utility but only within a limited range of problems. For analyses of the approach, see Abbott 1990b, 1990c. A better understanding of history can be found in sociology's relatively scarce formal temporal-modeling literature, begun by James Coleman, Harrison White, and others but never really strong in the discipline.

5   It is precisely this dual sense of history, I shall argue below, that has undone the historical sociologists. They have understood what the process theorists missed—the necessity of limiting generalization—but have ultimately missed the emphasis on contingency and process that those others understood.

6   This issue of causality versus description has proved central to relations between history, sociology, and their interdisciplinary offspring. For while social

science history believed in causality by conversion and historical sociology by ancestry, they meant very different things by the term. My short history of quantitative history comes from several sources. The principal ones are Bogue 1970, 1983, 1990; Kousser 1980; and various essays in Swierenga 1970. For a quantitative assessment of quantitative history, see Sprague 1978.

7 I thus disagree with Skocpol's (1987) assertion that the two came simultaneously. Quantitative history was the first wave of the "new social history" and clearly began without radical emphasis. See also Skocpol 1988.

8 Beyond the sources given in text, I have used Novick 1988, Wiener 1989, and Higham 1989 as background sources on radical history. I have also gone through the entire run of *History Workshop Journal* for relevant material.

9 Background sources on women's history include Vogel forthcoming, Dubois et al. 1985, Novick 1988, and Lerner 1989.

10 Of course, Tilly could not be ignored and was therefore one of the "masters" studied in the major stakeout of the historical sociology turf (the edited collection *Vision and Method in Historical Sociology* [Skocpol 1984b]). His institutional importance and his string of brilliant students made him inevitably central to historical sociology even if his work did not really fit the mold that came to be established for "comparative historical sociology."

11 This fact perhaps explains why there are seven closely tied ASA sections carrying out what is largely a common intellectual program. Different sections to some extent "specialize" in rejecting different parts of orthodoxy. The Marxist Sociology section rejects conservative politics, the Theory section rejects positivism, and so on. This specialization explains why historical sociology can be clearly anti-quantitative without ever having presented a deep analysis of the issues involved; the Theory section takes care of that subject (but see Skocpol 1984a). It also explains why there are sections as specialized as Political Economy of the World System.

12 Margaret Somers has questioned my use of the 1980s to establish the personnel of HS1 and HS2, arguing that the actual formation of historical sociology came in the late 1970s, at Harvard, in events like the Conference on Methods of Historical Social Analysis (reported in Skocpol 1984b). That may well be true, although without undertaking more detailed historical work I cannot evaluate the judgment. Since my aim is rather to document the existence of the two groups, the later period suits my purposes better.

13 Theda Skocpol has clearly been the dominant figure in defining historical sociology as a subdiscipline, as much by her institution building (in the 1979 Methods conference, for example) as in her brilliant work on revolutions (Skocpol 1979). It is for that reason, rather than because of some conspiracy theory on my part, that she figures so prominently in this essay. It is striking that Skocpol (1988) remarks that she has ultimately been persuaded of the importance of gender as a central social variable. This persuasion may be related to the presence of two historical sociologists of gender on the crucial list of four people active in both the ASACHS and the SSHA, as well as to the eventual arrival of gender as an ASACHS topic. Gender is without question the central issue in ASA politics generally, and

one of the four or five most central research topics in sociology. It is therefore not surprising that gender sociologists provide crucial links in historical sociology.

14   This concentration has also been remarked by Cornell (1987), although she sees even less work outside macropolitics than I do. See also Goldstone 1986: 83.

15   I should be clear about my own position. The SSHA, not the ASA, has been my venue for historical sociology. Since my substantive work involved professions—a micro topic, in ASACHS terms—it was of no interest to that section. It was of equally little interest to the labor historians of the SSHA, whose strong Marxism judged that professionals "aren't really workers." But my quantitative work on narrative was eagerly received by the SSHA, although perhaps it was less interesting to the ASACHS because it was quantitative rather than qualitative and narrative rather than causal. Nonetheless—and this foreshadows my later judgment that HS1 and HS2 are not totally distinct—my first paper in that area (Abbott 1983) appears in several of the bibliographies and syllabi in Roy 1987a.

16   It is striking that in studies of science, the interdisciplinary group shows far greater ability to merge perspectives from philosophy, sociology, and history than does historical sociology.

17   It is revealing that Samuel (1980) recalls Goffmanian interactionism as a decisive influence on the History Workshop; as we shall see below, HS1 saw Goffman as explicitly ahistorical.

18   Editorial boards provide a clearer indication of linkages than lists of authors do. There are journals in which HS1 and HS2 have been published side by side, *Comparative Studies in Society and History* and the *Journal of Interdisciplinary History* being the principal examples. In both cases, however, the coming together of the two schools has been mediated by an active editor outside either group, Raymond Grew in one case and Theodore Rabb in the other. I thank Charles Tilly for bringing this point to my attention.

19   Of course, there are lots of papers saying that it *ought* to be a subject of investigation, usually providing a few examples illustrating that necessity. Everyone in the area writes such a paper at least once in his or her career. My own version is Abbott 1983.

20   McDonald's (1990a) excellent paper discusses the prehistory of this issue at length. The notion that history provides facts and sociology theory is a very old notion, perhaps because it is not without a grain of truth to its mountain of falsehood.

21   It is worth recalling that Skocpol's argument was used by early social science historians to justify their turn from scaling to regression, both of which are of course anathema to HS1. That indicates the extent of misunderstanding between the two on what "causality" means.

22   From the point of view of standard sociology, this is essentially an argument that "taking time seriously" means "controlling for time and place"—in its simplest version a matter of control variables. By contrast, I shall later argue that taking time seriously means focusing on process rather than causality.

23   There is a standard empiricist answer to this problem, which is to break up the general phenomena or "large events" into sums of little ones. The change in knowledge becomes "now 20 percent of the people believe in Freudianism, now 30 percent, now 50 percent," and so on. Few serious historians think the problem can be conjured away by such means, and in any case, the empiricist solution has its own problems. See Abbott 1990c: 144.

24   Tilly, too, sometimes shows a disappointing contempt for the natural historians, even though the comparisons from which he expects so much are essentially comparisons of narratives. See Tilly 1984. At the same time, one should note that Tilly (1981: 100) opposed the creation of a specific "historical sociology" from the start, remarking, "I would be happier if the phrase had never been invented." Tilly has often argued that all sociology should be historical in the sense of attending to social processes.

25   By narrative I do not necessarily mean the telling of unformalized stories within a context of rhetoric, subjectivity, and so forth. The conflation of the narrative idea—that stories have an internal coherence—with subjectivity, intentionality, indeterminism, and so on, is just that, a conflation. A form of positivism based on narrative or process ideas is perfectly possible, and I have argued it at length elsewhere (Abbott 1990c). A superb example of the conflation of these issues is Richardson 1990.

26   As many people (e.g., Burawoy 1989) have noted, Skocpol's actual practice in *States and Social Revolutions* was in fact far more "narrative" and complex than her methodological prolegomenon promised. Skocpol herself pointed out the narrativity and complexity of her practice in commenting on this paper at the SSHA. This at least potentially reinforces my argument that her emphasis on "causal regularities" in methodological writing was in fact a matter of protective cover. Certainly the usual judgment on Mill's methods of agreement and disagreement is that they simply don't work. See, for example, Ragin 1987 or Burawoy 1989.

27   One is by an economist publishing in a sociology journal; the other is an editorial by symbolic interactionist D. R. Maines urging sociologists to take temporality seriously.

28   I would assert that there are no effective competitors to "narrativity" as new paradigms in social science. Positivist empiricism has lost its intellectual drive, although its practical applications are flourishing. Rational choice theory, after five generations of study by great economists, is surely not going to produce any surprises, except by getting serious about narrative and sequence as in the recent work of Peter Abell (1987, 1989, 1990). And postmodernism is rediscovering home truths about multiple realities familiar to every social scientist who took Berger and Luckmann (1967) seriously. As those of us who did that know, the problem is not to understand that reality is socially constructed but rather to articulate that insight with effective structural analysis. On that subject, postmodernism has little to offer.

References

Abbott, A. (1982) "The emergence of American psychiatry, 1880–1930." Ph.D. diss., University of Chicago.
——— (1983) "Sequences of social events." *Historical Methods* 16: 129–47.
——— (1988) "Transcending general linear reality." *Sociological Theory* 6: 169–86.
——— (1990a) "Positivism and interpretation in sociology." *Sociological Forum* 5: 435–58.
——— (1990b) "A primer on sequence methods." *Organization Science* 1: 373–92.
——— (1990c) "Conceptions of time and events in social science methods." *Historical Methods* 23: 140–50.
Abell, P. (1987) *The Syntax of Social Life*. Oxford: Oxford University Press.
——— (1989) "Games in networks." *Rationality and Society* 1: 259–82.
——— (1990) "The theory and method of comparative narratives." Unpublished manuscript, Department of Sociology, University of Surrey.
Abrams, P. (1982) *Historical Sociology*. Ithaca, NY: Cornell University Press.
Ad Hoc Committee on ASA Future Organization Trends (1989) "The future organizational trends of the ASA." Footnotes 17 (6): 1–6.
Alter, G. (1981) "History and quantitative data." *Historical Methods* 14: 145–48.
Barthes, R. (1974) *S/Z*. New York: Hill and Wang.
Berger, P., and T. Luckmann (1967) The Social Construction of Reality. New York: Doubleday.
Berkhofer, R. F. (1983) "The two new histories." *OAH Newsletter* 11 (2): 9–12.
Bernert, C. (1983) "The career of causal analysis in American sociology." *British Journal of Sociology* 34: 230–54.
Blumer, H. (1931) "Science without concepts." *American Journal of Sociology* 36: 515–33.
——— (1956) "Social analysis and the 'variable.'" *American Sociological Review* 21: 683–90.
Bogue, A. G. (1970) "United States: The 'new political history,'" in R. Swierenga (ed.) *Quantification in American History*. New York: Atheneum: 36–52.
——— (1983) *Clio and the Bitch Goddess*. Beverly Hills, CA: Sage.
——— (1990) "The quest for numeracy." *Journal of Interdisciplinary History* 21: 89–116.
Bonnell, V. E. (1980) "The uses of theory, concepts, and comparison in historical sociology." *Comparative Studies in Society and History* 22: 156–73.
Bourdelais, P. (1984) "French quantitative history." *Social Science History* 8: 179–92.
Burawoy, M. (1989) "Two methods in search of science." *Theory and Society* 18: 759–805.
Cappell, C. L., and T. M. Guterbock (1986) "Dimensions of association in sociology." *Bulletin de méthode sociologique* 9: 23–29.
Chatman, S. (1978) *Story and Discourse*. Ithaca, NY: Cornell University Press.
Chirot, D. (1976) "Thematic controversies and new developments in the uses of historical materials by sociologists." *Social Forces* 55: 232–41.

Cornell, L. L. (1987) "Reproduction, production, social science, and the past." *Social Science History* 11: 43–52.

Dubois, E. C., G. P. Kelly, E. L. Kennedy, C. W. Korsmeyer, and L. S. Robinson (1985) *Feminist Scholarship*. Urbana: University of Illinois Press.

Floud, R. (1984) "Quantitative history and people's history." *Social Science History* 8: 151–68.

Genette, G. (1980) *Narrative Discourse*. Ithaca, NY: Cornell University Press.

Gerschenkron, A. (1967) "The discipline and I." *Journal of Economic History* 27: 443–59.

Giddens, A. (1979) *Central Problems in Social Theory*. Berkeley and Los Angeles: University of California Press.

Goldstone, J. A. (1986) "How to study history." *Historical Methods* 19: 82–84.

Guterbock, T. L., and C. L. Cappell (1990) "Visible colleges." Unpublished manuscript, University of Virginia and Northern Illinois University.

Hall, J. A. (1989) "They do things differently here." *British Journal of Sociology* 40: 544–64.

Hall, S. (1978) "Marxism and culture." *Radical History Review* 18: 5–14.

Hamilton, G. G., and J. Walton (1988) "History in sociology," in E. F. Borgatta and K. Cook (eds.) *The Future of Sociology*. Newbury Park, CA: Sage: 181–99.

Hartz, L. (1955) *The Liberal Tradition in America*. New York: Harcourt Brace.

Higham, J. (1989) "Changing paradigms." *Journal of American History* 76: 460–66.

Hofstadter, R. (1968) *The Progressive Historians*. New York: Knopf.

Jarausch, K. H. (1984) "The international dimension of quantitative history." *Social Science History* 8: 123–32.

Johnson, R. (1978) "Edward Thompson, Eugene Genovese, and socialist-humanist history." *History Workshop Journal*, no. 6: 79–100.

Judt, T. (1979) "A clown in regal purple." *History Workshop Journal*, no. 7: 66–94.

Kammen, M. (1980) "The historian's vocation and the state of the discipline in the United States," in M. Kammen (ed.) *The Past before Us*. Ithaca, NY: Cornell University Press: 19–46.

Kimeldorf, H. (forthcoming) "Bringing unions back in." *Labor History*.

Knapp, P. (1983) "Can social theory escape from history?" *History and Theory* 23: 34–52.

Kocka, J. (1984) "Theories and quantification in history." *Social Science History* 8: 169–78.

Kousser, M. J. (1980) "History QUASSHED." *American Behavioral Scientist* 23: 885–904.

———— (1990) "The state of social science history in the late 1980s." *Historical Methods* 22: 13–20.

Lachmann, R. (1989) "In search of a comparative historical methodology." *Newsletter of the Comparative and Historical Sociology Section* 1 (2): 2–3.

Lerner, G. (1989) "A view from the women's side." *Journal of American History* 76: 446–56.

Lloyd, C. (1986) *Explanation in Social History*. Oxford: Basil Blackwell.

Lukes, S. (1975) *Emile Durkheim*. Harmondsworth, Middlesex, UK: Penguin.

McClelland, P. D. (1975) *Causal Explanation and Model Building in History, Economics, and the New Economic History*. Ithaca, NY: Cornell University Press.

McDonald, T. J. (1990a) "What we talk about when we talk about history." Paper presented at the CSST conference "The Historic Turn," University of Michigan, Ann Arbor, 5 October.

——— (1990b) "Faiths of our fathers." Paper presented at the conference "Modes of Inquiry for American City History," Chicago Historical Society, 25 October.

McMichael, P. (1990) "Incorporating comparison within a world-historical perspective." *American Sociological Review* 55: 385–97.

Marini, M. M., and B. Singer (1988) "Causality in the social sciences," in C. Clogg (ed.) *Sociological Methodology*. Washington, DC: American Sociological Association: 347–409.

Novick, P. (1988) *That Noble Dream*. Cambridge: Cambridge University Press.

O'Neill, W. L. (1986) *American High*. New York: Free Press.

Padgett, J. F. (1981) "Hierarchy and ecological control in federal budgetary decision-making." *American Journal of Sociology* 87: 75–129.

Propp, V. (1975) *Morphology of the Folktale*. Austin: University of Texas Press.

Ragin, C. (1987) *The Comparative Method*. Berkeley and Los Angeles: University of California Press.

———, and D. Zaret (1983) "Theory and method in comparative research." *Social Forces* 61: 731–54.

Richardson, L. (1990) "Narrative and sociology." *Journal of Contemporary Ethnography* 19: 116–35.

Ricoeur, P. (1984–85) *Time and Narrative*. 3 vols., Chicago: University of Chicago Press.

Roy, W. G. (1987a) *Comparative Historical Sociology: Teaching Materials and Bibliography*. Washington, DC: American Sociological Association.

——— (1987b) "Time, place, and people in history and sociology." *Social Science History* 11: 53–62.

Samuel, R. (1980) "On the methods of the history workshop." *History Workshop Journal*, no. 9: 162–76.

Scholes, R., and R. Kellogg (1966) *The Nature of Narrative*. London: Oxford University Press.

Schottler, P. (1989) "Historians and discourse analysis." *History Workshop Journal* 27: 37–65.

Schwartz, M. A. (1987) "Historical sociology in the history of American sociology." *Social Science History* 11: 1–16.

Selbourne, D. (1980) "On the methods of the History Workshop." *History Workshop Journal*, no. 9: 150–61.

Skocpol, T. (1979) *States and Social Revolutions: A Comparative Analysis of France, Russia, and China*. Cambridge: Cambridge University Press.

———— (1984a) "Emerging agendas and recurrent strategies in historical sociology," in T. Skocpol (ed.) *Vision and Method in Historical Sociology*. Cambridge: Cambridge University Press: 356–91.

———— (1987) "Social history and historical sociology." *Social Science History* 11: 17–30.

———— (1988) "An uppity generation and the revitalization of macroscopic sociology." *Theory and Society* 17: 627–43.

————, and M. Somers (1980) "The uses of comparative history in macrosocial inquiry." *Comparative Studies in Society and History* 22: 174–97.

Skocpol, T., ed. (1984b) *Vision and Method in Historical Sociology*. Cambridge: Cambridge University Press.

Sprague, D. N. (1978) "A quantitative assessment of the quantitative revolution." *Canadian Journal of History* 13: 177–92.

Stedman Jones, G. (1976) "From historical sociology to sociological history." *British Journal of Sociology* 27: 295–305.

Swierenga, R., ed. (1970) *Quantification in American History*. New York: Atheneum.

Sztompka, P. (1986) "The Renaissance of historical orientation in sociology." *International Sociology* 1: 321–37.

Tilly, C. (1981) *As Sociology Meets History*. New York: Academic.

———— (1984) *Big Structures, Large Processes, Huge Comparisons*. New York: Russell Sage Foundation.

Todorov, T. (1969) *Grammaire du Décaméron*. The Hague: Mouton.

———— (1977) *Poetics of Prose*. Ithaca, NY: Cornell University Press.

Tuma, N. B., and M. Hannan (1984) *Social Dynamics*. Orlando, FL: Academic.

Vogel, L. (forthcoming) "Telling tales." *Journal of Women's History*.

Wiener, J. (1989) "Radical history and the crisis in American history." *Journal of American History* 76: 399–434.

History, Behavioralism, and the Return
to Institutionalism in American Political Science

David Brian Robertson

The historical and comparative description of political institutions dominated political science when it emerged as a discipline a century ago. The self-consciously rigorous analysis of behavior inspired by psychology and the physical sciences began to eclipse historical analysis in the 1920s. By the 1950s and 1960s the behavioral revolution had altered the discipline's research agendas substantially. Questions that lent themselves to the cross-sectional analysis of current data largely displaced questions that required detailed study of singular events from the past. New research techniques and sources of evidence thrived in a unique period of relative stability and prosperity, a period in which ideological differences appeared relatively inconsequential and many political variables (such as institutions) appeared to be constants. Leaders of the discipline acknowledged that political science had assumed an ahistorical tone.

Since the 1960s, history has returned to American political science. Two currents in the discipline provide the sources of this return. First, behavioralist political scientists increasingly have investigated questions whose answers require historical evidence. Far from a very recent development, historical-behavioral research has flowed from questions posed in the 1950s and 1960s by such leading behavioralists as V. O. Key, Robert Dahl, and Walter Dean Burnham. Richer sources of historical data and the increased interest in long-term political change suggest that behavioral political science has "returned to history" independent of any other form of historical analysis.

The second source of the return to history among political scientists is the "new institutionalism," which is more a persuasion or an emphasis than a fixed blueprint for political analysis. This new form of historical institutionalism shares with behavioralism a concern for rigorously stated questions, empirical evidence, and the weighing of alternative explanations. But it departs from ahistorical forms of behavioralism by emphasizing questions about the impact of fundamental changes in political structures and processes, about critical political turning points and their effects on the present, and about the consequences of implicit circumstances such as institutional capacity and non-decision making.

The new interest in historical institutionalism flows from a number of perspectives, including criticisms of the ahistorical behavioralism of the 1950s and 1960s. Growing doubts about politics since the 1970s have coincided with fundamental uncertainty about economic and political relationships that had been taken for granted before Vietnam, Watergate, stagflation, and economic restructuring. These events stimulated a critical reappraisal of the nature of American political institutions, raising a set of questions that invited research into institutional history—a style of research rooted deeply in the discipline.

The Old Institutionalism

Political analysis traditionally explored the effects of political institutions on individuals and societies (March and Olsen 1989: 4). Drawing on classical, medieval, and contemporary events, political "realists" such as Machiavelli (1985) and the authors of the *Federalist* (Madison, Hamilton, and Jay 1961, especially numbers 6, 18, 20, 63) emphasized the ways that human ambition, power seeking, and political strategy play out in specific institutions.

As political analysis became professionalized in the late nineteenth century, the emerging political science discipline centered on describing political institutions across time and across polities. Political scientists worked in close proximity to historians. Political science was combined with history at eighty-nine institutions of higher education in 1914, and at sixty-seven additional institutions it was combined with history, economics, and in some instances sociology. Independent departments existed in only thirty-eight colleges and universities at that time. In the most prominent of these independent departments the dictum that "History is past Politics and Politics present History" became a guiding principle (Somit and Tannenhaus 1967: 56–57; Waldo 1975: 29).

Using contemporary standards of empirical social science theory, today's political scientists would judge much of the historical-institutional analysis in this era as either excessively philosophical or merely descriptive. W. W. Willoughby's *An Examination of the Nature of the State* (1896) offered a neo-Hegelian critique of various theories of the origin of the state, the nature of law, and the location of sovereignty. Woodrow Wilson's text *The State: Elements of Historical and Practical Politics* (1898) devoted eleven chapters to itemizing the structure of various political systems and generalized about the nature, forms, and functions of government. Descriptions of laws in various polities and speculation about these laws dominated volume one of the *American Political Science Review* (see, for example, Rose 1906).

It must be remembered that at the time describing these laws and political institutions was as challenging as it was important. Contemporary political scientists easily overlook the difficulty and necessity of this task.[1] The post–Civil War expansion of American government occurred in kaleidoscopically varied jurisdictions across the nation. The working rules of the American polity lay in the disparate acts of states and courts. The difficulty of simply compiling and keeping up with policy developments still challenges scholars who study policies that are not nationalized, such as workers' compensation and insurance regulation. Description was a daunting task in the United States compared to smaller, more centralized regimes in Europe.[2]

Today's "new" institutionalists would find common ground with at least three features of this "old" institutionalism. First, both give institutions a central role in political analysis by treating "political institutions as determining, ordering, or modifying individual motives, and as acting autonomously in terms of institutional interests" (March and Olsen 1989: 4). Second, both the old and the new institutionalism share the assumption that the historical development of political institutions merits particular attention. As James Bryce put it in his presidential address to the American Political Science Association (1909), "political institutions . . . are the principal subjects with which our science deals . . . [and] every institution . . . must be studied through its growth and its environment." Third, both assume a fundamentally coercive state capable of autonomous actions. Woodrow Wilson defined the state as an "organized force" whose "essential characteristic is authority," which may be dominated by either a "sovereign minority, or the sovereign majority" and which may regulate property "much as it pleases" (1898: 572, 623). Recent definitions by scholars who seek to "bring the state back in" to social science (Skocpol 1985) echo this realist view of the state's power.

By the 1920s dissatisfaction with historical and comparative description of institutions prompted an interest in more scientific alternatives. Advances in statistics and psychology inspired new research projects based on the quantitative study of political behavior. Charles E. Merriam at the University of Chicago became a central figure in the aspiration for a "new science" of politics (Karl 1974). The emphasis on hypothesis testing reduced history from a central source of information about political development to "a sometimes useful hunting ground for hypotheses, a convenient collection of illustrations, and a possible checkpoint for inferences derived in studies of the contemporary" (Waldo 1975: 30). According to Richard Jensen, Charles Beard kept his historical research on the Constitution almost entirely separate from his widely used textbook on American politics and his research on municipal administration. While Beard is remembered primarily as an historian today, he served as president of both the American Political Science Association in 1926 and the American Historical Association in 1933 (Jensen 1969: 11–12).

Although the institutional-historical tradition in American political science receded from the cutting edge of the discipline, it never completely disappeared. Quantitative analyses are inappropriate or prohibitively difficult for many questions about the presidency because of the small number and unique features of American presidential administrations. Many landmark studies of the presidency involve the qualitative comparison of several presidencies over time. Notable examples include Neustadt's (1960) argument that presidential power depends on persuasive skills, Tulis's (1987) analysis of changes in presidential rhetoric (which includes a content analysis of hundreds of presidential speeches), and Whicker and Moore's (1988) typology of political and managerial skills.

Historical-institutional research endured in every subfield in American political science while the behavioral movement flourished. Leonard White examined the roots of contemporary ideas about public administration in his three-volume study of the development of American public administration. Other leading analysts of the executive branch such as Herbert Kaufman, Samuel Huntington, and Francis Rourke emphasized the deep historical roots of contemporary administrative relationships and problems. Scholars interested in federalism studied the sources of cultural variation among the American states (notably Elazar 1970). Because of the importance of precedent in the development of the courts, the judicial system invited historical analysis from such political scientists as Edwin S. Corwin, Clinton Rossiter, Alpheus Thomas Mason, Wallace Mendelson, and Robert McCloskey.

The Behavioral Revolution and the Declining Role of Historical Research in the 1950s and 1960s

Several changes accelerated the trend toward a more self-consciously scientific—and a more ahistorical—political science after World War II (Dahl 1961a). Increasingly sophisticated technology for surveying public opinion and for processing data made a science of political behavior more practicable. Increasingly precise sampling enabled research on large populations. New interviewing, scoring, scaling, and statistical techniques permitted more rigorous hypothesis testing (Almond 1990: 142). Behaviorally oriented political scientists trained at schools such as the University of Chicago matured (including Herbert Simon, Harold Lasswell, Gabriel Almond, and David B. Truman, among others) while behaviorally oriented refugee scholars arrived from Europe. Foundation and government support enhanced interdisciplinary interest in behavioral science. Service in government agencies during World War II exposed many scholars to intense political maneuvering and revealed the empirical limitations of formal institutional depictions of government.

The behavioral "persuasion" that dominated political science in the mid-1960s (Waldo 1975: 61) could be described as an intellectual tendency united by several shared assumptions (Easton 1962; see also Eulau 1963, 1969; Somit and Tannenhaus 1967; Ricci 1984: 133–75). These assumptions tended to diminish the shrinking role of history in political science still further. Behavioralists assumed that there are discoverable regularities in individual political behavior, an assumption which for many implies that the scientific analysis of contemporary behavior yields adequate insight into political truth. They believed that research should be driven by empirical theories about these regularities, that the validity of these theories must be testable and subject to invalidation, and that rigorous (preferably quantifiable) data analysis be used to test these theories. Since it was much easier to gather new data that met these assumptions, historical information seemed less valid and useful (with exceptions for "hard" political statistics from the past). Thus Dahl (1961a) concluded that "the behavioral mood is ahistorical in character," and Easton conceded that it tended to dismiss factors (such as the importance of rules over time) that were difficult to measure (Easton 1990: 25).

The behavioral revolution has had a tremendous impact on all parts of American political science, including the new generation of historical-institutional scholars.[3] Many of the latter embrace behavioral assumptions about the rigorous statement of questions, the falsifiability of hypotheses, and the precise weighing of evidence. The new institutionalists explicitly identify and define dependent variables, evaluate alternative explanations of events, and seek to discern the necessary and sufficient conditions for an event to occur (see, for example, Weir, Orloff, and Skocpol 1988). Some institutional political scientists extensively analyze data (Bensel 1984; Tulis 1987), although, as earlier political scientists found, locating and developing suitable historical data sets is a time-consuming research accomplishment in its own right.

By the mid-1960s the widespread acceptance of behavioral assumptions shattered the link between history and political studies (Dahl 1961a). Landmark cross-sectional voting studies from the University of Michigan (Campbell, Converse, Miller, and Stokes 1960) virtually defined the notion of "science" in political science (see Asher 1983: 339; Eulau 1976: 122). Public opinion surveys became a dominant method in the discipline; more than a third of the articles published in three major American political science journals in 1979–80 involved survey results (Dryzek 1990: 155). Behavioral analyses of American government (Wahlke, Eulau, Buchanan, and Ferguson 1962) and comparative politics (Almond and Verba 1963) supplanted historical-institutional studies.

The relative stability and prosperity of the United States in the 1950s and early 1960s allowed ahistorical behavioralism to thrive. An APSA president (Lane 1965) could characterize the period as one of a "Politics of Consensus in an Age of Affluence." Change could be viewed as incremental, at most a slow-moving target exposed to mathematically powerful analytic techniques. Incrementalism seemed both rational and prudent (Lindblom 1959). The capacity of the American political system to make competent and responsive policy seemed unproblematic to many political scientists

(Ricci 1984: 149–57), particularly in comparison with totalitarian regimes. Questions about continuity and change receded among political scientists (even as the civil rights movement mounted fundamental challenges to the status quo).[4]

The ascendance of behavioralism in the 1950s and 1960s reduced interest in historical analysis by narrowing the scope of research questions and by focusing on individual decisions (in sufficiently large population samples) as the basic unit of analysis. The availability of statistical techniques and of a wealth of current data diminished interest in the broad, macrolevel questions that required historical answers. For many behavioralists scientific rigor required the decomposition of large questions into limited and specialized inquiry. Behavioralism assumes that politics can be reduced to individual behavior and that political outcomes result from individual decisions and actions (Somit and Tannenhaus 1967: 178; March and Olsen 1989: 4–5).

While even the most rigorous behavioralists conceded that past decisions tend to become institutionalized and to circumscribe current behavior (Eulau 1963: 18), most tended to disregard institutions because they constitute "an invisible force operating in the background of the political system" (Easton 1990: 3). Instead behavioralism emphasized "what we see" (Lindblom 1982). Questions about immediate individual behavior—what party an individual identifies with, how children are socialized politically, why citizens or legislators cast certain types of votes—could be tested in a way that "non-decision making" could not, because they involved overt action. Behavioralists attacked inquiries about the systemic limits on the political agenda that were untestable and inappropriate for scientific inquiry.[5] But such inquiries were destined to reemerge in the discipline when doubts about the performance of the political system became serious, as they did in the 1970s.

When political scientists define their central research question in terms of obvious and relatively small political changes that occur over a short period of time—marginal shifts in voting percentages for different parties' candidates or year-to-year public spending patterns—historical evidence is largely superfluous. Voting studies, the defining literature of behavioral political science, assumed the structure of voting rules as given and emphasized socioeconomic, cognitive, and psychological variables in explaining the outcome of elections. Thus in a major review of election studies, Herbert Asher (1983) limited himself to social psychological studies of voting choice, which hold "that an individual's attitudes are the most immediate determinants of voting behavior," while conceding in passing that "attitudes develop in, and their effects are shaped by, the social and institutional contexts within which a person lives" (339–40).

Naturally behavioralists exploited superior contemporary cross-sectional data at the expense of less accessible and precise historical information.[6] Heinz Eulau acknowledged the consequences of data availability on research agendas when he observed that

> Legislatures, it is said, have lost "power" over the last hundred years (though there is no theoretically satisfying explanation of just what this means), but one would not know it to judge from the great amount of research done on legislative behavior and processes since the early 1960's. Legislative bodies are of course as "open" as executive offices or courts are "closed" and therefore, natural hunting grounds for data-happy political scientists. (1976: 124)

Thus available data shaped many research projects, potentially distorting the relative significance of political institutions and historical trends.

Historical Behavioralism

Behavioralism did not and does not rule out historical analysis. In the 1950s and 1960s some behavioralist political scientists—and many of the most renowned leaders of the discipline—demonstrated that they could bring their rigorous methodology to bear on questions of continuity and change, that is, questions whose answers necessitated historical evidence.

Thus historical analysis in political science since the 1950s has taken two forms (Table 1). One form is the historical-behavioral study that applies behavioral assumptions to historical data. The second form is the historical-institutional study (see also Krasner 1984). The boundary between these types of studies necessarily is imprecise and is more fluid than Table 1 implies. For example, behavioral analysts of electoral realignment such as Burnham clearly track long-term change.

Much of the increased interest in historical-behavioral analysis follows from dissatisfaction with the inherent limitations of questions about cross-sectional variation at a single point in time. Questions about variations in political behavior over time necessitated historical answers. While cross-polity comparisons also can provide insights into the reasons for

Table 1 Comparison of Historical-Behavioral and Historical-Institutional
Political Science Research

	Historical-Behavioral Research	Historical-Institutional Research
Research Questions	Microlevel	Macrolevel
	Short- and medium-term change	Long-term change
	Observable events	Observable events and nondecisions
Unit of Analysis	Individual decisions	Institutional decisions and capacity
Number of units	Many	Few
Evidence	Discrete variables	Contextual case studies

divergence, historical comparison within one polity has the virtue of reducing (but not eliminating) complexities such as different constitutional, cultural, and socioeconomic contexts (Cooper and Brady 1981). As Dahl emphasizes, quoting the authors of the *American Voter*,

> It is evident that variables of great importance in human affairs may exhibit little or no change in a given historical period. As a result, the investigator whose work falls in this period may not see the significance of these variables and may fail to incorporate them in his theoretical statements. And even if he does perceive their importance, the absence of variation will prevent a proper test of hypotheses that state the relation of these factors to other variables of his theory. (Dahl 1961a)

Thus historical evidence became necessary when the questions asked involved the origins of variation and the location of contemporary behavior in long-term sequences of events (Tilly 1984).

History provides a developmental[7] perspective that permits insight into larger questions than those raised about behavior at a single point in time. Without such a developmental perspective, even the most rigorous explanations for political differences beg crucial questions about the causes of change. For example, deductive rational choice models of politics beg the question of how and why institutions were built in the first place (Shepsle

1989).[8] History also provides additional evidence for testing claims about politics and for building theories about politics (Kavanagh 1991; Swift and Brady 1991).

In the 1950s and 1960s, behavioralists interested in questions about long-term political stability and change began to develop longitudinal data to measure political variation over time. Behavioral studies based on historical data began to appear in the most prominent journals in the discipline (Key 1955; MacRae and Meldrum 1960; Hofferbert 1966; Walker 1969). As good historical data become ever more available, the number of historical-behavioral studies in political science has increased.

Circumstances enabled the Interuniversity Consortium for Political and Social Research (ICPSR), formed in the 1960s, to make historical data available to researchers. After a New Deal project assembled data on congressional election returns since the eighteenth century, the data languished until ICPSR director Warren Miller secured funding to archive the data and make it accessible for computerized analysis. Historians (including Lee Benson, Allan Bogue, and Jerome Clubb) as well as political scientists (including Walter Dean Burnham and Richard Hofferbert) helped ensure that the ICPSR would develop a formidable historical data base (Miller, 1989).

Since the 1960s historical census, voting, legislative roll call and state-level policy data has become more readily available. Sources include such publications as the *Congressional Quarterly* and individually developed projects now archived in the ICPSR (such as Jack L. Walker's data on American state policy innovations). Historical information about presidential administrations (King and Ragsdale 1988), Congress (Bibby, Mann, and Ornstein 1988), and the courts (Baum 1989) permit longitudinal analysis of incumbents. The sheer number of events that have now occurred in the behavioral era permit ever larger "Ns" for analysis of events previously thought appropriate only for cross-sectional analysis (for example, variations in partisanship; MacKuen, Erikson, and Stimson 1989) or case study (for example, incidents in which presidents use force; Ostrom and Job 1986).

Leading behavioralists, including V. O. Key, Robert Dahl, David Truman, and Walter Dean Burnham, contributed extensive historical research on such fundamental topics as the nature of American democracy and changes in the evolution of electoral coalitions. None of these scholars has had a more far-reaching impact on the discipline's research agendas than V. O. Key. In *Southern Politics* (1949), Key examined the question of

Southern political "exceptionalism" (that is, Democratic party dominance, intraparty factionalism, and suffrage restrictions).[9] His study provided a state-by-state, tour de force analysis of political organization, factionalism, and alignment in the former Confederacy. Where he felt it necessary for understanding the politics of a particular set of counties in a state, Key marshaled economic, political, and social data dating to the Populist and even antebellum eras. Sketches of individual political careers flesh out the data.

Contemporary scholars continue to cite Key's other writings because they raised questions about political development that remain so salient. In "A Theory of Critical Elections" (1955) Key examined voting patterns in New England towns to find patterns of "sharp alterations of the pre-existing cleavage in the electorate" (p. 4). Data from the 1880s to 1952 revealed significant breakpoints in the 1890s and in 1928. He argued that better understanding of such elections could provide a means for linking the study of electoral behavior to institutional processes and policy outcomes (p. 17), a theme later explored by Burnham and others. His posthumous book *The Responsible Electorate* examined the movement of voters across party lines from 1936 to 1960 and concluded that a significant part of the electorate votes retrospectively, that is, they are "moved by their perceptions and appraisals of policy and performance" (p. 150) to vote for candidates of the party that in retrospect best serves their interests.[10] The issues raised by the retrospective voting hypothesis still engage prominent behavioralists, including those at the cutting edge of the rational choice perspective (for example, Morris Fiorina 1981).

Walter Dean Burnham set out to more fully articulate and to test the notion of critical elections suggested by Key's provocative article in *Critical Elections and the Mainsprings of American Politics* (1970). Examining national and state data from as early as the 1820s (and examining county-level data in Pennsylvania from the 1840s), Burnham linked critical elections to massive social and economic upheavals and to major shifts in governance.

> The periodic rhythm of American electoral politics, the cycle of oscillation between the normal and the disruptive, corresponds precisely to the existence of largely unfettered developmental change in the country's political institutions. Indeed it is a prime measure of interaction between the two. The socioeconomic system develops but the institutions of electoral politics and policy formation remain essentially unchanged. . . . [When] entire classes, regions, or other major sectors of the population are directly injured or come to see themselves as threatened by imminent danger . . . the triggering event

occurs, critical realignments follow, and the universe of policy and of electoral coalitions is broadly redefined. (p. 181)

He asserted that American political parties were disintegrating over time, a development that was reducing the electorate's leverage in the political process (p. 192).

Hundreds of books and articles now examine aspects of electoral realignment (for a bibliography, see Shafer 1991). Sundquist (1973) emphasized the importance of the nature of issue cleavages and the ability of political leaders to exploit these cleavages. In Sundquist's view these new issues could bring about crises that result in realignment, or entirely new parties, or no change in alignment. Clubb, Flanigan, and Zingale (1980) argued that a change in voting behavior alone has been insufficient to bring about the far-reaching changes in the direction of American government associated with realignment. Instead, such changes follow from the acts of political leaders who take advantage of the opportunities provided by critical elections. These elections constitute a strong homogenous political force that brings unusual unity to the fragmented system of American government and unusual opportunities to alter the course of public policy. Among the major controversies that drive current realignment research, two of the most important are the relevance of realignment in the late twentieth century and the usefulness of current distinctions between historical party systems (Shafer 1991).

In *Who Governs?* (1961b), Dahl blended historical and behavioral evidence in answering the question of who ruled in New Haven, Connecticut. The first several chapters of Dahl's book traced the dispersal of elite power in that city over two centuries and the gradual transition from oligarchy to pluralism. In the second section he analyzed the historical development of and dispersion of power across the urban redevelopment and public education arenas.[11] His conclusions about democratic stability explicitly rest on established temporal patterns.

David Truman's analysis of interest groups in *The Governmental Process* (1953), while not utilizing electoral or attitudinal data, clearly is behavioral in its reliance on social psychology and sociological theories of group formation and behavior. To illuminate these theories Truman utilized remarkably broad historical knowledge of the formation and growth of trade unions, trade association, agricultural groups, and professional associations. As the critical election theorists understood disturbances as the source of electoral realignment, Truman saw socioeconomic disturbances as the engine of change in the interest group development. Like Dahl, Truman viewed the stability of the democratic political system as a topic of fundamental political importance. He found considerable merit in the dynamic stability of the interest group system in which multiple memberships "serve as a balance wheel in a going political system like that of the United States" (p. 514).

In addition to these research issues, behavioral political scientists increasingly have used historical evidence to address questions about institutional power and public policy. Scholars such as Nelson Polsby (1968) and Joseph Cooper and David Brady (1981a and 1981b) emphasize historical data about legislative expenditures, legislators' turnover, the seniority of the leadership and of committee chairs, contested elections and party strength in testing hypotheses about Congressional power and strategy (see also Davidson 1991). Presidential scholars have seized on historical data to develop propositions about change in the presidency (Quirk 1991). Ian Budge and Richard Hofferbert (1990) show that, from the perspective of four decades, there has been a closer relationship between political party platforms and policy outputs than conventional wisdom would suggest. Recent studies of divided partisan control of the legislative and executive branches in the United States since the 1930s (Jacobson 1990; Mayhew 1991; Fiorina 1992) are drawing considerable attention in the discipline.[12]

These historical-behavioral studies share an emphasis on research questions whose answers necessitate historical evidence. Given these interests, a returning to history would be evident in political science even if the behavioral consensus of the mid-1960s had gone unchallenged. Growing criticism of behavioralism itself began to lay the foundation for another source of the discipline's return to history by the late 1960s.

The Critique of Behavioralism and the Return to History

Interest in institutional themes, questions, issues, and variables revived as political and economic circumstances changed appreciably by the end of the 1960s. Postwar confidence about institutional stability and the predictability of the future waned. Critics attacked both the existing power structure and scholarly research agendas. More political scientists took an interest in a small number of critical events and in the nature of existing institutions and policies. These interests, in turn, motivated many to examine the historical development of these institutions and policies.

DISSATISFACTION WITH AHISTORICAL BEHAVIORALISM

By the mid-to-late 1960s unsettling changes inspired broader and deeper questions about the trajectory of politics. Social, economic, and political events in the late 1960s and 1970s turned what had been constants into variables. Stagflation, an upward drift in unemployment, international uncertainty, and fiscal stress cast doubt on the economic assumptions of the preceding generation. Faith in government ebbed under the pressure of urban riots, Vietnam, and Watergate. Welfare backlash and tax revolt paved the way for the success of the "new right" by the end of the 1970s. Voters announced their independence of political parties, and election after election seemed to undermine conventional wisdom. The "solid" Democratic South swung to George Wallace and Richard Nixon, and eventually to Ronald Reagan. Politicians altered campaigns and governing for television. In short, the ground shifted under the axioms of political science.

Under these conditions disenchantment with behavioralist research axioms fermented. By the end of the 1960s the leaders of the discipline acknowledged a self-consciously "postbehavioral" impulse (Easton 1969). Critics of behavioralism often faulted it as excessively narrow and in the context of social upheaval increasingly irrelevant. For some the profession had shirked its primary duty to criticize and help reconstruct the polity (Meehan 1972: 59). The normative attack on behavioralism often included an attack on pluralism, which seemed to combine ineffectual policy with a blind defense of the status quo.

Dissatisfaction with ahistorical behavioralism invited the use of historical evidence to critique existing institutions, public policy, pluralism, and political science.[13] Two notable historical critiques were *Regulating the Poor* (Piven and Cloward 1970) and *The End of Liberalism* (Lowi 1969). Piven and Cloward explicitly placed the reforms of the Great Society in the context of the historical development of American welfare policy. This historical context triggered more critical propositions about government action, notably the hypothesis that welfare policy is "initiated or expanded during the occasional outbreaks of civil disorder produced by mass unemployment, and are then abolished or contracted when political stability is restored" (1970: xiii).

Lowi analyzed the historical development of a broader range of American public policy and contrasted policy since the New Deal unfavorably with pre-New Deal initiatives. In his view pluralism, the American "public philosophy" since the 1930s, accounted for the contemporary inefficiency and injustice of national regulatory, welfare, and other policies. He explicitly attacked the political science profession, claiming that its ahistorical scientific pretensions made it an essentially conservative force that paid too little attention to existing institutional structures.

> Interest group liberalism produces an apologetic political science. . . . [Its] focus on realism, equilibrium, and the paraphernalia of political process is at bottom apologetic. The political scientist is not necessarily a defender of the status quo, but the result is too often the same, because those who are trying to describe reality tend to reaffirm it. Focus on the group, for example, is a commitment to one of the more rigidified aspects of the social process. Stress upon the incremental is apologetic as well. The separation of facts from values is apologetic (Lowi 1969: 312).

Criticism of behavioral political science was institutionalized in the Caucus for a New Political Science (formed in 1967) [14] and in the journal *Politics and Society,* founded in 1970 by several Caucus members.

REASSESSING THE ROLE OF THE STATE

While some political scientists used history to critique American public policy, analysts of the modernization of third world nations began to re-examine the history of modernization and the role of the state in developed countries such as the United States. In the 1950s and 1960s, scholars examining the modernization of African, Asian, and Latin American nations implicitly assumed that these countries would proceed along the same path as the industrialized nations (Migdal 1983: 319). But closer examination of historical and comparative evidence revealed the significant variations in the development of Western nations and reminded scholars of the sometimes wrenching events that accompanied the process (Huntington 1968; Moore 1966). The historical development of industrialized nations began to engage not only critics of behavioralism, but leading behavioralists as well (Almond, Flanagan, and Mundt 1973).

Both the historical public policy critiques and the reassessment of Western modernization sparked interest in the part that government plays in stability and change. Among Marxists, the role of the state in capitalist society had become a central issue in the 1960s (Carnoy 1984).[15] *Politics and Society* provided a forum for Immanuel Wallerstein (1971) and others to emphasize the important role of the state in economic development in capitalist nations. Marxists debated the degree to which the state was autonomous even in contemporary capitalist societies (Miliband 1969; O'Connor 1973; Poulantzas 1974; Offe 1975; Block 1977; Carnoy 1984). The manipulation of weak by strong states focused attention on the historical record of international exploitation (Wallerstein 1974) and the development of third world economic dependence (Cockroft 1972).

In a context in which government seemed less benign, this neo-Marxist debate on state autonomy influenced scholars beyond Marxist circles. Eric Nordlinger's *On the Autonomy of the Democratic State* (1981) expanded pluralist analysis to accommodate the independence of state officials. Public choice theorists (Niskanen 1971; Buchanan and Wagner 1977) provided conservative critics with a portrait of autonomous self-aggrandizing public officials.

Evidence of the rise of the "administrative state" even in the United States (Dodd and Schott 1979) caused some political scientists to reassess the nature of the American state. A study of the attitudes of administrators and legislators in the United States and several West European nations was premised on the larger question of the growth of bureaucratic power and the decline of legislative influence in public policy making in advanced capitalist nations (Aberbach, Putnam, and Rockman 1981). Authors of various persuasions made the case that American politics had become nationalized and thus transformed (Lowi and Stone 1978; Lunch 1987). Studies of bureaucratic power in industrial development (Armstrong 1973), in building the welfare state (Heclo 1974), in military crises (Allison 1971), and in the local implementation of policy (Pressman and Wildavsky 1973) gave credence to a view of government agencies as not only independent but also capable of manipulating elected officials and citizens.

The emerging public policy subfield suggested that government actors enjoyed considerable latitude in setting agendas (Kingdon 1984) and implementing policies (Mazmanian and Sabatier 1983). Public policy scholars such as Richard Rose (1990) began more explicitly to emphasize that because policy makers inherit many policy commitments and institutions when they take office, policy history is essential for understanding the constraints and opportunities that shape policy makers' actions (see also Ashford 1986).

The new interest in "political economy" in the 1970s marked the confluence of the critical "postbehavioral" impulse, introspection about the history of capitalism, the interest in policy outcomes, and the recognition of the timeless nature of the coercive powers of states. The term political economy came to have two meanings. One meaning of political economy emphasized that economic activity should be understood as an extension of the struggle for power and dominance. This form of political economy fostered institutional, critical, and historical comparative analyses. James O'Connor's *Fiscal Crisis of the State* (1973), one of the defining books of the new political economy, argued that the costs of managing the competitive (low-wage, economically insecure) and the monopoly sectors of the economy were pushing the government's fiscal burden to the breaking point. Other analysts drew attention to challenges to national sovereignty posed by international economic independence, multinational corporations, and powerful states (Katzenstein 1978; Krasner 1978).

Structural and historical political economy revealed the importance of non-decision making and political capacity. Historical and comparative evidence provided the only way to answer questions about politically important nonevents. Many of the most important political questions involved the failure of policy alternatives to receive serious discussion, the failure of political movements to emerge, and the failure of political systems to perform as expected. Evidence that these suppressed features exist can be culled from the historical record of counterfactuals, cross-national social movements, and unsuccessful alternatives.

These issues had surfaced early in the field of urban politics (Bachrach and Baratz 1970) and in the 1970s and 1980s influenced the analysis of urban problems such as dual markets (Berger and Piore 1980), class formation (Katznelson 1981), and the urban fiscal crisis (Judd 1979). It also prompted interest in the mobilization of economic interests, particularly labor and business. Corporatism, the formal interaction of government with peak trade union and employer organizations in functional policy areas, attracted both normative and empirical attention (Schmitter and Lembruch

1979; Diamant 1981). Corporatism along Swedish lines suggested a social democratic model for alleviating governability problems.

A second meaning of the term "political economy" applied economic, rational choice reasoning to political problems, characterizing political processes and outcomes in terms of optimizing, games, public goods, and the free-rider problem. This version—in the form of the contemporary "rational choice" perspective on politics—has even more profoundly affected contemporary political science than has the return to history. This approach tends to be very deductive and abstract, but its advocates have used historical data to demonstrate their claims. Examples include Robert Axelrod's (1984: 73–87) use of early twentieth-century military alliances to substantiate propositions derived from game theory and Terry Moe's (1987) analysis of the changing nature of the institutional politics of the National Labor Relations Board since World War II. Moe illustrated the need to bring institutional dynamics over time into accounts of political strategy.

Both forms of political economy examined government manipulation of the economy. Particularly in the American context such issues again drew attention to nondecisions. While the notion of private influence in public economic policy was hardly new among political scientists (McConnell 1966), the profession's leaders gave the notion of businesses' political prerogatives new currency. Charles A. Lindblom's *Politics and Markets* (1977), in which he reasserted the connection between market systems and pluralism, most forcefully assessed the "privileged position of business" in such systems. Lindblom, a leading pluralist thinker in the 1950s and 1960s, helped to shift the tone of the discipline toward a more critical and structural perspective on American political economy (see also Dahl 1985). At the annual American Political Science Association conventions, a new "Conference Group on the Political Economy of Advanced Industrial Societies" formed twenty panels in 1980. Its panels attracted large crowds through the following decade.

While Lindblom's analysis was not historical, the new interest in political economy and institutions stimulated interest in revisionist interpretations of the development of the American political economy. Some political scientists were drawn to the work of historians who blended these interests, including Gabriel Kolko (1963 and 1965), Robert Wiebe (1967), James Weinstein (1968), Alfred Chandler (1968), and Ellis Hawley (1969).

The literature of organization theory also attracted attention by highlighting hypotheses about the ways that organizations seek to maximize autonomy and minimize dependence and uncertainty (see the review of the literature in Scott 1987). The organizational theory literature accentuated the effect of past decisions, routines, and decisions on contemporary rules, standard operating procedures, and routines in institutions (Stinchcombe 1965).[16]

The new emphasis on the interaction of political and economic interests broadened the behavioral research agenda. By the 1970s darker portraits of manipulation of the economic cycle and transfer payments for reelection began to appear (Tufte 1978), sparking renewed interest in the history of government growth (Larkey, Stolp, and Winer 1981) and the viability of government itself (Rose and Peters 1978; Chubb and Peterson 1989). Mancur Olson (1982) argued that interest group competition for beneficial governmental policies contributed heavily to *The Rise and Decline of Nations*. American political scientists increasingly interested in rational choice began to incorporate economic variables into time-series analyses of voting in order to test the retrospective voting hypothesis and its alternatives (Alt and Chrystal 1983: 149–72). In outlining hypotheses about the life cycle of organizations (1967) and the dynamics of electoral coalitions (1957), Anthony Downs had suggested a research agenda that implied the necessity of historical evidence to examine conditions of political change.[17]

Together these circumstances—doubts about the performance of the political and economic system, a new concern about the role of the state, and interest in broader developmental questions as well as in questions about nondecisions, institutional capacity, and a small number of critical cases—brought historical institutionalism back into political science. But historical institutionalism did not return just as it pleased. The new historical institutionalism distinctly reflected the altered political economy of the 1970s and the postbehavioral thrust of social science.

The New Historical Institutionalism

While historical-behavioral political research has increased, much of the return to history in political science is associated with the "new" institutionalism. This "empirically based prejudice" (March and Olsen 1989) views institutions (usually understood as established patterns of political behavior including not only courts, legislatures, and bureaus but also long-standing electoral coalitions) as capable of autonomous action.[18] Since institutional variation occurs over the long term, this unit of analysis necessitates historical analysis.

Rather than a thoroughly detailed theoretical framework, the new institutionalism can be characterized as an intellectual persuasion in the way that behavioralism constituted a persuasion a generation earlier (Eulau 1963). Compared to behavioralism it emphasizes questions of relatively broad scope and long-term change, the relative autonomy of government institutions, and the complexity of historical development. While it is primarily their research questions that drive behavioralists to utilize historical evidence, new institutionalists are driven to history by both their research questions *and* by the central place of institutions in their theories. The practical constraints of the intensive study of institutions tend to limit the number of cases that they examine. Of critical importance for new institutionalists is the assumption that past decisions shape the institutional constraints and opportunities of later periods, including the present.

At the same time, its absorption of some behavioral principles helps explain why the new institutionalist approach departs from the "old" institutionalism and from Marxist analysis. In the first issue of the annual *Studies in American Political Development,* editors Karen Orren and Stephen Skowronek explicitly locate the new institutionalism in relation to turn-of-the-century political science.

> The new institutionalism has not returned to old formalisms. It has, instead, used the work of the recent past as a new point of departure from which to specify more closely the complex patterns of state-society relations. History provides the dimension necessary for understanding institutions as they operate under varying conditions. Beyond that, it is also the natural proving ground for the claim that institutions have an independent and formative influence on politics. . . . *Studies'* institutional perspective is defined broadly to encompass the social and cultural institutions that impinge on government as well as governmental institutions themselves. . . . Our editorial board ranges the spectrum of subfields, theoretical perspectives, and analytic methods. (Orren and Skowronek 1986)

THE IMPACT OF THE NEW INSTITUTIONALISM
IN POLITICAL SCIENCE

New institutionalist analyses gained prominence in political science in professional meetings, notable books, and historically oriented periodicals in the early 1980s. The program theme of the 1981 American Political Science Association meetings was "Restoring the State." In explaining this theme program cochairs Theodore Lowi and Sidney Tarrow of Cornell wrote that

> We do not reject the perspective that focuses on the political process, or on political behavior—even when it is *mass* behavior—but we argue that processes and behavior can best be studied within the context of institutions of the state and of citizens' concepts of it. . . . [W]e want to recognize that the state and the institutions of public control should be brought back in some form or another to the center of political science. . . . [W]e feel that the state is the one common thread in all subfields within the discipline, either as a direct force (as in the study of institutions, executives, and policies) or as an indirect force or "brooding omnipresence" significant only as a general context or even significant—as in the American past—by its absence from political discourse. (Lowi and Tarrow 1980)

Charles Lindblom's 1981 APSA presidential address, "Another State of Mind," argued that the "conventional" behavioralist theory of democratic politics lacked empirical grounding and that the "radical" model drawing attention to class struggle, the policing role of the state, and the importance of nonevents and agenda control should be brought back "in from the cold" (Lindblom 1982).

Many of these ideas had been fermenting in the 1970s among graduate students and faculty, particularly at Harvard University and the University of Chicago. Martin Shefter, Peter Gourevitch, Stephen Krasner, Peter Katzenstein, Charles Maier, and Theda Skocpol were graduate students at Harvard in the 1970s. With David Greenstone, Ira Katznelson, Philippe Schmitter, and Theda Skocpol on the faculty during the period, Chicago's graduates in the 1970s and early 1980s included among others Karen Orren, Amy Bridges, Donald Brand, Margaret Weir, John Ikenberry, and Edward Amenta.

Theda Skocpol and her associates are among the most central figures of the new historical institutionalism in political science. In *States and Social Revolutions* (1979), Skocpol argued that successful peasant revolutions have been predicated on the breakdown of state institutions of social control. This breakdown followed from the choices of self-interested state actors. Beginning in the 1980s Skocpol, her coauthors and students assessed the role of the American state in the development of social and economic policy (most notably Skocpol 1980; Finegold 1982; Skocpol and Finegold

1982; Skocpol and Ikenberry 1983; Orloff and Skocpol 1984; Weir, Orloff, and Skocpol 1988; Weir 1989; Amenta and Skocpol 1989). The impact of the Skocpol group's work is substantial. In a study of citations in political science journals, no individual who had received a Ph.D. since 1975 had been cited more frequently than Skocpol (Klingerman and Grofman 1989: 260). Skocpol served on the editorial board of *Politics and Society, Studies in American Political Development,* and the *Journal of Policy History.*

Equally influential is the work of Stephen Skowronek and a group of scholars in the orbit of Cornell University. Based on his dissertation at Cornell (where he worked with Lowi, Tarrow, and others), Skowronek's *Building a New American State* (1982) examined the development of the civil service, the army, and business regulation in the United States between 1877 and 1920 (the same period that Wiebe examined in *The Search for Order*). He argued that contemporary governability problems can be traced to the inability effectively to reconstitute "the state of courts and parties" that characterized American politics before the 1870s. In later work Skowronek (1988) related presidential effectiveness to stages of American political regime change. Other Cornell University political science faculty and graduates produced a steady stream of historical and comparative research dealing with such topics as working-class mobilization and party coalitions (Shefter 1986; Ginsberg and Shefter 1990; Mink 1986), policy outcomes (Bensel 1984, 1990; Sanders 1981), and corporatism as a strategy for dealing with economic change (Katzenstein 1985). Besides publishing Katzenstein's work, the Cornell University Press has published important historical-institutional work including Zysman's study (1983) of financial systems and Gourevitch's analysis (1986) of capitalist nations' responses to past economic crises.

By the mid-1980s the new historical institutionalism began to institutionalize itself within political science. March and Olsen's (1984) discussion in the *American Political Science Review* helped establish the new institutionalism as a significant force in the profession. Historical-behavioral and historical-institutional analysis began to appear more frequently in established journals, as new outlets for historically oriented political scientists appeared in the form of *Studies in American Political Development* (1986) and the *Journal of Policy History* (1989). The Social Science Research Council supported the movement's expansion through its Committee on States and Social Structures. This committee's 1982 conference on "States and Social Structures: Research Implications of Current Theories" resulted in the manifesto *Bringing the State Back In* (Evans, Rueschemeyer, and Skocpol 1985). Individual monographs multiplied through individual volumes and book series such as the Cornell Studies in Political Economy, Princeton's Studies from the Project on the Federal Social Role (and its forthcoming series on American Politics: Historical, International, and Comparative Perspectives), and Westview's Transforming American Politics series.

After two years of informal existence, the History and Politics section of the American Political Science Association was formed in 1990. By 1991 the section included over 400 members, ranking it twelfth in size among the twenty-seven organized sections in the association (Brintall 1991). The section self-consciously embraced diverse approaches to incorporating history in political research:

> Among us are social scientists who turned to history to expand the number of cases of phenomena of interest. For others, long-standing historical puzzles are appropriate foils for demonstrating the explanatory power of particular theories. Still others seek the deep structure or contours of contemporary political problems. Our group embraces—perhaps better than any other organized sections—competing epistemological attitudes. Some scholars use history to further scientistic objectives while others see it as the fit locus for interpretive approaches to the study of politics. These plural interests and perspectives were well represented in our Program last fall and were the focus of spirited but civil debate at a roundtable specially designed to explore the meaning of the turn to history. (Tulis 1990)

Thus the History and Politics section in the early 1990s aspired to bring about more interaction between historical-behavioralists and historical-institutionalists.

In November 1990 the appearance of a section newsletter edited by Kenneth Finegold and Elaine Swift helped formalize the section and define the field. The newsletter included a wide range of information about new books and articles, work in progress, syllabi, research queries, and fellowships. The section's breadth is indicated by its journal scan, which lists work published in major political science, history, and sociology journals by historical-institutionalists as well as behavioralists (Everett C. Ladd and Joseph Schlesinger) and game theorists (Terry Sullivan).

CENTRAL RESEARCH INTERESTS

The new historical-institutionalist research agenda focused on the consequences of government autonomy and structure for the distribution
of power and for public policy, primarily in the United States (but also
with elements of cross-national comparison). A central question turned
on American "exceptionalism," restated in a variety of forms. Many of
these themes carry forward the interests in political economy, bureaucratic
power, and social criticism that had sparked the renewed interest in historical analysis in the 1970s.

The exceptional social policies of the United States attracted considerable attention, particularly among the Skocpol group. Historical analysis of
policy development portrayed the nature of American welfare provision in
increasingly rich—but complex—tones. Skocpol, for example, noted the
extensive provision for the Grand Army of the Republic veterans and their
dependents in the late nineteenth century and the gender distinctions of
American social provision (Orloff and Skocpol 1984; Skocpol forthcoming). Several authors have drawn attention to the historical development of
the fragmented system of welfare provision between entitlement and short-
term programs and the resulting difficulty of maintaining political support
for these programs (Orloff 1991).

The exceptional nature of American economic management also has
attracted a good deal of new institutionalist research. A significant part of
Skowronek's analysis turned on antitrust and railroad regulation. Bensel
(1984) and Sanders (1986) argued that differences in sectional political
interests mediated by the constituent orientation of the Congress have
profoundly shaped economic regulations and other policies. Weir (1988)
explored the institutional and intellectual sources of the limited American interpretation of Keynesianism. Some authors have analyzed particular economic sectors (Brand 1988; Finegold 1988). Historical-institutional
analysis also influenced studies of employment policy (Weir 1992; Mucciaroni 1990), monetary policy (Woolley 1984), and the budget deficit
(Savage 1988).

Scholars conventionally emphasized political culture and tradition as
reasons for the exceptional social and economic policies of the United States
(Hartz 1955; King 1973; Lipset 1983), while a more recent literature in the
1970s emphasized the impact of left-wing political parties and the strength
of trade unions (Castles 1982).[19] Historical-institutionalist scholars began

to detail the ways in which the American working class mobilized at critical turning points in American history. Variations on this approach include the rise and fall of broad political-economic coalitions (Gourevich 1986), the relations among immigrant and native workers (Mink 1986), urban working-class development (Katznelson 1981: 7–17), comparison of political strategies of influential unions (Marks 1989; Hattam 1990), and the role of political patronage (Shefter 1986; Orloff and Skocpol 1984) for limiting the aspirations and strategies of organized labor. Bensel (1990) found that the political and economic disunity resulting from the Civil War and its aftermath debilitated social democratic forces in this century. The New Deal period has attracted special attention for the narrow areas in which corporatist arrangements took hold (Finegold 1982) and the political alignments of various industries (Ferguson 1984).

In all these studies, political structure plays a central explanatory role. The new historical-institutionalists emphasize that the capacity and coherence of the political system constitute formidable limiting conditions on public policy. Political capacity can be gauged on three dimensions: first, the formal boundaries of legitimate government intervention (that is, what is permissible for government to do); second, government's fiscal ability (the ability to raise revenues and fund policy initiatives); and third the professionalism and expertise of legislators and public administrators.

In addition to capacity, policy-making coherence constitutes another limiting condition imposed by political structure. Policy-making coherence refers to the degree to which various policy-making institutions are able to align their activity and produce definitive and consistent policy. It involves two dimensions. First, the degree to which authority *within* a level of government is unified or fragmented constitutes one dimension of policy-making coherence. Compared to more centralized systems, American government is marked by substantial fragmentation because of separate (but shared) powers, divided legislatures with coequal houses, and judicial review (and in the state governments, independently elected department executives). Second, the degree of autonomy possessed by different levels of government constitutes another dimension of policy-making coherence. In the United States state governments have traditionally exercised most of the nation's domestic policy-making powers, and new national policies usually have had to accommodate older state programs that already "occupy the field."[20]

Findings from these studies have stimulated interest in reexamining the nature of historical change. Political scientists traditionally viewed development as a process of "institutional change taking place incrementally, along a fairly smooth curve, at the margins" (Migdal 1983: 322). In this view existing political institutions were functional and efficient (March and Olsen 1989). But to new institutionalists the historical dynamics of institutional change appear to be much more a process of policy succession and learning whose trajectory is undetermined and hard to predict. Cycles of change seem to result from the inconsistency between existing conditions and institutions (Krasner 1984), and soon constitute a set of "working rules" whose existence and legitimacy influence politics more indirectly as political actors implicitly accept and adjust to their existence. The U.S. welfare state exhibits a zigzag pattern of development (Amenta and Skocpol 1989).

ANALYTICAL ISSUES

For the new historical-institutionalists, explaining political events depends on the historical analysis of well-chosen cases. Validating explanations often depends on counterfactuals and evidence that some conditions are necessary and sufficient for an event to occur, while others are not. Generalizations, then, have to be limited to specific sets of events.

Two important challenges for the new historical-institutional research involve analytical issues. One issue turns on operationalizing terms such as "state" and "institution." Critics such as Gabriel Almond (1988) suggest that the very open-endedness of these terms invites definitional battles and ambiguous findings. Many of Almond's criticisms can be answered (see the rejoinders to Almond following his article). Still, the boundary between the political actors who are part of the state and those who are not must be clear in order to draw conclusions about the direction and degree of political influence. Consequential and theoretically driven conceptual distinctions are especially important for organizing the contextual evidence necessary for rigorous qualitative historical studies.

The problem of defining the boundaries of the state is particularly vexing in the United States, where close functional relationships among ostensibly private and public actors substantially muddy relations of power and dependence. While independent action by a public official may constitute state autonomy in one sense, in another sense political constraints imposed by class dominance, the "privileged position" of business, or international economic competition (Przeworski and Wallerstein 1988) may render this autonomy meaningless. Timothy Mitchell (1991) argues that the analytical distinction between state and society oversimplifies the complex structural relationships between the two. For Mitchell a more constructive approach to the boundary problem lies in conceptualizing the state as a sum of structural effects that order social interaction and conflict. The important questions turn on the ways that actors manipulate these structural effects.

A second challenge involves the criteria by which events are selected for analysis and explanation. The selection of government actions to study must be theoretically driven. If events are chosen arbitrarily, even when the events obviously are important, the result is likely to be a patchwork of unrelated historical-institutional studies. Disagreements about findings already turn on sometimes implicit disagreements about what is important to explain, what alternative explanations exist, and what connections between causes are important (see, for example, Goldfield 1989, and Skocpol, Finegold, and Goldfield 1990). Selecting Mothers' Aid as characteristic of the American Progressive-era welfare state yields one set of conclusions about the sources of difference between the American and British welfare states, and notably emphasizes the importance of concerns about political patronage (Orloff and Skocpol 1984). An analysis of health insurance or workers' compensation laws in the same era leads to a somewhat different set of conclusions about the sources of these differences, in which federalism and interstate competition play a much more important role than patronage (Robertson 1988).

The Future of Historical Research in Political Science

Given these issues for the new institutionalism and given the rich sources of historical data now available for historical-behavioralists, it will be natural for some historically oriented political scientists to combine the institutional and behavioral approaches in future research.[21] Contemporary political science Ph.D.s are more likely than those of a generation past to have training in the use of behavioral techniques. Given that behavioral axioms have influenced the new institutionalism, historical-institutionalists may search out ways to combine the detailed, "closely grained" studies of particular cases with the statistical tests of selected hypotheses. Some historical-behavioralists recognize the crucial role that institutions play in theory building.

Studies such as David Brady's *Critical Elections and Congressional Policy Making* (1988) show the potential for blending the behavioral and institutional analysis of past politics. Brady investigated historical election and roll call data to examine the ways in which critical elections affected the distribution of partisan membership, committee membership, and voting patterns in the House of Representatives. He concluded that close partisan competition in House elections is essential for understanding realignment. The congressional turnover that usually is associated with realignment follows when the two parties compete closely in Congressional districts nationwide and an electoral surge for one of the parties occurs. The lack of this competition in most House districts in recent decades explains the absence of realignment in the 1960s and 1970s. Brady's results suggest that a fundamental change in the competitiveness of House elections occurred in the late nineteenth century, a change that must be explained in terms of "the structural changes in both electoral laws and institutions that have weakened the strength of and sanctions available to political parties" (p. 180).

A blending of behavioral and institutional interests also may inspire more interdisciplinary historical research. The interaction of history and political science constitutes an intellectual frontier of tremendous creative potential (Dogan and Pahre 1990). One such emerging interdisciplinary agenda is policy history (Critchlow 1988; Castles 1989). Research on the development of policies and outcomes has stimulated the interests of both historical-institutional and historical-behavioral political scientists, as well as historians, sociologists, and others. The interdisciplinary potential of such a research agenda suggests that history has the potential to become a unifying force in social science once again.

Since the rational choice perspective has achieved a dominant position in contemporary political science, the most intriguing possibility is a closer connection between the historical analysis of institutions and positive theories of institutions. Some rational choice theorists (Riker 1980; Shepsle 1989) argue that the lack of institutional theory marks the frontier of rational choice research, and Smith (1988) suggests that the new institutionalism provides an obvious bridge between the two perspectives on politics. Authors and publishers are beginning to describe the application of rational choice to institutional outputs as "neoinstitutionalism."

It is not clear that rational choice and the new institutionalist perspectives are compatible, however.[22] Because rational choice analysts use deductive logic and simplifying assumptions to analyze self-interest, strategic decision making and systemic equilibrium, institutional rules tend to be incidental to their analysis and may be of interest only in the roughest form (such as reelection or presidential cues; see, for example, Cameron, Cover, and Segal 1990). Contemporary historical institutionalists are much more inductive and tend to emphasize the constraints imposed on human choice by particular institutions at particular times, so that rules in all their empirical complexity are of inherent and central interest to them. Therefore historical-institutionalists are likely to caution against generalization and are likely to emphasize the constraints that institutions impose upon human action rather than the opportunities that general classes of rules provide for maximizing individual self-interest.[23]

A promising research agenda involves the political economy of particular sectors. The growing appreciation that political opponents mobilize in different ways in different industries (for example, Orren 1973; Ferguson 1984; Montgomery 1987; Sklar 1988; Marks 1989) suggests that middle-range theories about political and economic sectors promise new insights into politics. Such middle-range theories are likely to suggest insights that cannot be tapped either by macrotheoretical systemic regularities or by micropolitical strategic concerns, such as the effect of explicit institutions or implicit working rules on political behavior and strategy. The notion of "subgovernments" or more recent formulations such as Anton's (1989) benefits coalition obviously may be adapted to this approach.

The circumstances that have favored the return to history in political science should continue to reinforce historical analysis of all types in the 1990s. New global economic and political relationships, combined with increased openness, are very unlikely to produce the political and economic stability that characterized the heyday of ahistorical political science. Budgetary crises, political decentralization, and the proliferation of threats such as nuclear weapons and environmental abuse will keep reflection and criticism on the social science agenda. The enormous reconstitution of Eastern Europe and the Soviet Union will create unexpected political permutations likely to stimulate a reassessment of the meaning of domestic politics. These events may result in unprecedented changes in the central issues in the field: voting, elections, political parties, and patterns of behavior in institutions.

Such circumstances undoubtedly will increase interest in the existing historical questions in the discipline (such as electoral alignments) and across disciplines. Moreover, they should stimulate interest in expanding the scope of political inquiry, thus heightening interest in history as a tool for critically reassessing relationships now taken for granted. History is essential for political science (Kavanagh 1991; Swift and Brady 1991). History will be indispensable to the discipline's future.

Notes

Thanks to Eric H. Monkkonen, Dennis Judd, Alfred Diamant, Kenneth Finegold, Donald T. Critchlow, Eduardo Silva, Richard Pacelle, Tyler Fitch, and two anonymous reviewers for very helpful comments. The Public Policy Research Center at the University of Missouri-St. Louis helped to support this research.

1 Similarly, recent Ph.D.s can little appreciate the difficulty of computer use and the accomplishment of data analysis with 1960s computer equipment.

2 It would be far from accurate to describe policies in Britain or Germany as fully centralized or coherent in this period.

3 The empiricism of the behavioral movement heavily influenced even the approach of American Marxists (Carnoy 1984: 209).

4 While this paper argues that ahistorical behavioralism flourished in a period of relative stability and that instability contributed to the renewed interest in historical research since the 1960s, such an argument cannot be generalized to all periods of stability and change. The ahistoricism of the behavioral era owes much to the unique circumstances of new data to analyze and new tools to employ in social analysis. While historical analysis is one tool used to critique the status quo, it is not the only tool. Social reformers frequently use comparative evidence to stimulate interest in social change, for example.

5 For one such attack, see Merelman 1968. Some behavioralists took non-decision making seriously. Behavioralist literature on agenda setting (see Kingdon 1984) confronted the control of the decision agenda explicitly.

6 There are some significant methodological problems (notably compounded measurement error and collinearity) in longitudinal data analysis. In light of these problems, many political scientists assert that cross-sectional analysis frequently offers less problematic results than studies based on variable changes over time.

7 The term "developmental" is used in this paper to refer to studies that trace the transitions of political institutions across time. It is not meant to convey a judgment about the relative quality of institutions at different points of time. Some political scientists prefer to avoid the term development because of these judgmental connotations (Cooper and Brady 1981); others, including authors clearly concerned about or critical of institutional development, have used the term (Skowronek 1982). Today's authors who use the term "political development" appear to take for granted the neutrality of the term in a way many political scientists did not a generation ago.

8 Note, however, that congressional scholars such as Fiorina (1989) link

members of Congress as rational actors to the institutions that protect their incumbency.

9   In the book Key strongly implies that he agrees with contemporaries who viewed the Southern states' exceptional conservatism as a serious national problem; the book begins with the observation that "The South may not be the nation's number one political problem, but politics is the South's number one problem" (p. 3).

10   Or, in Key's own pithy words, "The premise and unorthodox argument of this little book is that voters are not fools" (p. 7).

11   Eulau cited Dahl's *Who Governs* to exemplify his point that "there is no necessary conflict between behavioral and historical methods." (1969: 7).

12   Obviously no exhaustive inventory of historical-behavioral studies in all areas of the discipline is possible here. Literature on the presidency, the courts (in the work of C. Herman Pritchett and others), the states (in the work of Richard Hofferbert, Jack Walker, and others) have all benefited from more rigorous testing of historical data.

13   Schattschneider (1960) argues that the key political strategy is to expand the scope of conflict. As had been true in the Progressive era, historical revision (Beard 1965) and comparative policy analysis aimed to persuade by challenging the factual basis of normative beliefs. By enlarging research questions, critics of mainstream political science necessarily are drawn into historical analyses.

14   Lowi was a founder of the Caucus but soon broke with it; see Lowi 1971.

15   In the context of police repression of dissidents and the use of the CIA to cover up the Watergate scandal, the definition of the state as the "monopoly of coercive power in a territory" had an instinctive persuasiveness to critics of behavioralism and pluralism.

16   "The primary problem of politics is the lag in the development of political institutions behind social and economic change" (Huntington 1968: 5).

17   However, Downs's research questions generated little study until interest in rational choice approaches to political science began to increase.

18   Whether an organization or institution can be said to "act" is controversial because it implies the reification of collective action. According to March and Olsen, "Whether it makes pragmatic sense to impute interests, expectations, and the other paraphernalia of coherent intelligence to an institution is neither more nor less problematic, a priori, than whether it makes sense to impute them to an individual" (1989: 18).

19   Robert Salisbury (1979) had provocatively restated the question as "Why No Corporatism in America?"

20   For a discussion of policy-making capacity and coherence, as well as a discussion of their impact on policy development in the United States, see Robertson and Judd (1989), especially pp. 9–14, 35–53, and 71–77. Skowronek (1982) examines these issues from the point of view of the executive branch.

21   The issue of the identity of political science is beyond the scope of this paper (but see Seidelman 1985, Farr 1988, and Almond 1990, among others who

have addressed the development and state of the discipline). The best predictor of political science's future is its past, which is decidedly pluralistic. I judge that heterogeneity to be not only inevitable but also a strength.

22   Lowi (1992) implies that the ascendency of rational choice perspectives in political science at least partially reflects the ascendency of neo-liberal, free-market conservatism in American politics in the 1980s.

23   Tilly aptly observes that

> So long as strategic interaction forms a significant part of the process at hand, game theory offers a promising way to shift from individual mental events toward social relationships without losing the precision of rational-action analysis. Nevertheless, game theory will not suffice. Eventually we must find the means of placing relationships rather than individuals at the very center of the analysis. Many of the relationships that constitute and constrain social life have so small a component of strategic interaction as to require other sorts of analysis. Communication networks, routine relations between bosses and workers, flows of tax money, spread of diseases, movements of capital, chain migrations, and promotion ladders all certainly involve strategic interaction at one time or another. But their crystallization into durable structures requires a specifically structural analysis. (1984: 33–34)

References

Aberbach, J. D., R. D. Putnam, and B. A. Rockman (1981) *Bureaucrats and Politicians in Western Democracies*. Cambridge, MA: Harvard University Press.

Allison, G. (1971) *The Essence of Decision: Explaining the Cuban Missile Crisis*. Boston: Little, Brown.

Almond, G. A. (1988) "The return to the state." *American Political Science Review* 82: 853–74.

———— (1990) *A Discipline Divided: Schools and Sects in Political Science*. Newbury Park, CA: Sage, 1990.

————, S. C. Flanagan, and R. J. Mundt (1973) *Crisis, Choice, and Change: Historical Studies of Political Development*. Boston: Little, Brown.

————, and S. Verba (1963) *The Civic Culture: Attitudes and Democracy in Five Nations*. Princeton: Princeton University Press.

Alt, J. E., and K. A. Chrystal (1983) *Political Economics*. Berkeley: University of California Press.

Amenta, E., and T. Skocpol (1989) "Taking exception: Explaining the distinctiveness of American public policies in the last century," in F. G. Castles, (ed.) *The Comparative History of Public Policy*. New York: Oxford University Press.

Anton, T. J. (1989) *American Federalism and Public Policy: How the System Works*. New York: Random House.

Armstrong, J. A. (1973) *The European Administrative Elite*. Princeton: Princeton University Press.

Asher, H. B. (1983). "Voting behavior in the 1980s: An examination of some old and new problem areas," in Ada Finifter (ed.) *Political Science: The State of the Discipline.* Washington: American Political Science Association.

Ashford, D. E. (1986) "Structural analysis and institutional change." *Polity* 19: 97–122.

———— (1991) "History *and* public policy vs. history *of* public policy." *Public Administration Review* 51: 358–63.

Axelrod, R. (1984) *The Evolution of Cooperation.* New York: Basic Books.

Bachrach, P., and M. Baratz (1970) *Power and Poverty.* New York: Oxford University Press.

Baum, L. (1989) *The Supreme Court,* 3d ed. Washington: CQ Press.

Beard, C. A. (1965 [1913]) *An Economic Interpretation of the Constitution.* New York: Free Press.

Bensel, R. F. (1984) *Sectionalism and American Political Development: 1880–1980.* Madison: University of Wisconsin Press.

———— (1990) *Yankee Leviathan: The Origins of Central State Authority in America, 1859–1877.* New York: Cambridge University Press.

Berger, S., and M. J. Piore (1980) *Dualism and Discontinuity in Industrial Societies.* New York: Cambridge University Press.

Bibby, J. F., T. Mann, and N. J. Ornstein (1988) *Vital Statistics on Congress.* Washington: CQ Press.

Block, F. (1977) "The ruling class does not rule." *Socialist Revolution* 7: 6–28.

Brady, D. W. (1988) *Critical Elections and Congressional Policy Making.* Stanford: Stanford University Press.

Brand, D. (1988) *Corporatism and the Rule of Law: A Study of the National Recovery Administration.* Ithaca, NY: Cornell University Press.

Bridges, A. (1984) *A City in the Republic: Antebellum New York and the Origins of Machine Politics.* New York: Cambridge University Press.

Brintall, M. (1991) "APSA organized sections: A status report." *PS* 24: 559–63.

Bryce, J. (1909) "The relations of political science to history and to practice." *American Political Science Review* 3: 1–19.

Buchanan, J., and R. Wagner (1977) *Democracy in Deficit.* New York: Academic Press.

Budge, I., and R. I. Hofferbert (1990) "Mandates and policy outputs: U.S. party platforms and federal expenditures." *American Political Science Review* 84: 111–31.

Burnham, W. D. (1970) *Critical Elections and the Mainsprings of American Politics.* New York: Norton.

Cameron, C. M., A. D. Cover, and J. A. Segal (1990) "Senate voting on Supreme Court nominees: A neoinstitutional model." *American Political Science Review* 84: 525–34.

Campbell, A., P. E. Converse, W. E. Miller, and D. E. Stokes (1960) *The American Voter.* New York: Wiley.

Carnoy, M. (1984) *The State and Political Theory.* Princeton: Princeton University Press.

Castles, F. G., ed. (1982) *The Impact of Parties*. Beverly Hills, CA: Sage.
——, ed. (1989) *The Comparative History of Public Policy*. New York: Oxford University Press.

Chandler, A. (1977) *The Visible Hand*. Cambridge, MA: Harvard University Press.

Chubb, J. E., and P. E. Peterson, eds. (1989) *Can the Government Govern?* Washington, DC: Brookings.

Clubb, J. M., W. H. Flanigan, and N. H. Zingale (1980) *Partisan Realignment: Voters, Parties, and Government in American History*. Beverly Hills, CA: Sage.

Cockroft, J. D. et al., eds. (1972) *Dependence and Underdevelopment: Latin America's Political Economy*. Garden City, NY: Doubleday.

Cooper, J., and D. W. Brady, (1981a) "Institutional context and leadership style: The house from Cannon to Rayburn." *American Political Science Review* 75: 411–25.

—— (1981b) "Toward a diachronic analysis of Congress." *American Political Science Review* 75: 988–1006.

Critchlow, D. T., and E. W. Hawley (1988) *Federal Social Policy: The Historical Dimension*. University Park, PA: Pennsylvania State University Press.

Dahl, R. A. (1961a) "The behavioral approach to political science: Epitaph for a monument to a successful protest." *American Political Science Review* 55: 763–72.

—— (1961b) *Who Governs: Democracy and Power in an American City*. New Haven: Yale University Press.

—— (1985) *A Preface to Economic Democracy*. Berkeley: University of California Press.

Davidson, R. H. (1991) "Legislative research: Mirror of a discipline," in W. Crotty (ed.) *Political Science: Looking to the Future, Volume IV: American Institutions*. Evanston, IL: Northwestern University Press.

Diamant, A. (1981) "Bureaucracy and public policy in neocorporatist settings: Some European lessons." *Comparative Politics* 14: 101–24.

Dodd, L. C., and R. L. Schott (1979) *Congress and the Administrative State*. New York: John Wiley.

Dogan, M., and R. Pahre (1990) *Creative Marginality: Innovation at the Intersection of Social Sciences*. Boulder, CO: Westview Press.

Downs, A. (1957) *An Economic Theory of Democracy*. New York: Harper and Brothers.

—— (1967) *Inside Bureaucracy*. Boston: Little, Brown.

Dryzek, J. S. (1990) *Discursive Democracy: Politics, Policy, and Political Science*. New York: Cambridge University Press.

Easton, D. (1962) "The current meaning of 'behavioralism' in political science," in J. Charlesworth (ed.) *The Limits of Behavioralism in Political Science*. Philadelphia: American Academy of Political and Social Sciences.

—— (1969) "The new revolution in political science." *American Political Science Review* 68: 1051–61.

—— (1990) *The Analysis of Political Structure*. New York: Routledge.

Elazar, D. J. (1977) *Cities of the Prairie: The Metropolitan Frontier and American Politics*. New York: Basic Books.

Eulau, H. (1963) *The Behavioral Persuasion*. New York: Random House.

—— (1969) "Tradition and innovation: On the tension between ancient and modern ways in the study of politics," in H. Eulau (ed.) *Behavioralism in Political Science*. New York: Atherton Press.

—— (1976) "Understanding political life in America: The contribution of political science," in C. M. Bonjean, L. Schneider, and R. L. Lineberry (eds.) *Social Science in America: The First Two Hundred Years*. Austin: University of Texas.

Evans, P., T. Skocpol, and D. Rueschemeyer, eds. (1985) *Bringing the State Back In*. New York: Cambridge University Press.

Farr, J. (1988) "The history of political science." *American Journal of Political Science* 32: 1175–95.

Ferguson, T. (1984) "From normalcy to New Deal: Industrial structure, party competition, and American public policy in the Great Depression." *International Organization* 38: 41–94.

Finegold, K. (1982) "From agrarianism to adjustment: The political origins of New Deal agricultural policy." *Politics and Society* 11: 1–28.

—— (1988) "Agriculture and the politics of U.S. social provision: Social insurance and food stamps," in M. Weir, A. S. Orloff, and T. Skocpol (eds.) *The Politics of Social Policy in the United States*. Princeton: Princeton University Press.

Fiorina, M. (1981) *Retrospective Voting in American National Elections*. New Haven, CT: Yale University Press.

—— (1989) *Congress: Keystone of the Washington Establishment*. 2d ed. New Haven, CT: Yale University Press.

—— (forthcoming, 1992) *Divided Government*. New York: Macmillan.

Ginsberg, B., and M. Shefter (1990) *Politics by Other Means: Institutional Conflict and the Declining Significance of Elections in America*. New York: Basic Books.

Goldfield, M. (1989) "Worker insurgency, radical organization, and New Deal labor legislation." *American Political Science Review* 83: 1257–82.

Gourevich, P. (1986) *Politics in Hard Times: Comparative Responses to International Economic Crises*. Ithaca, NY: Cornell University Press.

Hartz, L. (1955) *The Liberal Tradition in America*. New York: Harcourt, Brace, and World.

Hattam, V. (1990) "Economic visions and political strategies: American labor and the state, 1865–1896." *Studies in American Political Development* 4: 82–129.

Hawley, E. W. (1969) *The New Deal and the Problem of Monopoly*. Princeton: Princeton University Press.

Heclo, H. (1974) *Modern Social Politics in Britain and Sweden*. New Haven, CT: Yale University Press.

Hofferbert, R. I. (1966) "Ecological development and policy change in the American states." *Midwest Journal of Political Science* 10: 464–83.

Huntington, S. (1968) *Political Order in Changing Societies*. New Haven, CT: Yale University Press.

Jacobson, G. (1990) *The Evolution of Competition in House Elections, 1946–1988*. Boulder, CO: Westview Press.

Jensen, R. (1969) "History and the political scientist," in Seymour Martin Lipset (ed.) *Politics and the Social Sciences*. New York: Oxford University Press.

Judd, D. (1979) *The Politics of American Cities*. Boston: Little, Brown.

Karl, B. (1974) *Charles E. Merriam and the Study of Politics*. Chicago: University of Chicago Press.

Katzenstein, P. J., ed. (1978) *Between Power and Plenty: Foreign Economic Policies of Advanced Industrial States*. Madison: University of Wisconsin Press.

—— (1985) *Small States in World Markets: Industrial Policy in Europe*. Ithaca, NY: Cornell University Press.

Katznelson, I. (1981) *City Trenches: Urban Politics and the Patterning of Class in the United States*. Chicago: University of Chicago Press.

Kaufman, H. (1960) *The Forest Ranger: A Study in Administrative Behavior*. Baltimore, MD: Johns Hopkins University Press.

Kavanagh, D. (1991) "Why political science needs history." *Political Studies* 39: 479–95.

Key, V. O. (1949) *Southern Politics in State and Nation*. New York: Alfred Knopf.

—— (1955) "A theory of critical elections." *Journal of Politics* 17: 3–18.

—— (1966) *The Responsible Electorate: Rationality in Presidential Voting, 1936–1960*. Cambridge, MA: Belknap Press.

King, A. (1973) "Ideas, Institutions, and the Policies of Governments: A Comparative Analysis." *British Journal of Political Science* 3: 291–313, 409–23.

King, G., and L. Ragsdale (1988) *The Elusive Executive: Discovering Statistical Patterns in the Presidency*. Washington: CQ Press.

Kingdon, J. (1984) *Agendas, Alternatives, and Public Policies*. Boston: Little, Brown.

Klingemann, H.-D., B. Grofman, and J. Campagna (1989) "The political science 400: Citations by Ph.D. cohort and by Ph.D.-granting institution." *PS* 22: 258–70.

Kolko, G. (1963) *The Triumph of Conservatism: A Reinterpretation of American History, 1900–1916*. New York: Free Press.

—— (1965) *Railroads and Regulation, 1877–1916*. New York: Norton.

Krasner, S. D. (1978) *Defending the National Interest: Raw Materials Investments and U.S. Foreign Policy*. Princeton: Princeton University Press.

—— (1984) "Approaches to the State: Alternative Conceptions and Historical Dynamics." *Comparative Politics* 16: 223–46.

Lane, R. E. (1965) "The politics of consensus in an age of affluence." *American Political Science Review* 59: 874–95.

Larkey, P. D., C. Stolp, and M. Winer (1981) "Theorizing about the growth of government: A research assessment." *Journal of Public Policy* 1: 157–220.

Lindblom, C. A. (1977) *Politics and Markets: The World's Political-Economic Systems*. New York: Basic Books.

———— (1982) "Another state of mind." *American Political Science Review* 76: 9–21.

Lipset, S. M. (1983) "Radicalism or reformism: The sources of working-class politics." *American Political Science Review* 77: 1–18.

Lowi, T. J. (1969) *The End of Liberalism: The Second Republic of the United States.* New York: Norton.

———— (1971) "The politics of higher education: Political science as a case study," in G. J. Graham, Jr., and G. W. Carey (eds.) *The Post-Behavioral Era: Perspectives on Political Science.* New York: David McKay.

———— (1992) "The state in political science: How we became what we study." *American Political Science Review* 86: 1–7.

Lowi, T. J., and S. G. Tarrow (1980) "The 1981 APSA annual meeting program: Some thoughts and suggestions." *PS* 13: 339–40.

Lowi, T. J., and A. Stone, eds. (1978) *Nationalizing Government.* Beverly Hills, CA: Sage.

Lunch, W. (1987) *The Nationalization of American Politics.* Berkeley: University of California Press.

Machiavelli, N. (1985) *The Prince.* Chicago: University of Chicago Press.

MacKuen, M. B., R. S. Erikson, and J. A. Stimson (1989) "Macropartisanship." *American Political Science Review* 83: 1125–42.

MacRae, D., Jr., and J. A. Meldrum (1960) "Critical elections in Illinois: 1888–1958." *American Political Science Review* 54: 669–83.

Madison, J., A. Hamilton, and J. Jay (1961 [1788]) *The Federalist.* New York: Mentor.

March, J. G., and J. P. Olsen (1984) "The new institutionalism: Organizational factors in political life." *American Political Science Review* 78: 734–49.

———— (1989) *Rediscovering Institutions: The Organizational Basis of Politics.* New York: Free Press.

Marks, G. (1989) *Unions in Politics: Britain, Germany, and the United States in the Nineteenth and Early Twentieth Centuries.* Princeton: Princeton University Press.

Mayhew, D. (1991) *Divided We Govern: Party Control, Lawmaking, and Investigations, 1946–1990.* New Haven, CT: Yale University Press.

Mazmanian, D. A., and P. A. Sabatier (1983) *Implementation and Public Policy.* Glenview, IL: Scott Foresman.

McConnell, G. (1966) *Private Power and American Democracy.* New York: Alfred Knopf.

Meehan, E. J. (1972) "What should political scientists be doing?" in G. J. Graham, Jr., and G. W. Carey (eds.) *The Post-Behavioral Era: Perspectives on Political Science.* New York: David McKay.

Merelman, R. M. (1968) "On the neo-elitist critique of community power." *American Political Science Review* 62: 451–60.

Migdal, J. S. (1983) "Studying the politics of development and change: The state of the art," in Ada W. Finifter (ed.) *Political Science: The State of the Discipline.* Washington, DC: American Political Science Association.

Miliband, R. (1969) *The State in Capitalist Society.* London: Winfield and Nicholson.

Miller, W. E. (1989) "Research life as a collection of intersecting probability distributions," in Heinz Eulau (ed.) *Crossroads of Social Science: The ICPSR 25th Anniversary Volume*. New York: Agathon Press.

Mink, G. (1986) *Old Labor and New Immigrants in American Political Development: Union, Party, and State, 1875–1920*. Ithaca, NY: Cornell University Press.

Mitchell, T. (1991) "The limits of the state: Beyond statist approaches and their critics." *American Political Science Review* 85: 77–96.

Moe, T. M. (1987) "Interests, institutions, and positive theory: The politics of the NLRB." *Studies in American Political Development* 2: 236–99.

Montgomery, D. (1987) *The Fall of the House of Labor: The Workplace, the State, and American labor Activism, 1865–1925*. New York: Cambridge University Press.

Moore, B. (1967) *Social Origins of Dictatorship and Democracy Lord and Peasant in the Making of the Modern World*. Boston: Beacon Press.

Mucciaroni, G. (1990) *The Political Failure of Employment Policy, 1945–1982*. Pittsburgh: University of Pittsburgh Press.

Neustadt, R. E. (1960) *Presidential Power*. New York: Wiley.

Niskanen, W. A. (1971) *Bureaucracy and Representative Government*. Chicago: Aldine.

Nordlinger, E. *On the Autonomy of the Democratic State*. Cambridge, MA: Harvard University Press.

O'Connor, J. (1973) *The Fiscal Crisis of the State*. New York: St. Martin's.

Offe, C. (1975) "The capitalist state and the problem of policy formation," in L. N. Lindberg, R. Alford, C. Crouch, and C. Offe (eds.) *Stress and Contradiction in Modern Capitalism*. Lexington, MA: D. C. Heath.

Olson, M. (1982) *The Rise and Decline of Nations: Economic Growth, Stagflation, and Social Rigidities*. New Haven, CT: Yale University Press.

Orloff, A. S. (1991) "Gender in early U.S. social policy." *Journal of Policy History* 3: 249–81.

Orloff, A. S., and T. Skocpol (1984) "Why not equal protection? Explaining the politics of social spending in Britain, 1900–1911, and the United States, 1880s–1920." *American Sociological Review* 49: 726–50.

Orren, K. (1973) *Corporate Power and Social Change*. Baltimore, MD: Johns Hopkins University Press.

——— , and S. Skowronek (1986) "Editor's Preface," in *Studies in American Political Development* 1: vii–viii.

Ostrom, C. W., Jr., and B. L. Job (1986) "The president and the political use of force." *American Political Science Review* 80: 541–66.

Piven, F. F., and R. A. Cloward (1971) *Regulating the Poor: The Functions of Public Welfare*. New York: Vintage.

Polsby, N. W. (1968) "The institutionalization of the House of Representatives." *American Political Science Review* 62: 144–68.

Poulantzas, N. (1974) *Political Power and Social Classes*. London: New Left Books.

Pressman, J. L., and A. B. Wildavsky (1973) *Implementation: How Great Expectations in Washington Are Dashed in Oakland*. Berkeley: University of California Press.

Przeworski, A., and M. Wallerstein (1988) "Structural dependence of the state on capital." *American Political Science Review* 82: 11–30.

Quirk, P. J. (1991) "What do we know and how do we know it? Research on the presidency," in William Crotty (ed.) *Political Science: Looking to the Future, Volume IV: American Institutions*. Evanston, IL: Northwestern University Press.

Ricci, D. M. (1984) *The Tragedy of Political Science: Politics, Scholarship, and Democracy*. New Haven, CT: Yale University Press.

Riker, W. H. (1980) "Implications from the disequilibrium of majority rule for the study of institutions." *American Political Science Review* 74: 432–47.

Robertson, D. B. (1988) "Policy entrepreneurs and policy divergence: John R. Commons and William Beveridge." *Social Service Review* 62: 504–31.

———— (1989) "The bias of American federalism: The limits of welfare state development in the progressive era." *Journal of Policy History* 1: 261–91.

————, and D. R. Judd (1989) *The Development of American Public Policy: The Structure of Policy Restraint*. Glenview, IL: Scott, Foresman / Little, Brown.

Rose, J. C. (1906). "Negro suffrage: The constitutional point of view." *American Political Science Review* 1: 17–43.

Rose, R. (1990) "Inheritance before choice in public policy." *Journal of Theoretical Politics* 2: 263–91.

————, and G. Peters (1978) *Can Governments Go Bankrupt?* New York: Basic Books.

Salisbury, R. H. (1979) "Why no corporatism in America?" in P. C. Schmitter and G. Lehmbruch (eds.) *Trends Toward Corporatist Intermediation*. Beverly Hills, CA: Sage.

Sanders, E. (1981) *The Regulation of Natural Gas: Policies and Politics, 1938–1978*. Philadelphia: Temple University Press.

———— (1986) "Industrial concentration, sectional competition, and antitrust politics in America, 1880–1914." *Studies in American Political Development* 1: 142–214.

Savage, J. D. (1988) *Balanced Budgets and American Politics*. Ithaca, NY: Cornell University Press.

Schattschneider, E. E. (1960) *The Semi-Sovereign People*. Hinsdale, IL: Dryden Press.

Schmitter, P. C., and G. Lehmbruch (1979) *Trends Toward Corporatist Intermediation*. Beverly Hills, CA: Sage.

Scott, W. R. (1987) *Organizations: Rational, Natural, and Open Systems*. 2d ed. Englewood Cliffs, NJ: Prentice-Hall.

Seidelman, R., with the assistance of E. Harpham (1985) *Disenchanted Realists: Political Science and the American Crisis, 1884–1984*. Albany: State University of New York Press.

Shafer, B., ed. (1991) *The End of Realignment? Interpreting American Electoral Eras*. Madison: University of Wisconsin Press.

Shefter, M. (1986) "Trade unions and political machines: The organization and disorganization of the American working class in the late nineteenth century," in I. Katznelson and A. R. Zolberg, *Working-Class Formation: Nineteenth Century Patterns in Western Europe and the United States*. Princeton: Princeton University Press.

Shepsle, K. A. (1989) "Studying institutions: Some lessons from the rational choice approach." *Journal of Theoretical Politics* 1: 131–47.

Sklar, M. (1988) *The Corporate Reconstruction of American Capitalism, 1890–1916: The Market, The Law, and Politics*. New York: Cambridge University Press.

Skocpol, T. (1979) *States and Social Revolutions: A Comparative Analysis of France, Russia, and China*. Cambridge: Cambridge University Press.

———— (1980) "Political responses to capitalist crises: Neo-Marxist theories of the state and the case of the New Deal." *Politics and Society* 10: 155–201.

———— (1985) "Bringing the state back in," in P. Evans, T. Skocpol, and D. Rueschemeyer (eds.) *Bringing the State Back In*. New York: Cambridge University Press.

———— (forthcoming) *Protecting Soldiers and Mothers: The Politics of Social Provision in the United States*. New York: Cambridge University Press.

————, and K. Finegold (1982) "State capacity and economic intervention in the early New Deal." *Political Science Quarterly* 97: 255–78.

————, K. Finegold, and M. Goldfield (1990) "Explaining New Deal labor policy." *American Political Science Review* 84: 1297–1315.

————, and J. Ikenberry (1983) "The political formation of the American welfare state in historical and comparative perspective." *Comparative Social Research* 6: 87–148.

Skowronek, S. (1982) *Building a New American State: The Expansion of National Administrative Capacities, 1877–1920*. New York: Cambridge University Press.

———— (1988) "Presidential leadership in political time," in Michael Nelson (ed.) *The Presidency and the Political System*. 2d ed. Washington: CQ Press.

Smith, R. M. (1988) "Political jurisprudence, the 'new institutionalism,' and the future of public law." *American Political Science Review* 82: 89–108.

Somit, A., and J. Tannenhaus (1967) *The Development of American Political Science*. Boston: Allyn and Bacon.

Stinchcombe, A. L. (1965) "Social Structure and Organizations," in J. G. March (ed.) *Handbook of Organizations*. Chicago: Rand McNally.

Sundquist, J. L. (1973; rev. ed. 1983) *Dynamics of the Party System: Alignment and Realignment of Political Parties in the United States*. Washington: Brookings.

Swift, E. K., and D. W. Brady (1991) "Out of the past: Theoretical and methodological contributions of congressional history." *PS* 24: 61–64.

Tilly, C. (1984) *Big Structures, Large Processes, Huge Comparisons*. New York: Russell Sage.

Truman, D. B. (1953) *The Governmental Process: Political Interests and Public Opinion*. New York: Alfred A. Knopf.

Tufte, E. (1978) *Political Control of the Economy*. Princeton: Princeton University Press.

Tulis, J. K. (1987) *The Rhetorical Presidency*. Princeton: Princeton University Press.

———— (1990) "Section president's report." *History and Politics Section Newsletter* 1: 2.

Wahlke, J. C., H. Eulau, W. Buchanan, and L. C. Ferguson (1962) *The Legislative System: Explorations in Legislative Behavior*. New York: Wiley.

Waldo, Dwight (1975) "Political science: Tradition, discipline, profession, science, enterprise," in Fred I. Greenstein and Nelson W. Polsby (eds.) *Handbook of Political Science, Volume I: Political Science: Scope and Theory*. Reading, MA: Addison-Wesley.

Walker, J. L. (1969) "The diffusion of innovations among the American states." *American Political Science Review* 63: 880–99.

Wallerstein, I. (1971) "The state and social transformation: Will and possibility. *Politics and Society* 1: 359–64.

———— (1974) *The Modern World-System: Capitalist Agriculture and the Origins of the European World-Economy in the Sixteenth Century*. New York: Academic Press.

Weber, M. (1968) "The interpretive understanding of social action," in May Brodbeck (ed.) *Readings in the Philosophy of the Social Sciences*. New York: Macmillan.

Weinstein, J. (1968) *The Corporate Ideal in the Liberal State, 1900–1918*. Boston: Beacon Press.

Weir, M. (1989) "Ideas and politics: The acceptance of Keynesianism in Britain and the United States," in Peter A. Hall (ed.) *The Political Power of Economic Ideas: Keynesianism Across Nations*. Princeton: Princeton University Press.

———— (1992) *Politics and Jobs: The Boundaries of Employment Policy in the United States*. Princeton: Princeton University Press.

————, A. S. Orloff, and T. Skocpol, eds. (1988) *The Politics of Social Policy in the United States*. Princeton: Princeton University Press.

Whicker, M., and R. Moore (1988) *When Presidents Are Great*. Englewood Cliffs, NJ: Prentice-Hall.

Wiebe, R. H. (1967) *The Search for Order, 1877–1920*. New York: Hill and Wang.

Willoughby, W. W. (1896) *An Examination of the Nature of the State*. New York: Macmillan.

Wilson, W. (1898) *The State: Elements of Historical and Practical Politics*. Boston: D. C. Heath.

Woolley, J. (1984) *The Federal Reserve Bank and the Politics of Monetary Policy*. New York: Cambridge University Press.

Zysman, J. (1983) *Governments, Markets, and Growth: Financial Systems and the Politics of Industrial Change*. Ithaca, NY: Cornell University Press, 1983.

At the Intersection of Time and Space

Richard Dennis

In 1991, 512 out of 6,290 members of the Association of American Geographers (AAG) declared their allegiance to the Historical Geography Specialty Group: among thirty-nine AAG specialty groups, the historical geographers ranked fourth, albeit with barely half the members of the largest group, which was concerned with Geographical Information Systems (GIS) (AAG Newsletter March 1992). Membership of the latter, however, may be more a reflection of geographers' desire to identify with the fastest growing, best funded, and politically most acceptable branch of their subject, than of genuine commitment or expertise. Another question in the AAG's annual survey asks members to record their topical "proficiencies": while "Historical Geography" held firm at 547, and "Cultural Geography" attracted far more who were "proficient" (654) than subscribed to the Cultural Geography Specialty Group (335), the number of "proficient" GIS members (809) was two hundred fewer than the membership of the GIS Specialty Group (1,011). It seems as if historical and cultural geography is what American geographers actually do; GIS, and, to a lesser extent, gender issues (80 practitioners of "Gender" studies, but 213 members of the Geographic Perspectives on Women Specialty Group) is what they would like to be doing, or think they ought to be doing.

Does this indicate that "historical geography" is past its prime, no longer at the cutting edge of the subject, as, for example, Kay (1990) has argued? Kay charged that most historical geography appeared "antiquarian," by which she meant that it was narrowly focused on the past for its own sake, not designed to illuminate current concerns or events; that it had become a humanistic refuge from quantification, new technology (like GIS), applied geography and theory; and that it neglected major sections of society, particularly women and ethnic minorities, in part by ignoring the local and domestic scales of activity in which they had most influence or to which they were confined. Her onslaught attracted a predictable rebuttal from Meinig (1990), whose own lament for the neglect of historical geography (Meinig 1989) had provoked Kay's critique. Meinig emphasized the continuity between studies of past and present, the willingness of historical geographers to engage in theoretical debate, and the centrality of their teaching in many liberal arts degree programs. But Kay's comments are echoed more politely in Cole Harris' (1991) argument on the need for social theory in historical geography, and in David Harvey's (1990) agenda for "the construction of a historical geography of space and time." Neither Harris nor Harvey is much concerned with disciplinary boundaries among the humanities and social sciences, let alone with distinguishing between historical geography and the rest of geography.

Meanwhile, another prominent human geographer regards historical geography as "overdetermined," an "empty concept" conveying "few (if any) significant analytical distinctions" (Dear 1988: 270). Dear's argument, like Harvey's, is that by definition *all* geography should be historical because "the central object in human geography is to understand the simultaneity of time and space in structuring social process." So the only subdisciplines of human geography that have any intellectual coherence are those focused on distinct *processes*—political, economic, social. To me, even this distinction is unrealistic and impracticable for research purposes; and to Pile and Rose (1992: 124) it is seen as maintaining "the distinction between production and reproduction which feminist geographers have long since rendered obsolete." But Dear does not go as far as to argue that historical geography or other "overdetermined," "multidimensional," or "peripheral" subdisciplines are wrong, merely that they are incidental to geography's "intellectual identity."

In contrast to Dear, Radford (1990) expresses pride in historical geography's heritage of intellectual pluralism and in practitioners who have preferred constructive debate to dogma and individual curiosity to methodological bandwagons. Likewise, the collective of eighteen members of the Historical Geography Specialty Group who contributed to Gaile and Willmott's monumental *Geography in America* (Earle et al. 1989) rejoiced in the eclecticism of diverse paradigms, interpreting this variety as "a phase of remarkably creative experimentation." They recognized the need for theory (or, more likely, theories) in historical geography and paid particular attention to world-system theory—what, later in this chapter, I refer to as "big picture" historical geography—but at the last they remain committed to a postmodernist (though they never use that word) celebration of difference: "Each of us enjoys the challenge of making sense out of past geographies, of puzzling over them relatively unconstrained by doctrinal methodologies or philosophies. Let us trust that, even as we discipline ourselves to the imperatives of grand theory and the practice of applied geography, our liberating eclecticism will endure" (ibid.: 182).

No institutional net can be cast wide enough to embrace all of historical geography. Even Earle et al. omit any mention of David Harvey, despite Harvey's constant perception of his own work as "historical geography" (Harvey 1985b, 1990). Krim (1990), reporting on historical geography at the annual meeting of the Association of American Geographers, recorded sessions on environmental perception, rural landscapes and settlements, borderlands, and the historical geography of particular regions, including the American West. My own sampling of the same conference, taking in a wide range of papers with urban historical themes, hardly overlapped at all with Krim's, nor were many of the sessions I attended organized by the Historical Geography Specialty Group.

All this is by way of introduction to emphasize that what follows is a personal view from outside the American historical geography establishment; that the subject I have been asked to review is almost infinite in scope: that methods and research foci, even among self-confessed "historical geographers," vary from North America to Britain; and, consequently, that for some areas of research more central to North American geography what follows is necessarily a review of reviews.

Historical Geography, Quantification, and "Scientific Method"

A comparison of recent "progress reports" by British, American, and Canadian reviewers (Butlin 1987; Mitchell 1987; Wynn 1990) indicates very different reactions to recent intellectual trends in the social sciences and humanities, and within the whole discipline of geography. There is general agreement that historical geographers were marginalized during geography's quantitative revolution in the 1960s, despite that most research in historical geography was positivist and empirical. Indeed, one criticism of "traditional" historical geography was that it was too closely tied to the apron strings of archival data sources and field observation, producing meticulous reconstructions of past patterns but without either investigating the processes behind the patterns or evaluating the data themselves in their cultural and political context. Implicitly, historical geographers assumed that their sources were objective and neutral (Harley 1982). But their approach was atheoretical, at least in the sense of positivist spatial theory and a scientific method of hypothesis testing. Nor were many historical geographers quick to espouse computerized techniques to handle large datasets. For example, despite the extensive work of Darby and his associates, mapping and interpreting the information in Domesday Book (Darby and Versey 1952–77), it fell to a historian (Palmer 1985) to undertake the computerization of Domesday records.

In Britain, historical demographers (Wrigley and Schofield 1981) and a new breed of numerate urban historical geographers (Dennis 1984a) employed parish registers and nineteenth-century census enumerators' books, the latter linked to the testing of urban ecological theory through the technique of factorial ecology; a few more adventurous researchers experimented with computerized databases and made attempts to simulate missing data in records of medieval and early-modern agricultural innovation and productivity (Overton 1977, 1984); but the most fervent advocate of historical quantitative spatial analysis has been the Canadian geographer William Norton, who defines historical geography as the study of spatial form evolution, focused on the relationship between process and form, and whose methodological armory includes computer simulation models and counterfactual analysis (Norton 1984). Norton's mentors are the mathematician-turned-geographer Alan Wilson and the "new economic historian" Robert Fogel, rather than the traditional founding fathers of historical geography, Clifford Darby, Carl Sauer, and Andrew Clark.

But Norton has not carried many historical geographers with him. More commonly, there was a suspicion, often justified, that quantitative historical geographers were interested in the past not for its own sake but merely as a source of data on which to test elegant but abstract and contextless spatial models, or "selectively to explore the historical validity of current theories of human behaviour" (Mitchell 1987: 10).

Historical Geography in North America:
A Beleaguered Community?

Since the 1970s positivist human geography has been challenged by a variety of alternative approaches, especially those grounded in Marxism and humanism. Yet although some of the leading exponents of different kinds of radical human geography were based in North American departments (e.g., David Ley, Richard Peet, David Harvey), their ideas achieved more widespread attention in British historical geography. Consequently, American historical geographers still express a sense of beleaguerment, isolated in an unfriendly world of remote sensing, geographical information systems, and a narrow definition of relevance that encompasses only research that is geared to the *immediate* needs of policymakers. Thus Mitchell (ibid.: 9) observed that historical geographers "have acquired a status that is marginal to the contemporary scientific and ahistorical character of geography," while Meinig (cited in Rumney 1988) lamented the lack of academic jobs for young historical geographers despite (in Rumney's words) "the continuing strengths and vigor of historical geography." In the published version of his speech to the AAG, Meinig (1989: 85) noted the irony "that at a time when the achievements of historical geographers are being widely recognized [by non-geographers] . . . within our own house we are generally ignored."

This feeling of being undervalued has promoted a strong sense of community *within* North American historical geography. As already indicated, there is no shortage of sessions and papers devoted to historical themes at the annual meetings of the AAG, but many are cast in a traditional mold that has limited appeal to outsiders: local case studies; a concern for particular elements in the landscape, such as the distribution of different types of vernacular building; a continuing fascination with the frontier, a perspective that can be Eurocentric and that often goes along with an uncritical view of colonization or development as "progress" (Dennis 1984b). Earle et al. (1989) review a vast literature of colonial settlement models and frontier studies, concluding that nearly all research has emphasized the success of colonial expansion and the "accelerating years of prosperity." There has been an attempt to "simplify Europe overseas" (ibid.: 169), a theme also discussed by Cole Harris (1991) in illustrating how the ideas of Foucault and Giddens on power and modernity could be used to direct future studies of pioneer settlement. The question of status *within* colonial society deserves attention, as of course do the power relationships between settlers and native peoples and those between humankind and nature: "historical geographers have slighted environmental degradation" (Earle et al. 1989: 169). Geographers' woeful neglect of the dynamic relationship between people and their natural environment has also been exposed by William Cronon's widely acclaimed *Nature's Metropolis: Chicago and the Great West* (1991), which links the geography of capital, commodification, and exchange—one of David Harvey's principal themes—to ecological change in Chicago's prairie and forest hinterlands. Although a few historical geographers have continued to focus on change in the physical environment, pursuing Darby's grand themes of clearing woodland, draining wetlands, and reclaiming heathlands (Williams 1989, 1990), it has taken an environmental historian to demonstrate the connections between hitherto separate physical and human, rural and urban historical geographies.

On a more limited canvas, some historical geographers have recently approached questions of cultural transfer, immigration, and frontier settlement in more exciting and original ways. Ostergren's (1988) study of Swedish migration to Minnesota includes comparisons of origin and destination communities, as well as a discussion of a secondary destination in the different environment of South Dakota; Sauder (1989) extends the frontier into the "arid intermountain West," concentrating on the differing appraisals of the land made by explorers, surveyors, and settlers; and Mitchell and Newton (1988) offer contrasting perspectives on the Appalachian frontier. Most controversially, Jordan and Kaups (1989) link the cultural traits of the Upland South to a combination of Finnish and indigenous woodland Indian influences which facilitated successful forest colonization; yet there were few points of contact between Finnish settlers and the Scotch-Irish population of the area. Their interpretation raises critical questions about the kind and extent of contact necessary for the transmission both of skills and techniques and of belief systems and social structures.

North American historical geographers have also been prominent internationally, hosting meetings of English-speaking historical geographers in Los Angeles, Toronto, Baton Rouge, and Vancouver; since the late 1970s the only International Conferences of Historical Geographers outside North America have been in Oxford and Jerusalem (for reports on these meetings, see the *Journal of Historical Geography* and *Historical Geography* [formerly the *Historical Geography Newsletter*]). The interests of Israeli historical geographers are reflected in *The Land That Became Israel* (Kark 1990) and in the theme of the Jerusalem conference, on "Ideology and Landscape," embracing discussions on place making, cultural politics, iconography, and the reading of landscapes that have also been central to cultural-historical geography in Britain (Cosgrove and Daniels 1988). Landscape in this approach becomes *text* subject to the same conventions of critical interpretation as literature; indeed, the role models for cultural geographers include literary and artistic critics like Raymond Williams and John Barrell (Daniels 1989).

Postmodernism and Historical Geography

It is a short step from interrogating landscapes as texts to interrogating texts about landscapes. The works of poets and novelists thought to embody the character of particular places or localities, including "regional novelists," such as Thomas Hardy, Arnold Bennett, and D. H. Lawrence, have long attracted the attention of historical geographers (Pocock 1981) but, as Daniels (1985: 149) observes, most geographers have shown "little or no recognition of the literary conventions these novelists employ, for example their methods of narration or description." Yet the content of literary description—what we read about what places were like, or how authors or their characters perceived places—cannot be divorced from the form of representation, as Barrell (1982) demonstrated in a penetrating discussion of geographies of Hardy's Wessex.

More recently, geographers have also, and more successfully, begun to treat everyday language as text. In his interest in the vocabulary of the built environment Allan Pred (1990a) draws on both original strands of postmodernism: architecture and literary theory. Pile and Rose (1992) note that, among geographers, postmodernism has been assigned three critical characteristics: a critique of enlightenment rationality, a sensitivity to difference (hence, an interest in the geographies of genders and minorities and in the uniqueness of different localities), and—of immediate relevance here—the employment of innovative textual strategies. Pred's interest in language is not only as a key to understanding how past generations interpreted their world and imbued their environment with meaning, but also in how we represent *their* knowledge to *our* contemporaries. One chapter of *Lost Words and Lost Worlds* deals with the vocabulary of working-class popular geography: the words that were used to denote streets, landmarks, and districts in nineteenth-century Stockholm, often associated with folk humor or sexual slang. In the face of modernization and modernism, the transformation of the city by capital through acts of "creative destruction," an economic process elaborated in more detail in the case of Second Empire Paris by Harvey (1985b), Pred (1990a: 126) suggests that some aspects of Stockholm's "folk-geographic discourse" were probably "conscious and sub-conscious resistance to the attempt at ideological domination embedded in the street-name revision of 1885 and the street-naming policy of subsequent years." Ideological resistance to modernization included the continuance of old names and the subversion of new ones.

Pred's engagement with postmodernism is indicated in his celebration of different discourses and in his rejection of metanarrative: "There cannot be one grand history, one grand human geography, whose telling only awaits an appropriate metanarrative; . . . people make a plurality of histories and construct a plurality of human geographies" (Pred 1990b: 14, quoted in Gregory 1991: 29). Whereas Harvey remains committed to the metanarrative of Marxism, enlarged to explore the connections between political economy and cultural change but still, at root, progressing from an economic base to a cultural superstructure, as reflected in the structures of both his essay on "Paris 1850–1870" and his *Condition of Postmodernity* (Harvey 1985b, 1989), Pred "refuses to submit the multiple historical geographies of Stockholm to the discipline of a singular narrative" (Gregory 1991: 31).

In discussing Pred's textual strategy, Gregory invokes another hero of the new cultural geography, Walter Benjamin, whose interests in nineteenth-century Paris (Benjamin 1978b; Buck-Morss 1990), the experience of place (Benjamin 1978a), and mass culture, intersect with those of geographers, irrespective of his ambiguous but attractive combination of Marxism, messianic Judaism, and humanism. Much of Benjamin's writing survives as fragments, and even within the fragments, it often tails off uncertainly and incompletely. Pred's style can be just as fragmented, but consciously and deliberately so, an overt strategy in which fragmented representation parallels an "increasingly fragmented social life and rapid changes in impressions and relationships" (Pred 1990a: 186). Benjamin used the term "phantasmagoria" (a magic lantern of flickering lights and transient images); Pred flickers between "academic" and "artistic" language, as poetry and plays on words break into more conventional passages of analysis. Along with Gregory (1991: 32), I have to agree that "Pred's 'poetic forms' do not always enlarge my horizon of meaning. There is no question that his experiments are serious, but somehow his traverse across the typographical high-wire often seems to end in a tangle of thoughts and a pile of words."

In fact, it is this kind of experiment that has led some geographers to dismiss postmodernism as just concerned with play and frivolity, seeing its cultivation of ambiguity and relativism as an excuse for laissez-faire and a lack of commitment: the association of postmodernism with neoconservatism or, at best, the same kind of bleeding-heart liberalism that was all exposure and no action that Harvey condemned so vigorously in *Social Justice and the City* (1973). Rose (in Pile and Rose 1992), for example, argues that Harvey defines postmodernism as chaotic, barbaric, playful, elusive, and ambiguous and offers us a choice between a heroic modernism and an irrational postmodernism. To Rose, Harvey not only subordinates questions of race and gender to those of class and capital, but even genders postmodernism as feminine, thereby provoking the wrath of feminist geographers. Given postmodernism's concern for difference, for the marginalized, and for forms of "otherness" that are not simply opposites, it is not surprising that many feminist geographers are sympathetic to postmodernism.

However, Pile and Rose suggest that most geographers' understanding of "difference" is of a whole that has become fragmented; they acknowledge the importance of difference, but still try to put the pieces together again, to reconstruct a totalizing metanarrative, if not in the steps of Marx then, among historical geographers, applauding Braudel's concept of "total history." For Braudel (1980: 16): "Everything must be recaptured and relocated in the general framework of history, so that despite the difficulties, the fundamental paradoxes and contradictions, we may respect the unity of history which is also the unity of life" (cited in Hutcheon 1989: 63). British historical geographers writing on France have been most sympathetic to Braudel's ideas, particularly his integration of different scales of interpretation: changes of long duration (the history of environment), medium duration (the history of institutions), and short-term (the history of events) (Prince 1975). Thus Baker (1984a: 194) argued that "the personality of a place may be viewed as the outcome of *événements, conjonctures* and *structures* which involve both contingencies and causalities." But to postmodernists Braudelian narratives are totalizing, dissolving difference and contradiction; power masquerading as truth. The historian or geographer gives the impression that they are discovering the narrative, rather than constructing it, selecting "events" which are themselves only representations of what happened and, in the process of giving them meaning, converting them into "facts" (Hutcheon 1989).

For postmodern geographers, dismissive of metanarratives and all too conscious that in making geography they cannot avoid exercising power, enthusiasm is reserved for yet another nongeographical social theorist, Michel Foucault, who argued that *Reason* was inherently oppressive. The Enlightenment illuminated only some areas of interest, casting shadows over others, which then required mechanisms of surveillance and control: hence the definition of postmodernism as a critique of "the Enlightenment project" (Gregory 1989: 68); hence the particular research interest among British historical geographers concerned with the microgeography of institutions (Driver 1989), on the British workhouse system instituted under the Poor Law reforms of 1834 (Philo 1987), on concepts of mental illness and the organization and location of asylums, and on state regulation and policing (Ogborn, 1992); and hence the more general interest in Foucault's sensitivity to the relationship between power, truth, and experience (C. Harris 1991).

Perhaps as a result of this outward-looking stance, drawing on ideas from outside geography, as well as from other subdisciplines of human geography, the internal coherence of historical geography is less in Britain than in North America, certainly as measured by active support for regular conferences of "historical geographers," but this is balanced by the wider acceptance of historical perspectives throughout human geography. In the "new cultural geography," the work of Denis Cosgrove (1984, 1989, 1990), Peter Jackson (1989), and Nigel Thrift (1987) unself-consciously spans past and present; among economic geographers the same is true of Doreen Massey (1984) and David Harvey (1985a, 1985b, 1989, 1990), now returned to Britain as professor of geography at Oxford; and almost the only feminist geography that treats the past has been undertaken by geographers who would be reluctant to be labeled "historical" (e.g., McDowell and Massey 1984; Women and Geography Study Group 1984).

Geography and Gender

In fact, Rose and Ogborn (1988: 405) have berated historical geographers for their continuing neglect of women, "hidden from geography as they were once 'hidden from history.'" Kay (1989) makes a similar point, noting a growth of women's history unmatched by geographical studies of the experience of women or their influence on the making of American landscapes. In particular, she remarks on the gender-blindness of North American regional historical geographies, which have assumed that women's experience was subsumed in that of men and that women's activities were contingent, and therefore secondary, to those of men. As noted earlier, many landscape studies have emphasized themes of progress and improvement; they read like national epics, geographers' versions of *Exodus* (Kay 1991). But a reading of the diaries of pioneer women reveals more concern for "surviving" and "sustaining" than for "making landscapes" or "forging identities," the heroic language often used in epic interpretations. The *scale* of regional historical geographies also contributes to the neglect of women, whose "sense of place seems more rooted to the concept of home and relatedness, less to the staple export or political region" (ibid.: 449). We might expect studies of "community" or "locality" to be more sensitive to women's experience than studies at a continental or regional scale.

Among urban historical geographers, and starting from the perspective of time geography (see below), Miller (1983, 1991) has examined the implications for middle-class women of late nineteenth- and early twentieth-century suburbanization. He points to the double-edged, constraining as well as liberating, combination of suburbanization with new domestic technology. His argument connects better with those of feminist historians interested in the restructuring of suburbia (Wright 1980; Hayden 1981; Marsh 1990) than with traditional urban ecology. Closer to the latter, but also concerned with the impact of suburbia on the changing duties of women in and out of the home, is Harris's (1990) research on working-class suburbanization in turn-of-the-century Toronto.

In Britain, while there has been some attention paid to the role of women in different regional economies—sweated labor in the East End of London, female textile workers in Lancashire and Yorkshire, domestic servants drawn from rural districts to mainly middle-class suburbs, spas, and market towns, and the lack of waged work for women in steel towns and coal-mining areas—little of this research has been informed by feminist theory. Rose and Ogborn (1988) outline an agenda for feminist historical geography, exploring the interconnections between gender relations and spaces, places and landscapes, predicated upon the concept of patriarchy and investigative of the relations between patriarchy and capitalism. They suggest three areas for research: the importance of space in structuring the social relations of gender (e.g., considering how different spaces are associated with men or women and how space was used to control their lives, institutionally in the segregation and supervision of women and men in different wings of poorhouses, asylums, schools, and factories and domestically in the designation of gendered spaces within the home); spatial variations in the form of patriarchy, which connects with another major theme of current human geography—the importance of "locality"; and the role of gender in the cultural construction of landscapes (e.g., in iconography).

Although "mainstream," archive-based, British historical geographers may still feel uncertain how to relate their own unreformed research to these new ideas, at least a dialogue has been established; in North America there is less evidence that the historically oriented work of feminist geographers (e.g., Mackenzie and Rose 1983) has achieved an equivalent status among historical geographers still wedded to the reconstruction of past *landscapes*. Women, however, are not the only victims: Africans, Asians, and Native Americans have also been marginalized by Anglo-American historical geography (Earle et al. 1989).

Historical Geography and "New Human Geographies"

On the other hand, the links between historical and contemporary human geography in North America are maintained by their integration in the tradition of "cultural geography" as established by Carl Sauer. Here, past and present are united through an interest in relict features, architecture and artifacts from the past that have survived into the present landscape. However, there is still a failure to connect with contemporary social and economic geography, for reasons central to Sauer's methodology, for example, its nontheoretical and materialist emphasis, focusing on cultural practices and artifacts to the neglect of the values and habits that lay behind them (Mitchell 1987; Cosgrove and Jackson 1987). Nonetheless, landscape historical geographers are becoming more sensitive to political and social issues: Conzen (1990) introduces *The Making of the American Landscape,* a major new multiauthored text, with references to Cosgrove's dictum that "Landscape . . . is a construction, a composition . . . a way of seeing the world," as well as to Hoskin's (1955) more familiar ideas of landscape history.

If the problem of North American historical geographers is their marginalization, that of their British counterparts is the widespread acceptance of a historical approach among colleagues in human geography, giving a fresh meaning to Darby's famous observation that "all geography is historical geography," but leading some to question whether historical geography will, or need, survive as a distinctive part of the discipline (Butlin 1987). At present, historical research appears safe in the hands of "new" human geographers like those already listed, but there is the justifiable fear that research is now too closely linked to the "needs" of the present: justifying critiques of privatization by pointing to the inadequacies of Victorian laissez-faire or cultivating pride in a heroic interpretation of the past or supporting schemes for heritage conservation or, less ideologically, simply applying currently fashionable theories to test their validity in past situations. Much 1980s radical human geography in Britain was directed at a critical evaluation of "Thatcher's Britain," complemented by historical analyses of "Victorian values," the growth of homeownership, the relations between central and local government, and the rise of the welfare state, all evidently motivated by contemporary political debates. In response to the less strident conservatism of the early 1990s, a new generation of geographers, themselves "Thatcher's children," may prove less politically motivated than their welfare-state predecessors or seduced by postmodernism into celebrating difference without challenging inequality.

But if we accept that the essence of history is the reinterpretation of the past in the light of the present, it is difficult to see how things could be otherwise. Attempts by the Canadian geographer, Guelke (1982), to promote an idealist approach in historical geography—defining his subject as "the history of thought relating to human activity on the land" and seeking to rethink the thoughts of the colonists whose patterns of settlement provide the starting point for his research—are certainly more sophisticated than Ralph Brown's classic *Mirror for Americans* (Brown 1943), which described the geography of the Eastern seaboard in 1810 using only sources that were available in the early nineteenth century; but they have had as little success in establishing a new methodology for geographical research. Meanwhile, methodological debate has moved on. Guelke (1992) interprets the new language of structuration, on the interaction between structure and human agency, as the old possibilism, in which the environment was seen as fixing the boundaries of what it was possible for people to do. So he rejects structuration, just as he rejected possibilism, on the grounds that space itself has no power; what matters is "the preeminence of mind and its independence of the physical environment" (ibid.: 313). But to Cole Harris (1992) there is a crucial difference between possibilism and structuration. In the former, environment was considered separate from society, limiting freedom of action. In other words, structure was more important than agency. In structuration, space and environment are as socially constructed as human relationships. In fact, this is not so different from Guelke's view that the human mind creates the geographical context. For Guelke this is the only and the essential article of faith, but for most geographers it is too great a step to argue that *only* contemporaries' perceptions and ways of thinking are relevant to understanding and explaining their actions.

Nonetheless, perception studies of various kinds are still central to historical geography. Ward (1989) examines changing conceptions of the slum and the ghetto in American cities in the period 1840–1925, contrasting successive phases of interpretation by nineteenth- and early twentieth-century observers and social reformers with more recent ecological and structural reinterpretations. Harvey (1985b) stresses the experience and *consciousness* of urbanization among residents of Second Empire Paris, but only as one element in an impressive structural interpretation of the urbanization process. Bowden (1992) and his students focus on the invention of tradition and the development of perceptions which subsequently shaped geographical behavior—from the myth of the Great American Desert (Baltensperger 1992) to the perception of Los Angeles as un-urban (Krim 1992).

Yet for all the enthusiasm for the different varieties of "new human geography," the fact remains that in-depth applications of new approaches have been limited. Cole Harris (1991: 676) commented that structuration theory is "suggestively but not deductively useful," and that none of the social theories he reviews can be tested formally, while Butlin (1987) noted that there were actually very few applications of Marxist methods in historico-geographical research. The most notable were the books by Harvey and Dunford and Perrons's (1983) account, in their dogmatic *Arena of Capital,* of change in the structure of the British space-economy spanning the centuries from Domesday to 1945, all the way from feudalism to Fordism. Just as Harvey has little time for the hidebound empiricism of atheoretical urban historical geographers (Harvey 1988), so Dunford and Perrons preferred to draw on approved Marxist historians, like Hilton, Hobsbawm, and Stedman Jones, rather than the work of non-Marxist geographers.

Dunford and Perrons admitted that they had "not given much explicit attention to questions of human agency," thereby distancing themselves from other geographers who have employed Giddens's theory of structuration in an attempt to reconcile Marxist structuralism with a humanistic concern for individual human agency. Illustrations of a structurationist approach include studies by Gregory (1982a, 1982b, 1984), discussing regional transformation and class struggle in the late eighteenth- and early nineteenth-century West Riding textile industry; by Baker (1984b, 1990) in work on cooperatives, fraternal societies and cultural institutions in rural France; and by Pred (1984a, 1984b), whose studies of mercantile urban development in the Eastern United States and rural settlement in Sweden were intended to integrate the experiences and everyday activity patterns of actors such as merchants and farmers with their structural context. For example, in studying the effects of enclosure on "the becoming of place" in villages in southern Sweden in the late eighteenth century, Pred (1986) discussed the reflexiveness of dominant *projects* (enclosure, commercialization) and daily and life *paths* of individuals (the decline of cooperative agriculture, the growth of individualism, and how these trends are expressed in routine practices).

Pred's intellectual debts are also to Hagerstrand's time geography. Hagerstrand emphasized individuals' consumption of space through time, the routinization of much of everyday life, and the nature of "coupling constraints," limiting individuals' participation in different activities (Gregory 1989; Hagerstrand 1982). Time geography generated some fascinating case studies, typically illustrated by three-dimensional graphs depicting the paths of one or a handful of individuals through time and space; for example, studies of women's use of space, showing how the planning of the built environment worked to women's disadvantage by separating complementary land uses and functions in quite separate zones (Women and Geography Study Group 1984). Miller's (1982, 1983) studies of suburbanization demonstrate the conceptual value and potential of time geography, but it remained stillborn, partly because of the difficulties of making sense of more than a few paths at once and partly because a focus on describing how people used space seemed at odds with a growing concern for the production of space. More recently, Hagerstrand's ideas have been taken up by Giddens (1984) and Harvey (1990), who in different ways show how space and time are manipulated in the exercise of social power. Time and space are both socially constructed, and different conceptions of time

and space are integral to different modes of production. Industrial capitalism involved new ways of thinking about time and space, reflected in new
attitudes to property rights, and new disciplines of timekeeping. Control
of space depends on the "annihilation of space by time," which encapsu-
lates far more than the simple speeding up of communications. Giddens
discusses the emergence of writing and of money; Harvey emphasises the
role of credit.

The effect of "time-space compression" has not been to eliminate the
importance of space and place. On the contrary, geography matters more
than ever, both because particular places are associated with specialized
temporal regimes and because of peoples' needs to assert their identity
in a shrinking world: "the diminution of spatial barriers has provoked an
increasing sense of nationalism and localism, and excessive geopolitical
rivalries and tensions, precisely because of the reduction in the power of
spatial barriers to separate and defend against others" (Harvey 1990: 427).
Hence the growth of historical geographies of nationalism and of locality
studies.

Historical Geography and Locality Studies

"Locality studies" constitute the most tangible element of what Thrift (1983)
termed the "reconstruction of regional geography." Among British geographers, Gregory (1978) initiated a return to regional studies in the spirit
of Vidal de la Blache; while, from the left, Walker (1989) identifies several
strands in the displacement of "spatial fetishism" by a revived regional consciousness: a concern among industrial geographers for spatial divisions
of labor and the impact of economic restructuring, and an interest among
historical geographers in the *Annales* school of French economic and social
history, and in E. P. Thompson's variety of Marxist humanism, emphasizing how people (in Thompson's case, the English working class) make their
own history, albeit not in circumstances of their own choosing. Advocates
of "locality studies" argue that, however widespread the structures and processes of economic and cultural change may be, outcomes vary according
to the particular mix of local circumstances and historical context. Nor is
it just that global processes have local effects; local resistance and reaction
can also alter the course of global processes. Thus, industrial restructuring,

technological change, the transition from Fordism to flexible accumulation, and the impact of patriarchy, all have different effects in different localities. In Britain the Economic and Social Research Council has sponsored a series of locality studies, each of which involved historians, economists, and sociologists as well as geographers (Cooke 1989), but research elsewhere can equally well be classified under the "localities" banner. For example, Smith (1989) has compared the operation of paternalist strategies in the employer towns of Pullman, outside Chicago, and Bournville, in the suburbs of Birmingham; Thrift (1987) has contrasted the geography of class formation in nineteenth-century Sheffield and Leeds; Harris (1988, 1989) has examined the recent history of democratic political protest movements in Kingston, Ontario; and Parr (1990) has compared the ways in which patriarchy and gender divisions of labor operated in two small Ontario industrial towns—Paris, dominated by a single, large knitwear-goods factory, and Hanover, a furniture-making center. Paris is also compared with the English East Midlands, whence many female textile workers emigrated to Ontario in the early years of this century.

"Big-Picture" Historical Geography

While geographers have been at the forefront of localities research, they have made very little contribution to studies at an international or continental scale or to debates about long-term changes such as the transition from feudalism to capitalism. Robert Dodgshon, author of *The European Past* (1987), a rare attempt by a historical geographer to address questions of major social, structural, and spatial change, comments in a review of Michael Mann's *The Sources of Social Power* (1986) that "problems of direct interest to the historical geographer abound, yet Mann is unable to cite a single supportive study by an historical geographer" (Dodgshon 1988). Other examples of "big-picture history"—Wallerstein, Braudel, de Vries—are avidly consumed by geographers, but without reply. Perhaps, as Wynn (1990) suggests, historical geographers have become more interested in how people make places, while historians concentrate on what Darby once called "the geography behind history"—how places influence people and events. For example, Genovese and Hochberg (1989) argue that geography "intrudes into the drama of historical change itself" rather than merely providing "an arena of history" (Dodgshon 1990: 375). Their inspiration is the historian Edward Whiting Fox, who suggested critical differences between landlocked societies, which developed power structures based on land ownership, and societies with access to the sea or navigable waterways, where power was grounded in commerce. Most of the contributors to Genovese and Hochberg's *Geographic Perspectives in History* are historians, including *Annalistes* such as Le Roy Ladurie, but two American geographers, Meinig and Vance, also contribute chapters.

Recently, there have been attempts by geographers to paint on a bigger canvas—not only Dodgshon's work but also Corbridge's *Capitalist World Development* (1986), Agnew's *The United States in the World Economy* (1987), and Taylor's *Political Geography: World-Economy, Nation-State and Locality* (1985), which draws enthusiastically, although in Kearns's (1988) view, misguidedly, on Wallerstein's approach. Meinig (1989) applauds Agnew's work as "historical regional geography on a scale and of a kind we've not seen before," while in empire-building language that matches the subject matter of these studies Earle et al. (1989: 162) conclude that "such macro-perspectives promise geographers a prominent role in a reconstructed historical social science that is preeminently spatial."

However, Meinig's *Shaping of America* (1986: 1), an impressive and much-praised first volume bringing the story up to 1800, is perhaps the most original example of big-picture historical geography. As Cole Harris (1988) notes, Meinig is more impressive in his handling of social and cultural themes than in his treatment of economics and more interested in pattern than process. Nonetheless, it is a spectacular achievement, cartographically and in the quality of the writing. Indeed, the writing of historical geography has attracted comment, not only in Pred's textual experiments, but also in papers by Gregory (1982a), Meinig (1983), and Daniels (1985). Gregory quotes E. P. Thompson's advice that the form of the text should mirror the flow of history it represents; Daniels urges the use of narrative which conserves "a more seamless sense of the fluency of relations between people and between people and place than do systems or structural modes of temporal explanation." For Daniels, narrative "explicates meaning through context" and "can conserve theoretical concepts as it were in solution," as in the case of Harvey's essays on nineteenth-century Paris, informed by a Marxist theory of history. Writing in the early 1980s, Meinig observed that most historical geography was "scientific," analytical and logical; nonetheless he hoped for writing that would be "creative," not just reconstituting the past but also "evocative," deepening and extending our understanding.

Recent Historical Geography of Industrial and Urban Society

By focusing on theoretical and methodological issues, on the identity crisis of historical geography and its relations with other disciplines and other branches of human geography, I have so far neglected much of the most exciting recent empirical research by historically minded geographers. The final sections of this chapter attempt to redress some of these omissions.

Economic and social geographers have devoted considerable attention to successive phases of restructuring, associated with transitions from feudalism to capitalism and, within the latter, between mercantile, industrial, entrepreneurial, corporate, and state capitalism and with different forms of industrial organization—protoindustrialization, the development of the factory system and more recent movements from Fordism to flexible specialization. Harvey's (1982, 1985a, 1989) attempts at "putting the geography back in" Marxist economics, focusing on geographical strategies to counter accumulation crises—the opening up of new markets through colonial expansion and the promotion of new suburban lifestyles and habits of consumption, the acceleration of capital circulation through the creation of new credit systems and faster transmission of information—find echoes in a variety of recent empirical studies, by no means all by geographers who would accept Harvey's Marxist framework.

For example, Black (1989) has examined the increasing geographic movement of finance capital in early industrial England, thereby also contributing to an important ongoing debate on the effects of industrialization on regionalism. Did the industrial revolution first intensify regional differences, as Langton (1984, 1988) argued, or is it possible to regard regional integration and differentiation as complementary and coexisting forces (Gregory 1988)? On a larger scale, the same questions are relevant to American regional economic development in the nineteenth century (Earle 1987). Goheen's (1990a) study of the impact of the telegraph on the content of Canadian newspapers shows not only the emergence of a national information system, in which control over the dissemination of news was increasingly centralized and in which Canada's links with the United States were reinforced by a dependence on American news services, but also how the content of communication was influenced by technology: the telegraph was better suited to transmitting some kinds of information than others— prices, dates, quantities, not ideas and opinions.

The context for Goheen's work was communications theory rather than restructuring or socioeconomic transition; by contrast, Pudup (1989) examines the social and economic transformation of the Appalachian economy during the nineteenth century, questioning traditional views that the region's isolation led to arrested development. Her focus is on the links between external relations and internal social differentiation, especially the making of a local middle class, and her model is explicitly that of a big-picture historian, Robert Brenner, in his work on economic development and agrarian class structure in preindustrial Europe. Brenner is also invoked as the theoretical inspiration for Clarke's (1992) stimulating and provocative study of suburban development in late eighteenth-century London, conceptualized as a kind of protoindustrialization in the building trades and, in some respects, as a ruralization of the metropolis, perpetuating rural social relations and work practices in newly urbanized districts.

In his work on suburban residential differentiation, Walker (1978, 1981) has been the American urban geographer with historical interests most closely associated with Harvey. In more recent collaboration (Storper and Walker 1989), he and his coauthor reject the theoretical significance of a division between late nineteenth-century entrepreneurial capitalism and twentieth-century corporate capitalism in American industrial growth and regional development. Instead, they develop "a theory of territorial industrialization in which the essence of capitalism is its ever-shifting regional foundations" (Walker 1989: 633). In so doing, they seek to identify similarities across time and across different industries in geographical processes of localization, clustering, dispersal, and locational shifts. Most importantly, they emphasize the regional character of industrial technology and organization and the "passage of transitory economic landscapes" (Solot 1990). A good illustration of their ideas is Page and Walker's (1991) discussion of agro-industrialization in the Midwest.

British historical geographers have shown less interest in the location of industry, more in the geography of unionism and the origins of twentieth-century patterns of regional unemployment (Southall 1986, 1988, 1989) and in the role of the state, especially how "uneven development" was both a cause and a consequence of local and central government intervention. For example, Ward (1988) has explored both the origins of regional planning and the role of defense expenditure in interwar Britain, arguing that the state acted primarily to support the priorities of private capital, and Lee (1988) has considered the significance of place in the creation of social policy, as exemplified by local government funding of health care in England and Wales, again in the interwar period. Rose (1990) focuses on "contested concepts of community" in 1920s Poplar, in London's East End, contrasting two politicized views of community: the community of property taxpayers, composed of landlords and shopkeepers, anxious to stress personal responsibility and property interests, in conflict with the community of residents, as defined by the ruling Poplar Labour party, which was famous (or notorious) for its promotion of a local welfare state, protecting working-class residents from impoverishment as a result of unemployment, but necessarily dependent upon high levels of local taxation.

Rose makes two important points about community studies: the need for geographers to consider community as a contested idea, involving conflict and struggle, in contrast to benign views of community as harmony, consensus, and balance; and the need to avoid imposing our views of other people's community. The latter is reasonable enough if we can draw on a rich reservoir of oral history and autobiography, but this is seldom possible for studies of communities prior to World War I. Nonetheless, we can be more imaginative in reconstructing past communities, emphasizing the active nature of community life, expressed in patterns of marriage and friendship, church and club membership, voting behavior, and the interaction between residence and workplace (Dennis 1987, 1989a). For example, two papers by Schreuder (1989, 1990) demonstrate the importance of labor market processes in structuring immigrant residential communities in early twentieth-century America and also link the urban geography of ethnic neighborhoods to the issues of industrial restructuring and changing sources of capital, already discussed, thereby positing an alternative framework for urban social geography to either the Chicago School or some ill-defined notion of "modernization." Gilbert (1991) also presents a more politicized view of community, contrasting employer-miner relationships and their implications for local institutional structures and politics in late Victorian and Edwardian mining towns in South Wales and the English East Midlands. This is historical geography with critical implications for present-day politics, as Johnston (1991) shows in his study of the 1984–

85 British miners' strike, when regional variations in support for the strike mirrored long-standing cultural differences between mining districts.

An active view of urban structure is also evident in recent papers concerned with how city dwellers used their built environment to further cultural or political objectives, how space was appropriated and socially constructed. Several studies focus on landscapes of resistance or struggle. In the context of Bristol in the early 1800s, Harrison (1988) shows how public meetings and processions were located "both to give to and gain from their surroundings an extra representational significance." Streets acquired new symbolic meanings, and the ability to take control of a particular locality, however fleetingly, imbued a class or a social movement with new status and authority. Similarly, Marston (1989) has examined St. Patrick's Day parades in Lowell, while Goheen (1990b) has compared the routes, ordering, and composition of a Montreal funeral procession and a Hamilton labor parade. Of course, buildings, street patterns, and landscapes may be made with meaning, or they may have meaning thrust upon them: consider Harvey's (1979, 1985b) interpretations of the building of Sacre Coeur on Montmartre and of Haussmann's reconstruction of central Paris, Woolf's (1988) discussion of the Paris Opera, Cosgrove's (1982) interpretation of Ruskin's Venice, Domosh's (1987) analysis of the symbolism of American skyscrapers, or Duncan's (1990) reading of the landscape of precolonial Kandy.

Evident in all these studies is a convergence of the interests of historical geographers, architectural historians, and art historians, as the former place more emphasis on the experience of landscape and its visual aspects (Meinig 1979; Jakle 1987; Conzen 1990). Among studies of the representation, selective depiction, and distortion of landscape in art, see Prince's (1988) account of artists' renderings of agricultural change in England, Daniels's (1986) persuasive essay on J. M. W. Turner's painting of industrial Leeds, and Harvey's (1987) and Daniels's (1989) sympathetic but critical discussions of Clark's *The Painting of Modern Life* (1984).

The richness of current urban historical geography is also apparent in a shift away from the study of residential patterns, interpreted according to the precepts of human ecology, toward more comprehensive analyses of urban structure, including industrial and commercial districts and integrating social, economic, political, and architectural perspectives. Examples include Whitehand's (1984) work on English shopping centers, extending morphological studies far beyond their roots in the analysis of town plans and street patterns, Domosh's (1990) comparison of retail districts in New York and Boston, and Gad and Holdsworth's (1987a, b) series of papers on early twentieth-century high-rise offices in Toronto, financed speculatively by corporate capital, and thereby linking changes in the built environment to changes in the nature of capitalism. Even in studies of residential areas, much more attention is now paid to the financing of suburban development and the functioning of property markets, and to the social and political meaning as well as the extent of homeownership and private landlordism. Among an immense recent literature, the following contributions of geographers deserve mention: Hamnett and Randolph's (1988) work on the flat break-up market, comparing processes of institutional investment and disinvestment in apartment housing in London with similar processes associated with gentrification and conversion of rented apartments to condominiums in American cities; studies of housing tenure, landlordism, and homeownership in selected Canadian cities and comparing Britain and North America more widely (Doucet and Weaver 1991; Harris 1991; Harris and Hamnett 1987; Harris, Levine, and Osborne 1981; Hertzog and Lewis 1986; Kemp 1987; Levine 1988; Rose 1987). Several studies exemplify themes alluded to earlier in this essay, such as the centrality of geography to the making of social policy (Dennis 1989b) and the intersection of structure and human agency, exemplified in individual biographies (Allen and McDowell 1989).

"Geography Is about Maps"

I have made plenty of assertions that places matter—that geography causes as well as reflects social, economic, and political processes—but I have not made much reference to the geographer's traditional tool, the map. Yet the last five years have witnessed several major achievements in historical cartography. The beginnings of a major project on the history of cartography (Harley and Woodward 1987) indicate the subtlety with which we should treat maps; Harley (1989) argues that their production and interpretation are not the straightforward, scientific, objective processes they were once considered to be. Maps, like landscapes, are texts, not unambiguous mirrors of reality, and atlases are narratives, their story propelled by the selection of topics, their organization, and their presentation. Even computer-generated maps are value-laden representations, works of art as much as technical constructions. This is as true of the austere, but very useful *Atlas of Industrializing Britain* (Langton and Morris 1986) as of the magnificent *Historical Atlas of Canada* (Harris and Matthews 1987; Kerr et al. 1990), where *each* double-page plate constitutes a multilayered text equivalent to a research paper if not a whole monograph! Many of the plates are based on extensive new research and each embraces a variety of forms of representation; not only newly constructed maps at various scales, but also reproductions of contemporary maps, plans and pictures, architectural and archaeological drawings, graphs, charts, and imaginative reconstructions are included.

Conclusion

There still remain many omissions in this survey. I have concentrated on studies of the nineteenth and early twentieth centuries and deliberately omitted references to empirical studies of medieval society, to a recent upsurge of interest in the early modern period, or to research outside Britain and North America, for example, on the historical geography of colonization and imperialism and on Latin American societies. Much of this research has featured, or has been reviewed in the *Journal of Historical Geography*, or has appeared in the Research Series published by the Historical Geography Research Group of the Institute of British Geographers or, preeminently, in the series Studies in Historical Geography published by Cambridge University Press. Recent titles in the latter series have included edited collections on urban historical geography in Britain and Germany (Denecke and Shaw 1988; Kearns and Withers 1991) and migration in colonial Latin America (Robinson 1990) and single-authored texts on Australia (Powell 1988) and the West Indies (Watts 1987).

Essentially, I have been arguing that historical geography in North America is still more wedded to the reconstruction of past landscapes and less explicitly concerned with social theory than historical geography in Britain, which is more often focused on society and social change, on "place" (as opposed to the "space" of quantitative regional science) and "locality" (as opposed to a physically or culturally defined "region"), and on values and ideologies. This is reflected in a comparison of British and North American textbooks (Dodgshon and Butlin 1990; Mitchell and Groves 1987); like the atlases just discussed, each is a narrative constructed by its editors, exemplifying not only the histories of their respective landscapes and societies (such as the phases of Colonization, Expansion, Consolidation, and Reorganization identified by Mitchell and Groves) but also the character of national historical geographies.

In the past, historical geographers were sometimes guilty of being source-led, and some of us still spend too much time in the archives! A more recent danger is that of flirtation with a trendy social theory which may provide the flimsiest of wrapping: almost anything can be dressed up as "structure" and "agency"; some "locality studies" are just unreformed local history. As good postmodernists, we are supposed to eschew the idea that there might be a single "right" interpretation of events, and as I have already indicated, history is about the reinterpretation of the past in the light of new presents as well as new facts. But some interpretations are better than others, and there are limits to relativism. Obviously, we do not want to return to the days of empiricism uninformed by theory: rather, we should seek a reflexive relationship between theory, analysis, and archival and field research and between research undertaken at different scales.

At the height of the humanistic revolution in geography, Cole Harris (1978) advocated the practice of a historical mind that was open and eclectic with regard to method, for example incorporating both quantitative and qualitative forms of analysis. Numerate essayists and literate statisticians were thin on the ground during the 1970s and 1980s, but currently there is a tendency for Marxist analysis at least to become more statistical as well as more cultural. Earle et al. (1989: 161) anticipate a future for historical geography "at the intersection of macroscale theory and thick empirical description." Too often in the past the intersection has proved to be an overpass without an interchange. For a more exciting future, we need a grade crossing with no traffic signals.

Note

This is a much expanded and revised version of "History, Geography, and Historical Geography," first published in *Social Science History* 15:2 (Summer 1991): 265–88. I am grateful to Peter Jackson and Roger Miller for their efforts at getting me interested in time geography, social theory, and postmodernism; they are of course not to blame for what appears above.

References

Agnew, J. (1987) *The United States in the World Economy: A Regional Geography*. New York: Cambridge University Press.

Allen, J., and L. McDowell (1989) *Landlords and Property: Social Relations in the Private Rented Sector*. Cambridge: Cambridge University Press.

Baker, A. R. H. (1984a) "Reflections on the relations of historical geography and the *Annales* school of history," in A. R. H. Baker and D. Gregory (eds.) *Explorations in Historical Geography: Interpretative Essays*. Cambridge: Cambridge University Press: 1–27.

————— (1984b) "Fraternity in the forest: The creation, control, and collapse of woodcutters' unions in Loir-et-Cher 1852–1914." *Journal of Historical Geography* 10: 157–73.

————— (1990) "Fire-fighting fraternities? The *corps de sapeurs-pompiers* in Loir-et-Cher during the nineteenth century." *Journal of Historical Geography* 16: 121–39.

Baltensperger, B. H. (1992) "Plains boomers and the creation of the Great American Desert Myth." *Journal of Historical Geography* 18: 59–73.

Barrell, J. (1982) "Geographies of Hardy's Wessex." *Journal of Historical Geography* 8: 347–61.

Benjamin, W. (1978a) "A Berlin Chronicle," in W. Benjamin, *Reflections: Essays, Aphorisms, Autobiographical Writings*. New York: Harcourt Brace Jovanovich: 3–60.

————— (1978b) "Paris, capital of the nineteenth century," in W. Benjamin *Reflections: Essays, Aphorisms, Autobiographical Writings*. New York: Harcourt Brace Jovanovich: 146–62.

Black, I. (1989) "Geography, political economy and the circulation of finance capital in early industrial England." *Journal of Historical Geography* 15: 366–84.

Bowden, M. J. (1992) "The invention of American tradition." *Journal of Historical Geography* 18: 3–26.

Braudel, F. (1980) *On History*, translated by S. Matthews. Chicago: University of Chicago Press.

Brown, R. H. (1943) *Mirror for Americans: Likeness of the Eastern Seaboard 1810*. New York: American Geographical Society.

Buck-Morss, S. (1990) *The Dialectics of Seeing: Walter Benjamin and the Arcades Project*. Cambridge, MA: MIT Press.

Butlin, R. A. (1987) "Theory and methodology in historical geography," in M. Pacione (ed.) *Historical Geography: Progress and Prospect*. London: Croom Helm: 16–45.

Clark, T. J. (1984) *The Painting of Modern Life: Paris in the Art of Manet and His Followers*. Princeton, NJ: Princeton University Press.

Clarke, L. (1992) *Building Capitalism: Historical Change and the Labour Process in the Production of the Built Environment*. London: Routledge.

Conzen, M. P., ed. (1990) *The Making of the American Landscape*. London: Unwin Hyman.

Cooke, P., ed. (1989) *Localities: A Comparative Analysis of Urban Change*. London: Unwin Hyman.

Corbridge, S. (1986) *Capitalist World Development: A Critique of Radical Development Geography*. London: Macmillan.

Cosgrove, D. (1982) "The myth and the stones of Venice: An historical geography of a symbolic landscape." *Journal of Historical Geography* 8: 145–69.

———— (1984) *Social Formation and Symbolic Landscape*. London: Croom Helm.

———— (1989) "Historical considerations of humanism, historical materialism, and geography," in A. Kobayashi and S. Mackenzie (eds.) *Remaking Human Geography*. London: Unwin Hyman: 189–205.

———— (1990) "Environmental thought and action: Pre-modern and post-modern." *Transactions, Institute of British Geographers* 15: 344–58.

————, and S. Daniels, eds. (1988) *The Iconography of Landscape: Essays on the Symbolic Representation, Design and Use of Past Environments*. Cambridge: Cambridge University Press.

———— and P. Jackson (1987) "New directions in cultural geography." *Area* 19: 95–101.

Cronon, W. (1991) *Nature's Metropolis: Chicago and the Great West*. New York: W. W. Norton.

Daniels, S. J. (1985) "Arguments for a humanistic geography," in R. J. Johnston (ed.) *The Future of Geography*. London: Methuen: 143–58.

———— (1986) "The implications of industry: Turner and Leeds." *Turner Studies* 6: 10–17.

———— (1989) "Marxism, culture, and the duplicity of landscape," in R. Peet and N. Thrift (eds.) *New Models in Geography,* vol. 2. London: Unwin Hyman: 196–220.

Darby, H. C., and G. R. Versey (1952–77) *Domesday Geography of England*. 7 vols. Cambridge: Cambridge University Press.

Dear, M. (1988) "The postmodern challenge: Reconstructing human geography." *Transactions, Institute of British Geographers* 13: 262–74.

Denecke, D., and G. Shaw, eds. (1988) *Urban Historical Geography: Recent Progress in Britain and Germany*. Cambridge: Cambridge University Press.

Dennis, R. (1984a) *English Industrial Cities of the Nineteenth Century: A Social Geography*. Cambridge: Cambridge University Press.

———— (1984b) "Historical geography: Theory and progress." *Progress in Human Geography* 8: 536–43.

———— (1987) "Class, behaviour, and residence in nineteenth-century society: The lower middle class in Huddersfield in 1871," in N. Thrift and P. Williams (eds.) *Class and Space: The Making of Urban Society*. London: Routledge: 73–107.

———— (1989a) "Dismantling the barriers: Past and present in urban Britain," in D. Gregory and R. Walford (eds.) *Horizons in Human Geography*. London: Macmillan: 194–216.

────── (1989b) " 'Hard to let' in Edwardian London." *Urban Studies* 26: 77–89.

Dodgshon, R. A. (1987) *The European Past: Social Evolution and Spatial Order.* London: Macmillan.

────── (1988) "Review of M. Mann, *The Sources of Social Power*." *Journal of Historical Geography* 14: 324–6.

────── (1990) "Review of E. D. Genovese and L. Hochberg, *Geographic Perspectives in History*." *Journal of Historical Geography* 16: 375–77.

──────, and R. A. Butlin, eds. (1990) *An Historical Geography of England and Wales.* 2d ed. London: Academic Press.

Domosh, M. (1987) "The symbolism of the skyscraper: Case studies of New York's first tall buildings." *Journal of Urban History* 14: 321–45.

────── (1990) "Shaping the commercial city: Retail districts in nineteenth-century New York and Boston." *Annals of the Association of American Geographers* 80: 268–84.

Doucet, M., and J. Weaver (1991) *Housing the North American City.* Kingston, Ont.: McGill-Queen's University Press.

Driver, F. (1989) "The historical geography of the workhouse system in England and Wales, 1834–1883." *Journal of Historical Geography* 15: 269–86.

Duncan, J. (1990) *The City as Text: The Politics of Landscape Interpretation in the Kandyan Kingdom.* Cambridge: Cambridge University Press.

Dunford, M. and D. Perrons (1983) *The Arena of Capital.* London: Macmillan.

Earle, C. (1987) "Regional economic development west of the Appalachians, 1815–1860," in R. D. Mitchell and P. A. Groves (eds.) *North America: The Historical Geography of a Changing Continent.* London: Hutchinson: 172–97.

────── et al. (1989) "Historical geography," in G. L. Gaile and C. J. Willmott (eds.) *Geography in America.* Columbus, OH: Merrill Publishing Company: 156–91.

Gad, G., and D. Holdsworth (1987a) "Corporate capitalism and the emergence of the high-rise office building." *Urban Geography* 8: 212–31.

────── (1987b) "Looking inside the skyscraper: Size and occupancy of Toronto office buildings, 1890–1950." *Urban History Review* 16: 176–89.

Genovese, E. D., and L. Hochberg, eds. (1989) *Geographic Perspectives in History.* Oxford: Basil Blackwell.

Giddens, A. (1984) *The Constitution of Society: Outline of the Theory of Structuration.* Cambridge: Polity Press.

Gilbert, D. (1991) "Community and municipalism: Collective identity in late-Victorian and Edwardian mining towns." *Journal of Historical Geography* 17: 257–70.

Goheen, P. G. (1990a) "The changing bias of inter-urban communications in nineteenth-century Canada." *Journal of Historical Geography* 16: 177–96.

────── (1990b) "Symbols in the streets: Parades in Victorian urban Canada." *Urban History Review* 18: 237–43.

Gregory, D. (1978) *Ideology, Science and Human Geography.* London: Hutchinson.

────── (1982a) "Action and structure in historical geography," in A. R. H. Baker and M. Billinge (eds.) *Period and Place: Research Methods in Historical Geography*. Cambridge: Cambridge University Press: 244–50.

———— (1982b) *Regional Transformation and Industrial Revolution: A Geography of the Yorkshire Woollen Industry*. London: Macmillan.

———— (1984) "Contours of crisis? Sketches for a geography of class struggle in the early industrial revolution in England," in A. R. H. Baker and D. Gregory (eds.) *Explorations in Historical Geography: Interpretative Essays*. Cambridge: Cambridge University Press: 68–117.

———— (1988) "The production of regions in England's Industrial Revolution." *Journal of Historical Geography* 14: 50–58.

———— (1989) "Areal differentiation and post-modern human geography," in D. Gregory and R. Walford (eds.) *Horizons in Human Geography*. London: Macmillan: 67–96.

———— (1991) "Interventions in the historical geography of modernity: Social theory, spatiality and the politics of representation." *Geografiska Annaler* 73B: 17–44.

Guelke, L. (1982) *Historical Understanding in Geography: An Idealist Approach*. Cambridge: Cambridge University Press.

———— (1992) On "Power, Modernity, and Historical Geography," by C. Harris, *Annals of the Association of American Geographers* 82: 312–13.

Hagerstrand, T. (1982) "Diorama, path and project." *Tijdshrift voor Economische en Sociale Geographie* 73: 323–39.

Hamnett, C., and B. Randolph (1988) *Cities, Housing and Profits: Flat Break-Up and the Decline of Private Renting*. London: Hutchinson.

Harley, J. B. (1982) "Historical geography and its evidence: Reflections on modelling sources," in A. R. H. Baker and M. Billinge (eds.) *Period and Place: Research Methods in Historical Geography*. Cambridge: Cambridge University Press: 261–73.

———— (1989) "Historical geography and the cartographic illusion." *Journal of Historical Geography* 15: 80–91.

————, and D. Woodward, eds. (1987) *The History of Cartography Volume 1: Cartography in Prehistoric, Ancient, and Medieval Europe and the Mediterranean*. Chicago: University of Chicago Press.

Harris, C. (1978) "The historical mind and the practice of geography," in D. Ley and M. Samuels (eds.) *Humanistic Geography: Prospects and Problems*. Chicago: Maaroufa: 123–37.

———— (1988) "Taking on a continent." *Journal of Historical Geography* 14: 416–19.

———— (1991) "Power, modernity, and historical geography." *Annals of the Association of American Geographers* 81: 671–83.

———— (1992) "Reply to L. Guelke." *Annals of the Association of American Geographers* 82: 314–15.

Harris, C. (ed.) and G. J. Matthews (cart.) (1987) *Historical Atlas of Canada I: From the Beginning to 1800*. Toronto: University of Toronto Press.

———— (1988) *Democracy in Kingston: A Social Movement in Urban Politics 1965–70.* Kingston, Ont.: McGill-Queen's University Press.

———— (1989) "Synthesis in human geography: A demonstration of historical materialism," in A. Kobayashi and S. Mackenzie (eds.) *Remaking Human Geography.* London: Unwin Hyman: 78–94.

———— (1990) "Household work strategies and suburban homeownership in Toronto, 1899–1913." *Environment and Planning D: Society and Space* 8: 97–121.

———— (1991) "A working-class suburb for immigrants: Toronto 1909–1913." *Geographical Review* 81: 318–32.

Harris, C., and C. Hamnett (1987) "The myth of the promised land: The social diffusion of home ownership in Britain and North America." *Annals of the Association of American Geographers* 77: 173–90.

Harris, C., G. Levine, and B. S. Osborne (1981) "Housing tenure and social classes in Kingston, Ontario, 1881–1901." *Journal of Historical Geography* 7: 271–89.

Harrison, M. (1988) "Symbolism, 'ritualism' and the location of crowds in early nineteenth-century English towns," in D. Cosgrove and S. Daniels (eds.) *The Iconography of Landscape.* Cambridge: Cambridge University Press: 194–213.

Harvey, D. (1973) *Social Justice and the City.* London: Edward Arnold.

———— (1979) "Monument and myth." *Annals of the Association of American Geographers* 69: 362–81.

———— (1982) *The Limits to Capital.* Oxford: Basil Blackwell.

———— (1985a) *The Urbanization of Capital.* Oxford: Basil Blackwell.

———— (1985b) *Consciousness and the Urban Experience.* Oxford: Basil Blackwell.

———— (1987) "The representation of urban life." *Journal of Historical Geography* 13: 317–21.

———— (1988) "The production of value in historical geography." *Journal of Historical Geography* 14: 305–6.

———— (1989) *The Condition of Postmodernity.* Oxford: Basil Blackwell.

———— (1990) "Between space and time: Reflections on the geographical imagination." *Annals of the Association of American Geographers* 80: 418–34.

Hayden, D. (1981) *The Grand Domestic Revolution: A History of Feminist Designs for American Homes, Neighborhoods, and Cities.* Cambridge, MA: MIT Press.

Hertzog, S., and R. D. Lewis (1986) "A city of tenants: Homeownership and social class in Montreal, 1847–1881." *Canadian Geographer* 30: 316–23.

Hoskins, W. G. (1955) *The Making of the English Landscape.* London: Hodder and Stoughton.

Hutcheon, L. (1989) *The Politics of Postmodernism.* London: Routledge.

Jackson, P. (1989) *Maps of Meaning: An Introduction to Cultural Geography.* London: Unwin Hyman.

Jakle, J. A. (1987) *The Visual Elements of Landscape.* Amherst: University of Massachusetts Press.

Johnston, R. J. (1991) "A place for everything and everything in its place." *Transactions, Institute of British Geographers* 16: 131–47.

Jordan, T. G., and M. Kaups (1989) *The American Backwoods Frontier: An Ethnic and Ecological Interpretation*. Baltimore, MD: Johns Hopkins University Press.

Kark, R., ed. (1990) *The Land That Became Israel*. New Haven, CT: Yale University Press.

Kay, J. (1989) "Western Women's History." *Journal of Historical Geography* 15: 302–5.

——— (1990) "The future of historical geography in the United States." *Annals of the Association of American Geographers* 80: 618–21.

——— (1991) "Landscapes of women and men: Rethinking the regional historical geography of the United States and Canada." *Journal of Historical Geography* 17: 435–52.

Kearns, G. (1988) "History, geography, and world-systems theory." *Journal of Historical Geography* 14: 281–92.

———, and C. Withers, eds. (1991) *Urbanising Britain: Essays on Class and Community in the Nineteenth Century*. Cambridge: Cambridge University Press.

Kemp, P. (1987) "Some aspects of housing consumption in late 19th-century England and Wales." *Housing Studies* 2: 3–16.

Kerr, D., and D. Holdsworth, eds. and G. J. Matthews (cart.) (1990) *Historical Atlas of Canada III: Addressing the Twentieth Century*. Toronto: University of Toronto Press.

Krim, A. (1990) "Historical geography at the annual meeting of the AAG, Toronto, 1990." *Journal of Historical Geography* 16: 446–48.

——— (1992) "Los Angeles and the anti-tradition of the suburban city." *Journal of Historical Geography* 18: 121–38.

Langton, J. (1984) "The industrial revolution and the regional geography of England." *Transactions, Institute of British Geographers* 9: 145–67.

——— (1988) "The production of regions in England's Industrial Revolution: A comment." *Journal of Historical Geography* 14: 170–76.

———, and R. J. Morris, eds. (1986) *Atlas of Industrializing Britain 1780–1914*. London: Methuen.

Lee, R. (1988) "Uneven zenith: Towards a geography of the high period of municipal medicine in England and Wales." *Journal of Historical Geography* 14: 260–80.

Levine, G. J. (1988) "Class, ethnicity, and property transfers in Montreal, 1907–1909." *Journal of Historical Geography* 14: 360–80.

McDowell, L., and D. Massey (1984) "A woman's place?," in D. Massey and J. Allen (eds.) *Geography Matters!* Cambridge: Cambridge University Press: 128–47.

Mackenzie, S., and D. Rose (1983) "Industrial change, the domestic economy, and home life," in J. Anderson et al. (eds.) *Redundant Spaces in Cities and Regions?* London: Academic Press: 155–200.

Marsh, M. (1990) *Suburban Lives*. New Brunswick: Rutgers University Press.

Marston, S. (1989) "Public ritual and community power: St Patrick's Day parades in Lowell, Massachusetts, 1841–74." *Political Geography Quarterly* 8: 255–69.

Massey, D. (1984) *Spatial Divisions of Labour*. London: Macmillan.

Meinig, D. (1979) *The Interpretation of Ordinary Landscapes.* New York: Oxford University Press.

—— (1983) "Geography as an art." *Transactions, Institute of British Geographers* 8: 314–28.

—— (1986) *The Shaping of America: A Geographical Perspective on 500 Years of History, Volume 1, Atlantic America, 1492–1800.* New Haven, CT: Yale University Press.

—— (1989) "The historical geography imperative." *Annals of the Association of American Geographers* 79: 79–87.

—— (1990) "Reply to J. Kay." *Annals of the Association of American Geographers* 80: 621–22.

Miller, R. (1982) "Household activity patterns in nineteenth-century suburbs: A time-geographic exploration." *Annals of the Association of American Geographers* 72: 355–71.

—— (1983) "The Hoover® in the garden: Middle-class women and suburbanization, 1850–1920." *Environment and Planning D: Society and Space* 1: 73–87.

—— (1991) "Selling Mrs. Consumer: Advertising and the creation of suburban socio-spatial relations 1910–1930." *Antipode* 23: 263–306.

Mitchell, R. D. (1987) "The North American past: Retrospect and prospect," in R. D. Mitchell and P. A. Groves (eds.) *North America: The Historical Geography of a Changing Continent.* London: Hutchinson: 3–21.

——, and P. A. Groves, eds. (1987) *North America: The Historical Geography of a Changing Continent.* London: Hutchinson.

——, and M. B. Newton (1988) *The Appalachian Frontier: Views from the East and the Southwest.* Research Series No. 21. Cheltenham: Historical Geography Research Group.

Norton, W. (1984) *Historical Analysis in Geography.* London: Longman.

Ogborn, M. (1992) "Local power and state regulation in nineteenth century Britain." *Transactions, Institute of British Geographers* 17: 215–26.

Ostergren, R. C. (1988) *A Community Transplanted: The Transatlantic Experience of a Swedish Immigrant Settlement in the Upper Midwest, 1835–1915.* Madison: University of Wisconsin Press.

Overton, M. (1977) "Computer analysis of an inconsistent data source: The case of probate inventories." *Journal of Historical Geography* 3: 317–26.

—— (1984) "Agricultural revolution? Development of the agrarian economy in early modern England," in A. R. H. Baker and D. Gregory (eds.) *Explorations in Historical Geography: Interpretative Essays.* Cambridge: Cambridge University Press: 118–39.

Page, B., and R. Walker (1991) "From settlement to Fordism: The agro-industrial revolution in the American Midwest." *Economic Geography* 67: 281–315.

Palmer, J. (1985) "Domesday Book and the computer," in P. Sawyer (ed.) *Domesday Book: A Reassessment.* London: Edward Arnold: 164–74.

Parr, J. (1990) *The Gender of Breadwinners.* Toronto: University of Toronto Press.

Philo, C. (1987) "'Fit localities for an asylum': The historical geography of the nineteenth-century 'mad business' in England as viewed through the pages of the *Asylum Journal*." *Journal of Historical Geography* 13: 398–415.

Pile, S., and G. Rose (1992) "All or nothing? Politics and critique in the modernism-postmodernism debate." *Environment and Planning D: Society and Space* 10: 123–36.

Pocock, D. (ed.) (1981) *Humanistic Geography and Literature*. London: Croom Helm.

Powell, J. M. (1988) *An Historical Geography of Modern Australia*. Cambridge: Cambridge University Press.

Pred, A. (1984a) "Place as historically contingent process: Structuration and the time-geography of becoming places." *Annals of the Association of American Geographers* 74: 279–97.

——— (1984b) "Structuration, biography formation, and knowledge: Observations on port growth during the late mercantile period. *Environment and Planning D: Society and Space* 2: 251–75.

——— (1986) *Place, Practice and Structure*. Cambridge: Polity Press.

——— (1990a) *Lost Words and Lost Worlds: Modernity and the Language of Everyday Life in Late Nineteenth Century Stockholm*. Cambridge: Cambridge University Press.

——— (1990b) *Making Histories and Constructing Human Geographies*. Boulder, CO: Westview Press.

Prince, H. (1988) "Art and agrarian change, 1710–1815," in D. Cosgrove and S. Daniels (eds.) *The Iconography of Landscape*. Cambridge: Cambridge University Press: 98–118.

Pudup, M. B. (1989) "The boundaries of class in preindustrial Appalachia." *Journal of Historical Geography* 15: 139–62.

Radford, J. (1990) "Editorial." *Journal of Historical Geography* 16: 1–2.

Robinson, D., ed. (1990) *Migration in Colonial Spanish America*. Cambridge: Cambridge University Press.

Rose, D. (1987) "Home ownership, subsistence, and historical change: The mining district of West Cornwall in the late nineteenth century," in N. Thrift and P. Williams (eds.) *Class and Space: The Making of Urban Society*. London: Routledge: 108–53.

Rose, G. (1990) "Imagining Poplar in the 1920s: Contested concepts of community." *Journal of Historical Geography* 16: 425–37.

———, and M. Ogborn (1988) "Feminism and historical geography." *Journal of Historical Geography* 14: 405–9.

Rumney, T. (1988) "Historical geography at the annual meeting of the AAG, Phoenix, Arizona, April 1988." *Journal of Historical Geography* 14: 412–15.

Sauder, R. A. (1989) "Sod land versus sagebrush: Early land appraisal and pioneer settlement in an arid intermountain frontier." *Journal of Historical Geography* 15: 402–19.

Schreuder, Y. (1989) "Labor segmentation, ethnic division of labor, and residential segregation in American cities in the early twentieth century." *Professional Geographer* 41: 131–42.

————— (1990) "The impact of labor segmentation on the ethnic division of labor and the immigrant residential community: Polish leather workers in Wilmington, Delaware, in the early twentieth century." *Journal of Historical Geography* 16: 402–24.

Smith, D. (1989) "The perils of paternalism: Case studies from Chicago and Birmingham." Social Innovation Research Group Working Paper, Aston University, Birmingham, England.

Solot, M. (1990) "Review of M. Storper and R. Walker, *The Capitalist Imperative.*" *Journal of Historical Geography* 16: 358–59.

Southall, H. (1986) "Regional unemployment patterns among skilled engineers in Britain, 1851–1914." *Journal of Historical Geography* 12: 268–86.

————— (1988) "Towards a geography of unionization: The spatial organization and distribution of early British trade unions." *Transactions, Institute of British Geographers* 13: 466–83.

————— (1989) "British artisan unions in the New World." *Journal of Historical Geography* 15: 163–82.

Storper, M., and R. Walker (1989) *The Capitalist Imperative: Territory, Technology and Industrial Growth.* Oxford: Basil Blackwell.

Taylor, P. (1985) *Political Geography: World-Economy, Nation-State and Locality.* London: Longman.

Thrift, N. (1983) "On the determination of social action in space and time." *Environment and Planning D: Society and Space* 1: 23–57.

————— (1987) "Introduction: The geography of nineteenth-century class formation," in N. Thrift and P. Williams (eds.) *Class and Space: The Making of Urban Society.* London: Routledge: 25–50.

Walker, R. (1978) "The transformation of urban structure in the nineteenth century and the beginnings of suburbanization," in K. Cox (ed.) *Urbanization and Conflict in Market Societies.* Chicago: Maaroufa: 165–212.

————— (1981) "A theory of suburbanization: Capitalism and the construction of urban space in the United States," in M. Dear and A. J. Scott (eds.) *Urbanization and Urban Planning in Capitalist Society.* London: Methuen: 383–429.

————— (1989) "Geography from the Left," in G. L. Gaile and C. J. Willmott (eds.) *Geography in America.* Columbus, OH: Merrill Publishing Company: 619–50.

Ward, D. (1989) *Poverty, Ethnicity, and the American City, 1840–1925.* New York: Cambridge University Press.

Ward, S. V. (1988) *The Geography of Interwar Britain: The State and Uneven Development.* London: Routledge.

Watts, D. (1987) *The West Indies: Patterns of Development, Culture and Environment since 1492.* Cambridge: Cambridge University Press.

Whitehand, J. W. R. (1984) "Commercial townscapes in the making." *Journal of Historical Geography* 10: 174–200.

Williams, M. (1989) *Americans and Their Forests: A Historical Geography.* Cambridge: Cambridge University Press.

————— , ed. (1990) *Wetlands: A Threatened Landscape.* Oxford: Basil Blackwell.

Women and Geography Study Group (1984) *Geography and Gender.* London: Hutchinson.

Woolf, P. (1988) "Symbol of the Second Empire: Cultural politics and the Paris Opera House," in D. Cosgrove and S. Daniels (eds.) *The Iconography of Landscape.* Cambridge: Cambridge University Press: 214–35.

Wright, G. (1980) *Moralism and the Model Home: Domestic Architecture and Cultural Conflict in Chicago 1873–1913.* Chicago: University of Chicago Press.

Wrigley, E. A., and R. S. Schofield (1981) *The Population History of England 1541–1871.* London: Edward Arnold.

Wynn, G. (1990) "Introduction," in G. Wynn (ed.) *People, Places, Patterns, Processes: Geographical Perspectives on the Canadian Past.* Toronto: Copp Clark Pitman: 1–37.

Eric H. Monkkonen is Professor of History at the University of California at Los Angeles, specializing in the history of American cities and urban problems, especially crime and poverty. His research has focused on the larger issues of American urbanization, as reflected in his most recent book, *America Becomes Urban: The Development of US Cities and Towns 1790–1980.*

Andrew Abbott, author of *The System of Professions: An Essay on the Division of Expert Labor* is Professor of Sociology at the University of Chicago. In addition to his research on the division of labor he works on the problems involved of temporality in social structures.

Richard Dennis is Reader in Geography at University College, London. He is author of *A Social Geography of England and Wales* and *English Industrial cities of the Nineteenth Century,* and *Nineteenth-Century Cities: Culture, Economy and the Built Environment.*

Susan Kellogg is Assistant Professor of History at the University of Houston, where she is a specialist in the ethnohistory of Pre-Columbian and colonial Latin America. She is author of *Law and the Transformation of Aztec Society, 1500–1700* and co-author of *Domestic Revolutions: A Social History of American Family Life.*

David Brian Robertson is Associate Professor of Political Science at the University of Missouri at St. Louis. He is Associate Editor of the *Journal of Policy History* and is co-author of *The Development of American Public Policy: The Structure of Policy Restraint.*

Hugh Rockoff is Professor of Economics at Rutgers University at the State University of New Jersey, and Research Associate at the National Bureau of Economic Research. He is author of books on the history of price controls in the United States as well as on the free banking experiment in the nineteenth century.